Organizational Betrayal

Organizational Betrayal

How Schools Enable Sexual
Misconduct and How to Stop It

CHAROL SHAKESHAFT

HARVARD EDUCATION PRESS

CAMBRIDGE, MASSACHUSETTS

Paperback ISBN 9781682539286

Library of Congress Cataloging-in-Publication Data

Names: Shakeshaft, Charol, author.
Title: Organizational betrayal : how schools enable sexual misconduct
  and how to stop it / Charol Shakeshaft.
Description: Cambridge, Massachusetts : Harvard Education Press, [2024] |
  Includes bibliographical references and index.
Identifiers: LCCN 2024016169 | ISBN 9781682539286 (paperback)
Subjects: LCSH: Child sexual abuse by teachers—United States. |
  Sex crimes—United States—Prevention. | Education and state—
  United States. | School personnel management—United States. |
  Corporate culture—United States.
Classification: LCC LB2844.1.C54 S53 2024 | DDC 362.76/7—dc23/eng/20240718
LC record available at https://lccn.loc.gov/2024016169

Published by Harvard Education Press,
an imprint of the Harvard Education Publishing Group

Harvard Education Press
8 Story Street
Cambridge, MA 02138

Cover Design: Endpaper Studio
Cover Image: Bloomberg Creative via Getty Images

The typefaces in this book are Sabon and Myriad Pro.

This book is dedicated to

- all targets of sexual abuse, those who work to keep them safe, and those who help them heal;
- Emma Shakeshaft and Sarah Meyland, who have been on this journey with me the whole way;
- Dale Mann, who has supported my work for decades and helped me make this a better book than it would have been without his counsel.

Contents

PART I
A Culture of Organizational Betrayal   1

1   Sexual Abuse Happens in All Types of Organizations   3

2   The Scope of School Employee Sexual Misconduct   19

3   Who Is Harmed?   33

PART II
Who, What, Where, and How   45

4   Abusers   47

5   Victims, Targets, Survivors   65

6   Patterns   83

PART III
Standard of Care for Preventing School Employee Sexual Misconduct   105

7   A Model for Prevention   107

8   Policies and Training   135

9   Personnel Management   163

PART IV
Going Forward   199

10   Institutional Courage and Societal Change   201

Appendix 1: Methodology   213

Appendix 2: Training Programs   217

Notes   231

Acknowledgments   245

About the Author   247

Index   249

PART I

A Culture of Organizational Betrayal

Sexual Abuse Happens in All Types of Organizations

I have been working on this book for thirty years, through employment at two universities, two publishers I disappointed by failing to finish, three full drafts of the manuscript, and thousands more abuses of children. I'm not entirely sure I know what kept me from finishing. Perhaps it is because I thought I would not be done until I knew everything. Or perhaps it was the trauma of those children that paralyzed me instead of pushing me, fearing my account of their stories wouldn't be as compelling as they deserved.

Despite not knowing everything about school employee sexual abuse of students, I have come to realize that I know more about the subject than anyone else. I have examined hundreds of cases and interviewed parents, victims, offenders, detectives, police officers, attorneys, and school officials. I have evaluated hundreds of school policies, examined countless hiring procedures, and taken and critiqued increasingly more training programs as they have come on the market. I have been awarded three federal grants to help me understand educator sexual misconduct and spent personal funds for the rest.

I have served as an expert witness in both criminal and civil cases on the sexual abuse of children in schools and youth organizations. I have worked on more than three hundred cases involving sexual abuse of students in the United States by trusted others, particularly teachers and other school employees. I have written nearly three hundred expert assessments of organizational compliance with Title IX and other standards related to preventing the sexual abuse of children by adults employed in youth-serving organizations in forty-five states and the District of Columbia.

I have presented expert testimony in over 150 depositions and testified in nearly forty trials in state and federal cases concerned with sexual abuse in K–12 independent and public schools, child-care facilities, youth organizations, institutions of higher education, and religious organizations that serve children and youths.

I am a Title IX hearing officer at Virginia Commonwealth University. I served as the federally appointed monitor for compliance of a settlement agreement between the parties in the USC/Tyndall class action suit, *Sutedja v. University of Southern California et al.*, as well as the Report of the Equitable Relief Committee.[1]

I have spoken to hearing officers who determine whether an employee can be fired for boundary crossing and misconduct. I have served as an expert witness in civil cases where parents sued schools for not protecting their children.

I have learned that there are far more people complicit in the continuing sexual abuse of children by school employees than just the offending employee. There are the teachers who see something odd but don't do anything; the school administrators who ignore an allegation because they believe that none of their teachers would do such a thing; the school superintendents who fear controversy and leave these issues to others in the district; the school boards who approve the resignation of abusers, passing them on to the next school; the parents who trust the school too much; and the friends who have been sworn to secrecy by the victim, so they don't tell. We are all complicit.

I'm often asked why school employees sexually abuse students. My answer: because they can. Despite our claims that we love children and do everything for them, when push comes to shove, we care about protecting the adult more than protecting the child.

A combination of lack of training, adult protectionism, and indifferent leadership have left millions of children vulnerable to sexual abuse by an employee in a school.

I realize I cannot wait to publish this book, even if there are components of this tragedy that are not yet fully documented. I know enough to stop educator sexual misconduct and to protect children. That is what this book is about.

There are a lot of people who care about the safety of children—educators and employees in youth-serving organizations, legislators, policy makers, attorneys, law enforcement officials, parents, students—they all care about the safety of children, and yet these crimes continue. What we have been doing and not doing has not protected children. We are all complicit and we all must change. Now.

I first became interested in the topic in the 1980s when a local high school principal, who was also one of my doctoral students, came to me with a problem. He said, "I think that one of my teachers is having sex with a student. What should I do?" At this time, I hadn't thought much about teacher-student sex. Prodded by this call for help from my student, I began talking with my colleagues and friends. I learned that they had stories from their middle and high school days. My search of newspaper articles in the microfilm collection at the university library at the time confirmed that abuse of students by school employees had been reported in newspaper stories since at least the 1960s. Books and professional articles had been published detailing the experiences of students as prey. An article in the *Executive Educator* in 1981 by an assistant superintendent in Iowa looked back at his career and described dealing with teachers sexually abusing students.[2]

This wasn't a new story. Nor was it a problem solved, as the principal who came to me documented. Students were still being sexually targeted by those employed to teach and support them.

I wanted to know more and maybe stop this harm. So, starting in the 1980s, I began studying school employee sexual misconduct; collecting national data using surveys, interviews, and document analysis; and documenting more than two hundred case studies of what happens and doesn't happen in schools when an employee crosses the line with a student.[3] Identifying the patterns of grooming and abuse and understanding how the institution responds when a child is the target of sexual misconduct by a school employee has led me to develop a model of prevention.

School employee sexual misconduct is real. Students are harmed. Prevention is not complicated. But school leaders and legislators aren't doing enough to keep children safe. Many school organizations and those who work at every level have betrayed students by refusing to see and act. Some have called this willful blindness. While this betrayal may not be conscious or premeditated, it happens because it puts the interests of adults over the safety of children.

School employee sexual misconduct encompasses verbal, visual, and physical behaviors that cross personal boundaries with students. Future chapters will provide more explicit examples and discuss the difference between a behavior that is a safe interaction with a student and one that could be identified as sexual misconduct. Sexual misconduct can be hugs, kissing, oral/anal/vaginal intercourse, playing with a student's hair, emails, telephone calls, texts, photographs, and other interactions that have a sexual intent. And it is worth mentioning that sexual activity between an adult and a student can never be consensual, not only because of the age of the student, but also because of the custodial in loco parentis status of school employees.

Sexual misconduct isn't an isolated or rare happening. A study commissioned by the US Senate and published in 2004 documented that nearly one out of ten students report that at least once, and often many times, during their kindergarten through high school career, they were targeted by a school employee with some form of sexual misconduct.[4] In chapter 2, you will see that in the twenty years since this study was published, the number of K–12 students who were targets of sexual misconduct each year, as well as the proportion of students targeted, has increased. This abuse, widely reported in the media, has been available to the public and the education establishment for more than sixty years. It is time for this assault to be recognized, documented, deconstructed, and stopped.

The solutions aren't complicated, and yet they haven't been universally implemented. Ironically, much of current practice aimed at preventing school employee sexual misconduct requires the victims to take the responsibility for their own safety (for example, resistance and reporting) and for the offenders to police themselves. While these approaches are important, they have not been enough and do not address the root causes or the patterns of abuse that facilitate sexual misconduct in schools. This book provides an ecological model of prevention as an organization-wide responsibility.

In the following chapters, I (1) describe how existing school organizations enable employees in their sexual misconduct with students, (2) identify intervention points to change these cultures, and (3) provide strategies to change the culture of enablement. This is a guide to prevention, a path to safety, a prescription to increase the caring that we all profess to value.

How does school employee sexual misconduct happen?

The problem is acute in schools, and it goes beyond schools to all the organizations that serve children and youth—summer camps, religious groups, voluntary and community-based associations like the YMCA and scouting organizations. I examine the decisions and practices of all the organizations that serve children and youth. I focus on the responsibilities and behaviors of all actors, but particularly those who might be described as bystanders—administrators, teachers, aides, custodians, lunchroom personnel, coaches, nontargeted students—who see things but don't understand what they are seeing or don't act to stop the sexual abuse of students by adults.

Seeing but not acting is epidemic. If a custodian found a handgun in a stairwell, they would act on the "See Something: Say Something" maxim. If the custodian finds a classroom door chronically locked after school and knows that the math teacher is inside with the same lone female student, what does the custodian do? Nothing.

If school personnel have a suspicion that something isn't "right," why don't they report? There are many reasons: self-protection, fear for their job, lack of care, lack of clarity about their responsibility, insecurity about accusing someone who might be popular or powerful. Power in schools is relative. There is formal power, but also imputed power given to people who are well-liked or well-connected. People who are perceived as having power or as being morally responsible are not likely to be reported even though they may be observed crossing teacher-student boundaries.[5] In schools, support staff are less powerful than teachers, and teachers are (in general) less powerful than administrators. All of those groups are more powerful than students. In the case of an observation or an allegation, who is less likely to be believed? The student or the employee?

School employees who are inclined to sexually abuse get away with it because no one stops them. It is as simple as that. By stopping them, I mean providing protections such as policies, training, supervision, and reporting.

In the cases I have studied where sexual misconduct and abuse have occurred, a child has been harmed, and the offender is charged and prosecuted. What isn't fully understood and acknowledged is that the organization has "allowed" and sometimes encouraged and facilitated boundary-crossing behaviors by the offender. At each boundary crossing, the adult receives no consequences or restrictions. Therefore, the "offender-to-be" tries something else, crosses another boundary. Step by step, the school employee keeps crossing boundaries until the child is sexually exploited. Stopping boundary crossing early keeps the adult from becoming an offender and the student from becoming a victim. Stopping boundary crossing is an organizational responsibility. When the organization fails to do that—in the absence of policies, training, supervision, feedback, reporting, investigation, and reinforcement—the organization has betrayed the students it serves.

Each time an adult crosses a boundary with a student and isn't stopped, the behavior becomes normalized, rationalized, and accepted, not only by the boundary crosser but also by others in the organization, and tragically, by the students. A person who starts to talk to a student alone and listens to the student's personal problems in a private isolated setting might start out as someone who was just trying to help that student who has come with a problem or who seemed upset or who asked for help. This leads to the adult and the student spending time alone together. The adult sees this as "helping"; the student interprets it as care.

Often students report in the beginning that they felt special because an adult they respected or admired was paying a lot of attention to them. As these interactions continue and more boundaries are crossed, the adult might offer a ride home after school; the adult might suggest they stop and get something to eat; the adult might compliment the student—"You're really smart," or "You're so mature. You're not like the other students." The adult might find a growing attraction to the student, something the adult hadn't anticipated. The student might find a growing attraction to the adult. The adult might suggest more activities. The student might be responsive. The adult is then primed to cross further personal, physical, and sexual boundaries.

After that happens a few times and no one intervenes or reminds the adult about policies prohibiting one-on-one closed-door student time, the offending adult has normalized the behavior as acceptable. But it's not only that adult. Students and colleagues begin to code the behavior as acceptable. Without training, policies, and enforcement, everyone comes to see these boundary crossings as "what some people do," not as red flags that require immediate action.

In this scenario, the adult didn't become a teacher to have sex with students, but—with vulnerable children and lax supervision—that's exactly what happens. This scenario is typical in the cases I have studied.

There are 3.1 million full-time-equivalent teachers and 92,000 principals in American education. They work in 129,000 public and private K–12 schools.[6] The vast majority don't abuse students. They help, they don't harm. Teachers have jobs that are overdemanding and underrewarding. They still have noble motives, and they still provide a critical service.

At the same time, in the case of sexual misconduct by a colleague, they are bystanders to the abuse who fail to notice, speak up, or intervene. Passivity becomes permission. However, it can be corrected. Educators of goodwill can change a culture of unconscious or conscious protecting and enabling of abusers to one of calling them out and removing them, and that is what most people who work in schools endorse.

The case narratives shared in this book provide examples of how people of good will miss—either consciously or not—the opportunity to intervene and stop behaviors that can lead to sexual boundary crossing and misconduct. Good intentions without action are not enough, and they leave the organization responsible for harm to children.

Documenting this pattern over and over, across schools, gender, race, and other student and adult characteristics, I began to ask, "Where were the adults? Where were the professionals? Where were the organizational actors? Why didn't they step in?"

"ORGANIZATIONAL BETRAYAL": THE IMPORTANCE OF NAMING

As I began to try and understand how and why school children continued to be sexually abused by those in positions of trust, I came across the germinal work of Jennifer Freyd and her colleague Carly P. Smith. In the 1990s, Jennifer Freyd began a series of studies that inform my understanding of institutional or organizational betrayal. Freyd named the abuse, and its aftermath, by someone who is trusted and has power over a person as betrayal trauma.[7] Along with Smith, Freyd documented the physical and mental harm from abuse by a trusted other. School employees, coaches, and others who work with children fall into this category. Using betrayal trauma theory, Freyd extended her research into our understanding of institutional betrayal as a failure to protect when protection would be a reasonable and expected response. Betrayals perpetrated by institutions can stem from failures to protect their members from experiencing harm in the first place or failures to respond supportively after members have already been harmed.[8] The responsibility for protection and prevention is on the organization—its leaders and its members.

Her research also documents the harm from institutional betrayal. Smith and Freyd developed the Institutional Betrayal Questionnaire (IBQ) to document both the culture in which betrayal abuse occurs and the harm done by the institution for not preventing or remedying the abuse and the trauma.[9]

Smith and Freyd's 2017 study documented a link between experiences of institutional betrayal and health outcomes.[10] Their work establishes that it is not just betrayal trauma from a trusted abuser that affects later health outcomes of a sexual abuse target; it is also institutional betrayal—the culture and the actions of the organization—that damages health and provokes dissociation.

In a 2020 study of undergraduate college students reflecting upon their high school experiences, Lind, Adams-Clark, and Freyd measured the level of high school gender harassment experienced by the respondents as well as the institutional betrayal they experienced (Gender Experiences Questionnaire [GEQ], IBQ). Their findings support the relationship between gender harassment, to include sexual harassment and misconduct, and trauma that continued into the college years. An important implication of this study is that gender harassment and sexual misconduct may "hurt students regardless of whether the student experiences gender harassment directly."[11] A climate that tolerates or is indifferent to sexual misconduct traumatizes students beyond those who are targeted.

Other studies have documented the relationship between institutional betrayal of a sexual abuse victim and the level of the victim's trauma. The harm comes from a culture in which sexual misconduct is tolerated or even encouraged and from the failure to respond to an allegation of misconduct.[12] The research on institutional trauma and betrayal has guided the research for this book and serves as the conceptual framework for understanding why sexual misconduct continues to occur and how to stop it. The tragedy of educator sexual abuse is not simply a matter of an indifferent individual; it is an organizational responsibility.

Smith and Freyd documented the effects of sexual misconduct and institutional betrayal to include PTSD, depression, anxiety, trauma-related symptoms, and negative physical health outcomes (headaches, sleep issues, shortness of breath, and problematic sexual functioning).[13] Monteith et al. documented suicide as a risk of institutional betrayal.[14]

The effects of institutional betrayal where the school has not protected the student from sexual abuse go beyond the student involved and have been named secondary institutional betrayal.[15] Survivors of rape who reported experiencing institutional betrayal by the organization that was supposed to protect them from harm were interviewed and identified lack of trust of other institutions in addition to the one that betrayed them.

Smith and Freyd provide examples of secondary institutional assault from the media, governmental agencies, the legal system, and university public responses.

MEDIA:
- sensationalized stories of sexual assault
- cover-ups of assaults by men in positions of fame or power
- focus on stories where institutions failed survivors, which reinforces institutional betrayal
- perpetuation of rape culture through language and stereotypes

US GOVERNMENT:
- Allowing men in office who are accused of sexual assault to deflect accountability by discrediting survivors (examples include Clarence Thomas and Brett Kavanaugh's hearings for Supreme Court appointments and the election campaigns of Donald Trump)

US CRIMINAL LEGAL SYSTEM:
- light sentences, delayed prosecution, and not-guilty verdicts for perpetrators

- failure to bring charges, even when police investigations identify a possible crime

UNIVERSITIES:
- betrayal by universities such as Michigan State, Penn State, University of Michigan, and University of Southern California in allowing prominent employees to sexually abuse students and athletes for decades

Survivors pointed out that instances of institutional betrayal have follow-on consequences. Employees became hesitant to report; they feared recrimination; they doubted that higher-level officials would act. In other words, institutional betrayal affects even those not betrayed because they come to believe that they can't trust the institution.

DATA FOR THIS BOOK

After the school principal asked me what to do about an allegation of educator sexual misconduct in his school, he involved law enforcement, and the abusing teacher was arrested and convicted. I persuaded Audrey Cohan, then a graduate research assistant, to work with me to understand how organizations were responding—or not—to sexual misconduct by an employee. In the late 1980s, we sent postcards to eight hundred superintendents of public school districts in New York State asking if they had ever had an incident of sexual abuse of a student by a staff member and, if they had, would they talk with us. We heard from 225 superintendents that, yes, they had responded to at least one allegation of employee-to-student sexual misconduct, and yes, they would talk to us. This study provided a peek into organizational response patterns.

The cooperating superintendents provided revealing anecdotes about how schools handled sexual misconduct of students by employees. But it was also clear that superintendents, school boards, and their attorneys weren't about to open employee files or let me interview those administrators, students, and other personnel who played a role in offending, preventing, or stopping.

I believed that if we could (or would) do postmortem examinations each time a student is sexually abused by an adult in a school, we would be able to identify the trigger points where better policies, training, supervision, and reporting might have increased prevention. These are volatile issues for school administrators and communities. Admitting that a school is vulnerable to employee abuse of children—or even that abuse has occurred—is perceived as an admission of failure and incompetence. The counsel to leaders has been to focus on the myth that every person who becomes a teacher is a professional motivated only to help children. The child-related counterpart is to blame the victim—"She had a crush on her teacher," or "They are teenage boys, the teacher just made them happy." Blaming the victim is far less risky for a school administrator than blaming a teacher or, even more explosive, blaming the administrators and the school board for creating and tolerating a culture that looks the other way. Most of the time, the administrative stakeholders just want to put the ugly incident behind them, a response which does not prevent future abuse and may even enable it.

An additional barrier to action-oriented postmortems is getting access for data collection to a critical mass of school districts. However valuable direct inquiry might be, it turns out not to be feasible to get permission to interview teachers, administrators, victims, parents of victims, other students, and predators when and where abuse has occurred. Very few, if any, sites allow such scrutiny. And thus, we have had little research on the organizational components that enable the sexual abuse of students by school employees.

In thinking about how it would be possible to achieve the same end—a 360-degree inquiry of a case of sexual abuse of a student by a staff member in a school—I realized that the documentation from civil cases where a parent or child files a suit against a school district for not preventing the abuse of the child by an employee would provide detailed, valid, and vetted information for a study that would include the perspectives of the school district, the school, the victim, the predator, the faculty, the student body, and staff bystanders.

Thus, when I was first contacted to be an expert witness in a civil legal case, I jumped at the chance. Not only might I have an opportunity to evaluate the actions of those involved, but I might also be able to use my reports to better understand organizational actions and responses in cases where a student had been the target of school employee sexual misconduct.

Civil suits and questions of liability require institutional information: policies, regulations, procedures, police reports, and depositions of victims, school administrators, and bystanders. Depositions are sworn testimony in a sustained and pointed question-and-answer process conducted by lawyers. The information shared is as close to a participant's "truth" as is likely to be available. People being deposed swear an oath to tell the truth, and the penalties of perjury apply, just as they would in trial testimony. Further, in these cases, child-serving organizations are legally required to provide their relevant school policies and practices, including information about hiring and managing personnel, training, reporting, investigating, supervising students and staff, and resolving and remedying allegations. In addition, the records often include expert witnesses who comment on the documentation of the harm done to the victims. In sum, the case records of civil lawsuits provide a 360-degree picture of educator sexual misconduct.

The content of this book is based upon the analysis of these documents from the K–12 civil cases of school employee sexual misconduct in which I have served as an expert witness. Most of the materials are now in the public domain, and I also have permission from plaintiff attorneys to use materials from all cases to study sexual abuse in schools under the following conditions: (1) only pseudonyms for school districts, people involved, case names, and attorneys would be used; (2) my case descriptions would be edited to protect the identity of individuals and locations. My use of case material is to document the patterns across cases and to provide examples of how the abuse occurs and how the school community responds. My findings are aggregate findings or descriptions that were stripped of any possible identifiers prior to my analysis.

For each of the hundreds of cases I have analyzed—whether hired by plaintiff's or defendant's attorneys—I examined the same organizational components: (1) policies in place and followed; (2) training of staff, students, and parents; (3) practices for hiring and managing the employee; (4) reporting of the allegation; (5) investigating of the allegation; (6) supervision practices for both staff and students; (7) organization responses to red flags; and (8) remedying. The basic records typically include police incident reports, witness statements, and depositions from the victims, the alleged perpetrators, central office and building administrators, faculty colleagues, students, and parents. Some of the most illuminating evidence often comes from the testimony of school superintendents, school board members, building administrators, teacher union officials, and other school staff. My analysis of every case has been guided by a template of organizational actions and expectations. Appendix 1 provides more detail on the research methods for this analysis.

For this book, I am using a sample of 132 cases selected from my expert reports of school employee sexual misconduct. The most important information from these cases comes from the qualitative descriptions in depositions and the content analysis of policy, training, and reporting documents and narratives.

Since we continue to lack a comprehensive empirical analysis of educator sexual abuse, these cases cannot be generalized to the population of all students who have been sexually abused by a school employee. They are only generalizable to the cases that I have studied and from which I identified both patterns of abuse and levers for prevention. In all, 88 percent of the cases involved male perpetrators: of those, male-to-female abuse constituted 58 percent; male-to-male, 27 percent; and male-to-both, 3 percent. Female-to-male abuse accounts for 10 percent of the cases and female-to-female, 2 percent of the abuse. The average number of victims who brought a lawsuit against the same perpetrator is three. The case records for many of the suits identify additional victims of the perpetrator who were not party to the lawsuit. The majority of cases occurred in public schools (76 percent), followed by independent nonreligious schools (14 percent) and religious schools (10 percent). A total of 3 percent involve pre-K students who were sexually abused by a school employee; 21 percent, elementary students; 29 percent, middle school students; and 41 percent, high school students. The remaining 6 percent deal with perpetrators who pursued their misconduct across more than one level of schooling—elementary and middle or middle and high school.

WHY I WROTE THIS BOOK

When Rebecca Auburn was eleven and in the sixth grade, she was sexually abused by her teacher, Mr. Conroy. This book is for the Rebeccas and the Seo-Juns, the Isabellas, the Juans, the Sanjays, and the approximately six million students who have been the targets of sexual misconduct by a school employee.

The first time Rebecca told anyone what had happened to her was when she was twenty-one and seeing a therapist to help her with her anxieties and fears. The second person she told was her mother, Frances. Frances was stricken. She knew herself to be a caring and careful mother. And yet, her daughter had been sexually exploited by an adult right under her nose. What had she missed? Did her divorce from Rebecca's father distract her? Frances remembered that Rebecca's behavior changed during sixth grade. Her daughter had become secretive and moody. Rebecca was angry a lot of the time and didn't want anyone, especially her father, to touch her. Frances had assumed this behavior was a combination of Rebecca's reaction to the divorce and a normal part of Rebecca's adolescent transition. But was that all it was? Could she have known? Should she have known? Was it her fault?

Parents rarely know what is happening in the schools their children attend. They are also not taught about appropriate employee-to-student boundaries and what might signal a boundary crossing by an adult. This book is for the parents of all children who have been sexually abused, who struggle to understand what happened.

The next person Rebecca talked to was the current superintendent of schools, Dr. Arlene Hamer. Dr. Hamer had been a teacher in Rebecca's school with a classroom next to Mr. Conroy's. As she listened to Rebecca's story, Dr. Hamer searched her memory for evidence that what she was hearing might be true. Mr. Conroy, now close to retirement, was still a sixth-grade teacher in the district. If there was any truth to these allegations, it would end his career and probably deny him a pension. These were serious charges, both for the well-being of one of the most popular elementary teachers in the district and for the safety of the children.

Dr. Hamer remembered that Mr. Conroy always decorated the door to his classroom with student artwork. The pictures were colorful and creative, and everyone liked to see what new work would be posted each week. As she pictured these sixth-grade artistic masterpieces, Dr. Hamer realized that Conroy had always covered the window in the classroom door with the students' work and that the door was always shut. Dr. Hamer also remembered that in the years that she had worked next door to Mr. Conroy, she had often seen female students staying late to help Mr. Conroy. As a young teacher, Dr. Hamer had been impressed by Mr. Conroy's dedication to teaching and to his students. He came early and left late. He met individually with students and took an interest in their lives. But as she thought about it, Dr. Hamer realized that Mr. Conroy had not been equally interested in all of his students. Each year there was a special student who was the focus of Mr. Conroy's attention. As she thought about these students, Dr. Hamer realized they were always shy girls who didn't have many friends or who were from disrupted homes. Dr. Hamer began to put the pieces together and pondered the conclusion that much of what she had seen as dedication might really have been sexual grooming and exploitation. How had she missed it?

In most cases of educator sexual abuse, there are teachers and administrators who would never harm a child but who are also witness to these acts—they just don't recognize what they see. They don't know what the warning signs are. They don't know how to read those signs and interpret what they are seeing. This book is for the Dr. Hamers, who care deeply about students and who have spent their lives building what they believe are safe learning communities.

Once the allegations were brought to Dr. Hamer's attention, she opened an investigation. The statute of limitations had run out on the possibility for Rebecca to bring a criminal charge, but when word got out through

Dr. Hamer's investigation, others who had been more recent students stepped forward with their stories and reported to both the school and the police. Eventually, Mr. Conroy was found guilty of child sexual abuse and sentenced to prison.

Rarely does a school district open an investigation on past abuse, even if the perpetrator is still employed. Even more rarely is a public statement made and an open process put in place. This book is for those administrators and school board members who quietly pass the trash and allow the abuser to move to another group of children. It is also for the courageous administrators who investigate and are open about the abuse and the steps that will be taken to make sure it doesn't happen again.

The school and police investigations as well as the criminal prosecution cost hundreds of thousands of dollars. Incarcerating Conroy cost the public even more. This book is for the taxpayers who pay for our criminal justice system.

Some students who were abused were able to bring a civil suit against the district for failing to protect them. The cost of attorneys for the district and the company that insured the district was high. In the end, the district reached a settlement of $7 million with several students and their families. This book is for insurance providers and for citizens in the school district whose taxes are used to pay for increased costs for insurance.

Dozens of girls shared their experiences of depression and the feelings of worthlessness they had experienced through the years after Mr. Conroy had abused them. Many grew into women with drug and alcohol problems. Some had trouble sustaining intimate relationships. The emotional and physical health of the victims were much worse than for the population in general. There was more obesity, diabetes, and cancer. More money was spent on therapy and other mental health programs. Several had tried to commit suicide. Treatment for the victims was expensive and ongoing.

This book is for the children who grew into adults who have spent years trying to repair the damage; for their pain; for the time and money spent with therapists and doctors; for their early deaths. It is also for citizens who pay the taxes necessary to provide a physical and mental health infrastructure in our country to help those who need it.

As Mr. Conroy's conviction became a certainty and as the insurance company briefed the board on the likely settlement costs, the board chair made a private but pointed suggestion to Dr. Hamer that she should seek employment elsewhere. This book is for the courageous school administrators who do the right thing and who are punished for their leadership.

Educator sexual misconduct. That's what happened to Rebecca. This book examines the behavior from an educator, directed at a student, and intended to sexually arouse or titillate the educator or the child. These behaviors constitute educator sexual misconduct and might be physical, verbal, or visual. Examples include touching breasts or genitals of students; oral, anal, and vaginal penetration; showing students pictures of a sexual nature; and sexually related conversations, jokes, or questions directed at students.

This book is not about "relationships," "affairs," or "consensual sex" between a student and an adult in the school. Although that's what the abuser wants the public to believe, there is no such thing as consensual sex between a school employee and a minor student or, in most states, a non-minor K–12 student. Educator sexual misconduct is sexual abuse and exploitation of a minor. It is sexual abuse and exploitation by a person in a position of trust. It is a violation of professional ethics. It is a breach of professional licensure and certification standards. It is a violation of federal law, and in most states, it is a criminal act. And yet it persists.

WHAT'S TO COME

This book is organized into four parts. The first part, "A Culture of Organizational Betrayal," consists of three chapters and describes a school culture that enables and permits sexual misconduct by documenting the extent of the abuse and the many populations who are harmed. The second part, "Who, What, Where, and How," looks at who abuses, who they abuse, and how they go about grooming and manipulating students to participate in their own abuse. This section is followed by part III, "Standard of Care for Preventing School Employee Sexual Misconduct," which describes the components of prevention and how to put them in place. Finally, in part IV, "Going Forward," I offer strategies that move beyond the school and provide examples of structural and societal changes that build institutional courage and defeat institutional betrayal.

The nasty but unavoidable conclusion to our current circumstances is that childhood sexual abuse, whether in schools or in the larger society, is culturally and institutionally supported. Institutions are complicit in their continued construction and maintenance of a culture of power differentials that are uninterrupted and that harm children.

Sexual misconduct of students by employees cannot be stopped unless we address these power differentials and the shared responsibility of all adults for putting the safety of children before the comfort of employees. Decades ago, Spiegel pointed out that "knowledge of the social environment . . . is essential as it holds the socially constructed attitudes and beliefs that foster the existence of sexual abuse in the first place."[16] This book asks us to protect children by confronting the culture of schools.

CHAPTER 2

The Scope of School Employee Sexual Misconduct

'm often asked why I use the term *school employee sexual misconduct* and what does it mean? I selected the term to include all sexualized behaviors from school employees directed at students, both criminal and noncriminal behaviors, that are sexualized and inappropriate in adult-student interactions. *Sexual harassment* is often used to describe inappropriate behavior that is short of physical interaction. *Sexual abuse* usually comes with a legal definition. Neither are comprehensive enough to bracket *misconduct*, the more inclusive adult-to-student sexualized behavior that doesn't belong in schools.

Sexual misconduct may be physical, verbal, or visual behaviors directed toward a student. In addition to *sexual harassment* and *sexual abuse*, other terms include *boundary crossing* and *inappropriate behavior*. Sexual misconduct may be physical contact such as full-body hugs or playing with a student's hair or kissing or touching intimate body parts such as breasts, buttocks, or genitals or oral, anal, or vaginal sexual intercourse.

Sexual misconduct is also visual, such as sending nude pictures, sharing pornography, masturbation, or other sexual performative acts in person or through video/photos. Misconduct can be face-to-face or through technology to solicit, send, or share pictures and videos. Employees use cellphones, the internet, texts, snapchat, and other digital platforms to groom and abuse students.

Sexual misconduct is also verbal: sexualized language and sexual discussions in person and via email, Twitter (now X), Instagram, and other messaging platforms.

A 2023 review of technology-mediated child sexual abuse identified four types of technology-assisted (TA) abuse: (1) the creation of visual material that exploits or abuses the child; (2) sexual abuse via live streaming;

(3) confronting children with pornographic material (pictures, drawings, films, DVDs, magazine); and (4) soliciting children to send pictures, videos, or voice notes of themselves.[1]

What all these variations have in common is that they are from an adult to a student, they cross accepted boundaries between the adult in the school and the student, and they are sexualized behaviors.

The following sections provide some examples. I have edited the vignettes from real events and real people; some are composite accounts. Names and locations have been changed. These examples do not exhaust the entirety of the types of sexual abuse school children have experienced and for which I have documentation. I have chosen them because they are representative of what is done to students. The list is not exhaustive primarily because I don't wish to cause further trauma to readers or those who have experienced sexual misconduct, abuse, and trauma. All the acts below were carried out by many different school employees in different schools and districts. Some employees enacted a few of the behaviors toward a student and others enacted many of these behaviors toward a student. These are typical acts, not just a one-off by a single actor.

PHYSICAL SEXUAL MISCONDUCT

- A male junior high school physical education teacher-coach would delay after-sport showering so that a selected boy was alone with him. The coach would join the male athlete in the shower and masturbate him.
- A female high school English teacher invited male students to her home for small parties that included drinking. She would select individual students to join her in the bedroom, where she engaged in sexual intercourse with them.
- A male third-grade teacher sat at the back of the room during classroom movies and placed a female student on his lap. During the film, he would pull down the student's underpants, touch her vagina, and rub his penis against her buttocks and vagina.
- A male high school art teacher stood behind female students, looking at and discussing their work while playing with their hair, massaging their shoulders, and leaning over with his hands around their necks and close to their breasts. He also hugged and kissed them on the lips when congratulating them on a project done well.

VISUAL SEXUAL MISCONDUCT

- A male teacher for special-needs students met with the boys in the class after school. He told them they needed to learn how to masturbate and had them stand in a circle, with their pants down, and masturbate while he watched.
- A middle school teacher sent text message pictures of his penis to twelve-year-old female students in his class and asked them to text back pictures of their "privates."
- A female high school teacher sent pictures of her breasts to male students in her classes. She requested return texts of their penises.
- A social studies teacher used his telephone (with a special device under his desk) to take videos of female underwear and crotches while the females were at his desk asking questions or getting help with schoolwork.

VERBAL SEXUAL MISCONDUCT

- A school resource officer stopped girls in the hallway and accused them of violating some behavior. He called them into his office. He interrogated the girls about their sexual practices and shared his own.
- A coach forced male athletes to tell him about their sexual practices with their girlfriends, insisting on details and demonstrations.
- An assistant principal discussed the bodies of female students with other adults in the school. He also pointed out which students he thought were having sex.
- A music teacher regularly asked students about what sexual acts they did with their boyfriends or girlfriends.

Many of the cases involved escalating misconduct: an adult might start with verbal harassment, add visual misconduct, and then move to physical abuse. School employees targeted students for sexual contact (see chapter 6 on how this happens) and engaged them in oral, anal, and vaginal penetration in classrooms, closets, locker rooms, music rooms, outdoors, indoors, and in cars, buses, vacation houses, and the residences of both the abuser and target.

HOW WIDESPREAD IS SCHOOL EMPLOYEE SEXUAL MISCONDUCT?

Surprisingly, in a country that counts the number of reindeer (Alaska Caribou) in Alaska, we don't have a federal data collection system that keeps track of the number of students who are abused by school employees.[2]

Counting is important:

- As a country, we document what we care about.
- If we document the extent of a problem, there is more likelihood that we will address the issue.

Persuading lawmakers, school boards, administrators, and others to act requires compelling evidence. Without metrics (and even with them) policy makers, administrators, school board members, and others fail to support prevention.

Why then are there so few studies that document the number of students who are targeted?[3] This is a question I'm asked often and have asked myself for decades. Nobody likes topics that are controversial and upsetting. The lobbies for schools and teachers are powerful. Studies are expensive. All this is true. But I have concluded that there is no societal will to know. Children neither vote nor pay taxes. Pressing allegations against educators makes parents feel vulnerable for themselves and their children. Documenting the prevalence of educator sexual misconduct might compromise support for schooling.

Educator sexual abuse has been ignored for years. Why start now? If protecting children had broader support, we would collect data. Questions about school employee sexual misconduct would be added to existing, regularly scheduled federal data collection efforts, or government or foundation funding would be available for new studies.[4]

In the absence of regularly collected data that could not only track abuse but also gauge whether this abuse is increasing or decreasing, there are at least four primary studies that provide a nationwide estimate of the extent of school employee sexual misconduct in K–12 schools.[5] These studies are important because (1) they approximate a national sample and (2) the data is drawn from the reports of students, who are the most reliable reporters of what has been done to them.

LANDMARK STUDIES ON SEXUAL HARASSMENT OF STUDENTS

AAUW 1997, 2001, and Shakeshaft 2004

The American Association of University Women (AAUW) surveyed a representative sample of students asking about their experiences of sexual harassment. In the early 2000s, Congress amended the Elementary and Secondary Education Act of 1965, mandating the conduct of a study of sexual abuse in US schools. The US Department of Education contracted me to do the study.

My job was to produce a synthesis of empirical research on the topic of sexual abuse of students by school employees.

It soon became clear that to be comprehensive and useful, I would need to broaden my search beyond documentation of a very narrow federal definition of sexual abuse which, at the time, was an act where one knowingly "causes another person to engage in a sexual act by threatening or placing that other person in fear" or "engages in a sexual act with another person if that other person is–(A) incapable of appraising the nature of the conduct; or (B) physically incapable of declining participation in, or communicating unwillingness to engage in, that sexual act."

While that definition described two of the several patterns of school employee sexual interactions with students, it left out many that would be inappropriate or criminal between an adult in a position of power and authority and a child. Therefore, I followed the lead of colleagues to the north, at the Ontario College of Teachers, who recommended using the term educator sexual misconduct, which is more inclusive of the behaviors that harm children and that must be prevented. I now use educator sexual misconduct and school employee sexual misconduct interchangeably.

The first task was to document the scope of the problem. As someone who naively assumed that there must be federal and state education and law enforcement data available on prevalence, I was stunned at how little empirical information existed. I found seven informative studies, none of them funded or supported by federal or state agencies or entities. Each used different methods, definitions, and samples. The results ranged from 3.1 percent of students to 50.3 percent of students who experienced educator sexual misconduct by school employees.[6]

The American Association of University Women: 2001

I knew that the AAUW had commissioned an analysis of girls who reported having been abused. The AAUW gave me permission to reanalyze the data that had been collected on their behalf by Harris International in fall 2000.[7]

Using the 2000 Harris data, I found that 9.6 percent of all students in grades 8–11 reported contact or noncontact educator sexual misconduct that was *unwanted*: 8.7 percent reported only noncontact sexual misconduct and 6.7 percent experienced only contact misconduct. (These total to more than 9.6 percent because some students reported both types of misconduct). Because the question asked only about unwanted interactions, these responses probably underestimated the number of students involved in a sexual encounter with a school employee.

In 2015, Frank Hernandez, Jonathon McPhetres, and Jamie Hughes surveyed 1,203 secondary students from three high schools in one Texas school district. The author wrote, "The survey asked about 'consensual sexual relationships between a student and a teacher.'" The authors specified "consensual sexual relationships" because they did not want to confound "willing" interaction with sexual harassment, abuse, and rape.[8] Of the students reporting a "consensual" sexual relationship, 1.5 percent reported they were currently in such a relationship with a school employee, and another 3 percent reported being asked by an employee but declined.

Nearly twenty years after AAUW's path-breaking documentation, two additional studies have provided updates.

Grant et al. 2023

Grant and her colleagues contacted university professors, Title IX officers, and sexual harassment organizations and asked them to distribute the survey to their students and student organizations. Students were asked to think back to their experiences in K–12 schooling—and from the safe distance of post-secondary education. In all, 511 students completed the 8-question survey. There is no information on the region of the country where respondents lived. The researchers surveyed young adults about their experiences of school employee sexual misconduct. Slightly more than half of the students reported they "either knew someone who experienced sexual harassment by a school employee or experienced it themselves."[9] Slightly more than 17.4 percent of students reported experiencing sexual misconduct from a school employee themselves.

Of those who reported being the target of sexual misconduct by a K–12 school employee, 42.9 percent were the targets of verbal sexual misconduct; 39 percent, inappropriate touching; 8 percent, physical sexual contact; 6.4 percent, sexual messages or images; and 3.7 percent, spying. Of the abusers, instructional personnel accounted for 57.1 percent; coaches (who might also be teachers), 33.3 percent; administrators, including principals and district administrators, 1.7 percent; and bus drivers and custodians, 1.4 percent.[10]

These students were primarily abused on school property (82 percent)—classrooms, hallways, athletic facilities, cafeterias, locker rooms, and parking lots. Nearly 15 percent were abused on a field trip, in a driver's education car, or on school transportation; 3 percent report the abuse outside the school but still on school grounds.

In this same study, 40 percent of students were friends with a school employee on social media; of those, 82 percent did not know there was a rule that prohibited school employees from using social media to contact students. Of those who knew about the rule, nearly 58 percent of the students reported that the school district nonetheless allowed students access to an employee's private phone number.

Jeglic et al. 2023

Elizabeth Jeglic and her colleagues also surveyed college students in four state colleges in the United States, asking them to think about their experiences in their K–12 education.[11] The Jeglic team's survey questions were the same or nearly the same questions as those I analyzed from the 2000 AAUW analysis. With 6,632 responses, 11.7 percent of respondents reported experiencing at least one form of educator sexual misconduct in their K–12 school career. Most of the abusers (63.4 percent) were academic teachers; the second most common group was coaches and gym teachers (19.7 percent). Nearly 90 percent were male abusers, and females were 72 percent of those who were abused.[12]

SO WHAT DO WE KNOW NOW?

Both Grant et al. and Jeglic et al. document an increase from the 2000 data I used.[13] The only difference in the three studies was that my analysis of the 2000 results came from eighth- to eleventh-grade students, while the Grant et al. and Jeglic et al. studies asked college students to think back to their K–12 experiences.

These three studies detailed in tables 2.1 and 2.2 provide evidence of an increase in school employee sexual misconduct in the past twenty years. Using US Department of Education K–12 public school enrollment data from fall 2023, I calculated the number of students in each of these studies who would have been the target of sexual misconduct by a public school K–12 employee at some time in their school career.[14] This calculation doesn't include projections for the five million students who attend nonpublic schools or for homeschool students who receive much of their education from vendors and other education service providers.

These are responses from students to surveys that ask about their experiences in K–12 schooling. Most students did not report their abuse to anyone in the school. Reports to friends and family occurred more often, while reports to police were nearly nonexistent. This explains partly why "official" reports of sexual misconduct made to police don't tell the whole story.

TABLE 2.1 Student reports of at least one incident of employee sexual misconduct during K–12 schooling in 2020–2021

Study	Year data collected	Percent reported ESM	Number of K–12 students this represents
Grant et al.	10/2018–4/2019	17.4%	9,430,800
Jeglic et al.	2018–2019	11.7%	6,341,400
Shakeshaft	2000	9.6%	5,200,000

Sources: Billie-Jo Grant, Jeffrey Haverland, and Jessica Kalbfleisch, "Title IX Policy Implementation and Sexual Harassment Prevalence in K–12 Schools," *Educational Policy* (2023): 1–38; Elizabeth L. Jeglic et al., "The Nature and Scope of Educator Misconduct in K–12," *Sexual Abuse* 35, no. 2 (2023): 188–213; Charol Shakeshaft, "Educator Sexual Misconduct: A Synthesis of Existing Literature" US Department of Education, 2004, https://files.eric.ed.gov/fulltext/ED483143.pdf.

TABLE 2.2 Abused students who reported school employee sexual abuse by report recipients

Study	To school officials (includes teachers)	To police, child services	To friends, family
Shakeshaft	6%	Data not collected	69.7% told friends; 31.8% told parents
Grant et al.	4.7% reported to a school employee; 1.9% reported to the Title IX coordinator; 29.6% knew how to report or file a complaint; 6.1% knew who Title IX officer was; the employees who received a report were mandated reporters; only 21.4% filed a complaint	Data not collected	51.9% told friends; 11.9% told parents or other family members
Jeglic et al.	0% disclosed kissing or intercourse/oral sex; 2% reported sexual images/messages; 9% disclosed being sexually touched; 16% who reported sexual touching said that an educator used threats to prevent them from reporting	2% disclosed	49% reported sexual intercourse/oral sex

Sources: Charol Shakeshaft, "Educator Sexual Misconduct : A Synthesis of Existing Literature" US Department of Education, 2004, https://files.eric.ed.gov/fulltext/ED483143.pdf; Billie-Jo Grant, Jeffrey Haverland, and Jessica Kalbfleisch, "Title IX Policy Implementation and Sexual Harassment Prevalence in K–12 Schools," *Educational Policy* (2023): 1–38; Elizabeth L. Jeglic et al., "The Nature and Scope of Educator Misconduct in K–12," *Sexual Abuse* 35, no. 2 (2023): 188–213.

Note: These results also include sexual abuse by peers. The data on who a student tells includes both those who were targets of school employees and those who were targets of peers.

HOW DOES THIS COMPARE WITH NATIONAL AND INTERNATIONAL DATA?

Gewirtz-Meydan and Finkelhor (2020) analyzed data from three US studies of children zero to seventeen years old.[15] Parents answered the questions for children aged zero to nine, and children aged ten to seventeen answered the questions themselves. Of children who reported sexual abuse, the sexual abuse took place in a school or day care/afterschool facility for 11.1 percent of respondents. Of those who reported abuse by an acquaintance (which includes teachers and other school personnel), 6.9 percent of males and 15.4 percent of females reported sexual abuse by an adult acquaintance, for an overall rate of 11 percent.[16]

These national percentages represent students who, when asked, report that they have been the victim of sexual misconduct by an adult working in a school. The proportion of students reporting abuse is far smaller than the number of adults who are reported and investigated. Because one adult might abuse several students, it would make sense that the number of adults reported would be fewer than the number of students who have experienced adult sexual misconduct in schools. But just how different?

We have no US or local studies that answer that question. Certainly, we know that there have not been 9.6 million adults arrested on charges of sexual abuse of students (the Grant study estimate of the number of students who have been abused). Fox News, for instance, reported that in the first 9 months of 2022, 199 public educators in the United States were arrested for sex-related crimes against students. Using that rate, the number arrested over a 13-year period of K–12 schooling would be 318,396, and that is nowhere near the 5.2 million to 9.6 million students who would have been sexually abused during the same period.

A Canadian report indicates that 252 current or former school personnel committed or were accused of committing sexually based offenses against 548 children over a 5-year span. What that tells us is that the average number of students abused per offender *when there is a report* is slightly more than two.

I analyzed numbers in two examples of "best-case" scenarios, meaning school districts that have a special unit to investigate and uncover sex crimes in the schools. In this analysis, I'm making the assumption that such districts are more likely to receive and investigate reports than a district that does not have a designated department for prevention of school employee sexual misconduct.[17] I used the Jeglic et al. finding of 11.7 percent reporting sexual misconduct some time in their K–12 education as the most likely expected proportion of students who were targets of sexual misconduct. I then compared that to the number of reports in the year.

New York City Public Schools

Unlike most cities, the New York City Public Schools established a special commissioner of investigation (SCI) and the Office of the Special Commissioner in 1990. It was created as "a result of the findings and recommendations of the Joint commission on Integrity in Public Schools" and was "entrusted with autonomy in investigations concerning the New York City Department of Education, the largest school district in the nation."[18] The office is separate from the New York City Department of Education and The New York City Department of Investigation. The office of the Special Commission has an investigative capability and is empowered to obtain testimony and records by subpoena.

Edward F. Stancik was the first special commissioner and remained commissioner until his death in 2002, at age 47. A former Manhattan deputy chief attorney, Ed was committed to identifying and stopping corruption in New York's public schools. I had the privilege of membership in an advisory council working with him on school employee sexual misconduct. His investigations were numerous and carefully conducted. This was the first such unit in the United States that specifically included identifying sexual abuse of students by employees, bringing the offenders to justice, and preventing abuse in the future.[19]

In 2021–2022, New York City public school K–12 student enrollment was 957,438 in more than 1,800 schools.[20] If 11.7 percent of students experienced school employee sexual misconduct sometime in their K–12 career, the number would be 112,020. If we divided by 13 for an annual estimate of cases, the most conservative estimate would be 8,617 different students each year.[21]

In 2022, 136 cases of sexual misconduct by Department of Education employees or vendors were reported to the SCI: 40 of those were substantiated.[22] These 40 substantiated cases are very many fewer than the 8,617 students who are projected to have experienced sexual misconduct.

Chicago Public Schools

In 2017, an investigative team comprising Jennifer Smith Richards, David Jackson, Gary Marx, and Juan Perez Jr. from the *Chicago Tribune* obtained data from the police through the Freedom of Information Act on the number of sex crimes in Chicago Public Schools. The team compared police reports with criminal court dockets and civil lawsuit information and then acquired district records on how the allegations had been handled internally. In addition, they interviewed more than one hundred people, including victims and families.[23] They refined the data and focused on the number of police reports between 2008 and 2017.

This investigation opened a window on the extent of school employee sexual misconduct. The reporters found 108 cases that identified 72 school employees.[24] These data include only those reports that were made to the Chicago Police and only those where the sexual abuse occurred on school grounds. Following the *Chicago Tribune*'s exposé, an investigative unit—the Sexual Allegations Unit (SAU)—was established by the Chicago Board of Education Office of the Inspector General (OIG).

In its first year, the office opened over five hundred cases. During its first four years in operation, SAU received 1,735 allegations and closed 1,384 cases alleging adult sexual misconduct with students. Not all those who were determined to be guilty of criminal conduct were criminally charged. SAU provided six circumstances for the seemingly paradoxical outcomes:

- There is a higher burden of proof in the criminal justice system for a conviction than in a school system for removal from the school and loss of license.
- A jury acquits under the higher burden of proof in criminal proceedings.
- The conduct does not meet a criminal definition of sexual abuse but is behavior that violates professional norms between adults and students in schools.
- Victims often deny the abuse, even when the evidence is otherwise. Victims may believe they are in love. They may want the abuse to stop but do not want punishment for the abuser. They may fear harm to themselves or their families if they admit the abuse.
- The victim is unavailable or uncooperative and does not testify.
- The victims come forward after the statute of limitations has expired and criminal charges cannot be brought.[25]

A failure to convict does not mean that harm was not done to a student and does not mean that a school or district cannot deliver consequences to include loss of job and license.

Assuming that each case represented one student (which is a conservative estimate since abusers often target several students at the same time or several students serially), that would be 470 reports of possible sexual misconduct of a student by an employee in 2021–2022. Because we don't know what types of conduct is included as sexual misconduct (hugging, kissing, picture taking, sexual talk, penetration), this too is a high bar that would result in a conservative estimate of actual abuse.

Using the prevalence rate reported by Jeglic et al., we might expect that 39,934 Chicago students would be targets of some form of sexual misconduct in 2021–2022. If we believe that the students in Jeglic's study had only one incident and that it happened in only one grade, and thus looked at a yearly rate, the number would be 3,072 students who were targeted, nearly 6.5 times the number reported to the SAU.[26]

Using New York City and Chicago Public Schools as an example, a conservative estimate of the actual number of cases of school employee sexual misconduct is well above the numbers being investigated. For the sake of this example, I am estimating the number of students in each case who might have experienced school employee sexual misconduct using 11.7 percent as the proportion. I am then dividing that number by thirteen to get an annual estimate. This is, of course, imprecise. We don't know when in their K–12 school career the abuse happened. And for most, it happens over several years. But this method provides the lowest estimate by year for comparison and, therefore, a better understanding of what these numbers mean, as seen in table 2.3.

These numbers are instructive. Most incidents are not reported and therefore not investigated and not stopped. We need to change that pattern.

Other School Districts

A search of sexual abuse cases brought against school districts makes it clear that all types of districts in all states experience school employee sexual misconduct. Henschel and Grant have been following newspaper reports of school employee sexual misconduct since 2014. They report that school

TABLE 2.3   Estimates of actual annual abuse versus investigated abuse (New York City and Chicago)

District	Enrollment K–12	In K–12 career (11.7%)	Annual number abused	Most recent annual reports of incidents of school employee sexual misconduct
NYC	957,438	112,020	8,617	136
Chicago	341,312	39,934	3,072	470

employee sexual misconduct was described in newspaper articles in all states during this period and that 52 percent of all incidents reported were in the southern region of the country. A third of these offenders targeted multiple victims.[27]

A Note on Investigating and Reporting

Comparing the likely large numbers of students who suffer misconduct from school employees each year to the much smaller number of investigations that some districts commission, investigate, and resolve each year demonstrates how big the problem is and how small the responses are. But districts can only investigate what is reported, and the lack of reporting handicaps the ability of investigations to protect children. If educator sexual misconduct is underinvestigated, it is also underreported. This problem is examined in chapter 9.

Homeschool

Critics of homeschooling worry that without oversight, sexual abuse of students by parents might increase. Without a complete understanding of the way homeschool works, these criticisms rarely examine the many other adults with whom homeschooled children interact. Homeschool isn't just children at home with their parents directing their learning. Homeschooling includes private tutors, online educators, cooperative instructors from universities and K–12 schools, and in some cases, intermittent attendance at brick-and-mortar schools. Thus, while the concern might be that parents have free reign to sexually abuse their children without any "outside" oversight, these charges seem more likely to be motivated to protect public school enrollments than to advance the safety of homeschooled children.

Brian Ray and M. Danish Shakeel were curious about whether homeschool represented a safety threat and surveyed a nationally representative sample of homeschooled versus conventionally schooled students.[28] They developed a nine-item sexual abuse variable and analyzed responses where abuse occurred in school by a teacher or other school employee. They then compared the level of sexual abuse in homeschooled versus conventionally schooled settings. They found that for homeschooled children, as for those not homeschooled, the learning done outside the home in organizations and schooling pods is the determining factor for sexual misconduct toward students.[29]

Because homeschool students also attend other organizational learning events—as do conventional school students—there is concern about oversight and the safety of students who work with tutors, organized groups (Boy Scouts, youth organizations), and university instructors. Homeschool parents and children need training about the risks of inappropriate conduct and boundary crossing by adults in these settings, as do public school parents and students.

International Data

A 2022 report from the Canadian Centre for Child Protection examined the number of disciplinary, court, and media public records on teacher discipline. Based on these reports, "252 current or former school personnel working in Canadian K–12 schools . . . committed or were accused of committing offenses of a sexual nature against a minimum of 548 children between 2017 and 2021." At the same time, "38 current or former school personnel were criminally charged for stand-alone pornography-related offenses."

With more than 5.6 million public and private school students in Canada, a conservative estimate would be that nearly 271,000 students were sexually abused by a school employee in that five-year period.[30]

SUMMING UP

School employee sexual misconduct is widespread and occurs across state, national, and international boundaries. The documentation that is available is persuasive and compels action. The following chapters continue to describe the sexual misconduct directed toward students as well as effective prevention actions.

CHAPTER 3

Who Is Harmed?

The effects of school employee sexual misconduct cast a wide net. The individual and organizational costs are great.

Organizations that "allow" sexual misconduct by employees are causing widespread harm by not following prevention practices—harm that extends beyond the target of the abuser to families, peers, the school building, the school district, and the community.

Harm from educator sexual misconduct is often discounted. "It's only a kiss." "She was into me and wanted sex." "Boys always want sex." "It was only a picture." And even if there is a recognition of the injury, it most often is assigned only to the victim.

Of course, the victim is the primary recipient of harm, but others, too, are damaged. In addition to the targeted student, that student's family is disrupted and distressed, often resulting in a breakdown of the relationship between the target student and parents. Other students distrust their perceptions of who in the school they can trust. School employees feel guilt for not noticing and lack of confidence in their own judgments. School resources such as employee time and district funds are spent responding to lawsuits, community upset, and press inquiries instead of educating students. The reputation of the school and district suffers, and that increases resistance to school budgets. Members of the community are at odds with each other, especially when the accused teacher or coach is popular. Insurance companies lose money in court decisions and settlements, and they increase premium costs to schools.

Schools rely on the trust that families and communities provide them. They earn that trust by providing education in a safe environment. The sexual abuse of students by school employees—if unchecked—violates that trust, harms the organization, and diminishes its ability to serve.

TARGETS/VICTIMS

Most estimates of the harm to students who are victimized by school employees have come from generalizing from studies of childhood sexual abuse, not specifically from abuse by school employees. A 2021 systematic review and meta-analysis of studies examining the relationship between child sexual abuse and PTSD found a high risk of PTSD among child sexual abuse survivors. In this study, PTSD was defined by DSM-III, IV, and V (the *Diagnostic and Statistical Manual of Mental Disorders*) to include anxiety disorders, nightmares, disturbed sleep, numbing of responsiveness, insomnia, startle response, irritability, hypervigilance, panic, being easily angered or upset, and difficulty concentrating.

In another review, in 2021, Maria Nagtegaal and Cyril Boonmann examined 261 studies of the problems that survivors of child sexual abuse face and identified five domains: medical, psychological, sexual, repeated (self) harm, and other problems.[1]

Strong relationships between child sexual abuse were found with sleep disorders, psychological nonepileptic seizures, and self-injury (suicide attempts). Medium-strong relationships were identified between child sexual abuse and gynecological problems, distress such as anxiety or depression, psychosis, adolescent pregnancy, risky sexual behavior in adolescent boys, multiple sexual partners and pregnancy involvement, self-injury (other injuries), suicidal ideation, and interpersonal dependency. A medium relation was found for chronic pelvic pain, fibromyalgia, and HIV in men who had sex with men.

The following is from a 2023 victim statement in court. She is a 33-year-old woman who had been raped by her teacher. She had attended a private school until her sophomore year, when she sought safety in a public school. She recounted her personal harm and told a story that generalizes across other cases of school employee sexual misconduct:

> As a child . . . I was an exemplary student, always maintaining a high GPA. I was an avid ballet dancer, played piano for years, and dabbled in a number of other extracurricular activities. I recall stepping onto the campus [of her new public school] the first day and thought it was "so cool" to see that we had a police officer just for our campus. I believed it to be the safest place besides my home or parents' business, as every school I had attended prior was safe. [I believed the] campus was filled with trustworthy people: teachers, administrators. . . . Instead, [name of school] being a safe haven for me, it became the location of my death.

You see, I died on [date of rape]. Not in the literal sense obviously, but the person I was before that day no longer existed and regardless of my actions, she would never come back. I stopped dancing, stopped playing piano, became extremely withdrawn all the while trying to keep a smile on my face so no one would know what you did to me. My love of school and education quickly withered and, at fifteen, I was faced with grown-up decisions because you decided to hurt me. I tried to "protect" myself by wearing layers of clothing, but your attacks became more violent and two weeks before my sixteenth birthday, you decided that molesting and fondling was no longer enough. I remember opening my mouth to scream and nothing came out. I remember trying to fight, but it was impossible. Every day after school, I would scrub my skin hard enough, trying to erase anything you touched. My nighttime prayers changed from "Now I lay me down to sleep, I pray the Lord my soul to keep, if I die before I wake, I pray the Lord my soul to take" to begging and pleading with God that each night would be my last.

This victim continued to explain that since the rape, every decision she made was based on the safety of herself and her parents. She panicked over the smallest changes in plans. From that time to when she made her statement, she "didn't party, didn't enjoy life," never drank alcohol, dressed extremely conservatively, didn't wear makeup, and "kept myself as plain looking as possible just to be sure I'm not targeted and sexually assaulted. . . . My parents watched as their happy, innocent, intelligent daughter was changed into a cold and withdrawn shell."[2]

The after-effects of the years of abuse from the teacher left her with "chronic PTSD, severe depression, and anxiety" along with a disease that requires "around the clock attention." She reminded the court and the abuser that "your selfish actions" affected not only her and those who love her, but also her entire immigrant community.

She not only pointed out the harm from the abuser but also from those administrators and teachers who stood by and did nothing. "You [abuser] took my life from me, but you also had help along the way. You raped me at school, where I should have been protected. Your school colleagues knew you were dangerous, yet they never did a thing about it." Even after the arrest, school personnel blamed her and took revenge on her throughout her last two years of high school.

None of what this courageous survivor related in her victim statement is unusual. Unfortunately, it is a valid litany of the harm to the victim, the family, the school, and the community. It makes clear that what was done to her, although primarily the fault of the abuser, was also enabled by school professionals who not only did nothing to stop the teacher's sexual misconduct and rape, but also did nothing to help her recover from trauma. In addition to the harm sexual abuse does to a child, there is harm from the way the child is treated by the organization that allowed the harm to occur.

Sexual assault is one of the adverse childhood experiences (ACEs) that have been studied since the mid-1980s. These are childhood traumatic experiences such as witnessing or experiencing violence, abuse or neglect, witnessing violence in the home or community, having a family member attempt or die by suicide, and environmental stressors such as substance abuse, mental health problems, and instability because of parental separation such a divorce or prison.[3]

The ACE studies examine the relationship between the type and number of adverse childhood experiences and the health and well-being of the adult. The first large-scale study, which has been replicated hundreds of times, indicates that adverse childhood experiences are more common than acknowledged, and they have a powerful impact on adult health, even up to a half-century later.[4] These adverse childhood experiences have a compounding effect on child and adult wellbeing. The more ACEs experienced, the higher the risk for adverse outcomes. While not everyone who experiences trauma as a child ends up with mental and physical health outcomes as an adult, the relationship is strong.

The Centers for Disease Control and Prevention notes that the chronic health outcomes of ACEs include chronic obstructive pulmonary disease, asthma, kidney disease, stroke, coronary heart disease, cancer, diabetes, and obesity.[5] Depression and suicide or attempted suicide are mental health conditions that arise from ACEs. The health risk behaviors more common among those with high ACE scores are smoking, alcohol abuse, substance abuse, physical inactivity, and risky sexual behavior. Social outcomes are failure to complete high school, unemployment, and lack of health insurance.[6]

ACEs, such as sexual abuse, have been linked to higher levels of shame.[7] Shame is a self-conscious and aversive emotion and is exhibited through withdrawal, avoidance, attack of self, and attack of others. The most likely scenario of shame from sexual abuse is to attack oneself. There is a relationship between the amount of shame and the amount of self-harm.[8] As an adult looking back, a woman who was sexually abused by her teacher for two years described her shame:

Shame has a way of piercing the heart and crushing the soul. Perhaps more damaging than the causal event, shame isolated me from my peers and made me feel confused, alone, and disconnected. I became terrified of people and always assumed that they were judging me like they did in high school. The isolation of high school led to the isolation in college, medical school, residency, and beyond. How could I explain to others that my first sexual relationship was with my 39-year-old high school English teacher.

Shame differs from guilt. Guilt is concern with one's responsibility for a harmful attitude or behavior, while shame is a negative self-evaluation.[9] For instance, a person who is feeling guilt might say, "What I did was bad." A person feeling shame would say, "I am bad."

One survivor, trying to account for the effects of sexual abuse from a teacher, related:

It wasn't until many years later that I realized how profoundly wrong this experience was. I just pushed it down, pretending it didn't happen, but it continued to haunt me. . . . As an adult, I continued to isolate myself and had trouble with confidence, self-esteem, and forming relationships with others. I kept my pain well-hidden and have struggled with depression, anxiety, and an eating disorder that went on for many years. After graduation . . . I made a suicide attempt. I came to believe that something was profoundly wrong with me and that my self-worth was dependent on my appearance and sexual desirability. . . . I have been hiding out and holding back most of my life, burying myself in my work.

ORGANIZATIONAL BETRAYAL COMPOUNDS HARM TO VICTIMS

A number of researchers have documented the harm to children when the institution they trusted fails to protect them. Walsh and Krienert note that realizing "the relationship was exploitive or formed through manipulation, may cause deep-seated victimization."[10] Smith and Freyd have studied institutional betrayal, the identification of victims with the institution, and posttraumatic symptoms such as dissociation, anxiety, depression, sleep problems, sexual problems, and other impacts on victims.[11] They concluded that "added betrayal surrounding sexual assault exacerbates what is already a traumatic experience."[12] These authors also noted that betrayals leading up to sexual assault, "such as creating an environment that is conducive to sexual assault," were most commonly reported as betrayal of the student by the organization. One factor of an environment that is conducive to sexual assault is the failure to listen to students, to ask questions, or to credit or inquire into their responses.

Self-Inflicted Harm to Offenders and Their Families

Sexual misconduct with a student also harms the offender and the offender's family. It interferes with relationships with spouses, children, friends, and colleagues. Kurt Brundage, a high school English teacher, wrote about his experience as an offender who was arrested and spent "two years, one month, and three days in prison":[13]

> I was a 35-year-old man living with my parents, sleeping in the bedroom I grew up in, unable to live at home with my wife and daughter; the state decided my charges somehow automatically meant I was a danger to anyone under the age of eighteen, and I was therefore prohibited from having any contact with any minor, including my own daughter. I had . . . earned supervised visitation rights—but I could not spend the night in my own house where my wife and daughter lived. We were not allowed to be a family. This is what a ruined life looks like.[14]

Although this child offender detailed the effects of having sexually abused a minor student and described the grimness of life in jail and then in prison, he wasn't able to take responsibility for his own ruin. He blamed the state for not being able to live at home with his wife and daughter. There is something pitiful in his charge that "no one ever seems to contemplate what the lives of these teachers . . . look like after all the headlines have passed and sentences expire." But a fair assessment of his life is that he harmed himself and his family.

Often the offender's children attend the same school or school district in which the offender taught. The children have to continue to come to a school where their parent been accused of abuse and most often arrested and convicted. The conflicting emotions of shame, anger, and love that the children of offenders experience are seldom addressed.

The Harm to the Organization's Reputation

A 2022 report on school employee sexual misconduct in Canada identifies erosion of trust: "The failure to keep children safe from educator sexual misconduct erodes trust in our school system. Public trust is further eroded when cases are mismanaged, downplayed, or covered up in attempts to protect the school's reputation."[15] The erosion of trust is attached not only to the school where the abuse took place, but to schools in general.

Financial Costs to Victims of Sexual Abuse

I could find no studies specifically calculating the financial costs to students who have been sexually victimized by school employees, but there are many studies about the costs to victims and society in general. Students who are sexually abused have a higher than average likelihood of dropping out of school and missing more days of school each year than students who aren't abused. These risks may be exacerbated when the abuser is a school employee. Sexual abuse victims incur medical and psychological costs throughout their lifetime. The adult outcomes of substance abuse, obesity, diabetes, and other mental and physical health outcomes related to childhood sexual abuse accrue costs to the individual as well as society. Victimization is also associated with increased child welfare needs and costs, both for the victim as a child and for the victim as a parent of a child.[16]

A 2018 study by Letourneau et al. of the costs of child sexual abuse during the victim's lifetime notes that at the time of their study, they found only three other studies—one in 1996, one in 2003, and another in 2015—estimating the economic burden of child sexual abuse.[17] Based on research of the effect on victims of child sexual abuse, Letourneau et al. calculated the average lifetime costs for female and male victims of child sexual abuse.[18] This calculation includes costs for childhood health care, adult health care, lifetime productivity loss, child welfare, violence/crime, special education, and suicide death. Children with special needs are more likely to be sexually abused than children who do not receive special services. These services increase after sexual abuse occurs.[19] The risk of suicide among those sexually abused as children is higher than those not sexually abused. Letourneau et al., using Cutajar et al. as a base, estimated those costs.[20] They also developed and included an estimate of quality-adjusted losses (QALY). They did not include this in the average lifetime cost total but pointed out the importance of understanding the impact and cost of child sexual abuse through a lifetime.

Productivity Costs

Letourneau et al. relied upon two studies that estimated the effect of child sexual abuse on the wages of adult females to result in 20.3 percent lower wages than those of women who weren't sexually abused as children (productivity losses).[21] There were no differences in estimates of male productivity between those who had been abused and those who had not.

A Canadian collaboration of twelve researchers from six institutions analyzed data from the Quebec Longitudinal Study of Kindergarten Children (QLSKC), which had collected data from 3,030 children every two years between 1986 and 2017.[22] In the last data collection period, the sample responded to questions from the Adverse Childhood Experiences Questionnaire and the Sexually Victimized Childhood Questionnaire. Federal government income tax returns were collected between the ages of eighteen and thirty-seven. Earnings were calculated using the mean of the five most recent tax returns when the earners were between the ages of thirty-three and thirty-seven.

Bouchard et al. found that those who had been sexually abused as children had $4,382 lower annual earnings at age thirty-three, adjusted for sex, than those who were not victims of child sexual abuse.[23] The average earnings of those who experienced interfamilial sexual abuse as children were less than the earnings of those experiencing extrafamilial sexual abuse (which would include sexual abuse by a school employee), except in cases where the extrafamilial abuse included penetration.

Bouchard et al.'s 2017 lost productivity costs of $4,382 a year were calculated for forty-six years and converted to the value of 2015 and 2023 dollars for comparison with Letourneau.[24] I have provided both the Letourneau et al. and the Bouchard et al. productivity costs in table 3.1.

Average Lifetime Cost per Victim

The calculations in table 3.1 provide a comprehensive picture of the average costs that those who are sexually abused as children "pay" because of the psychological, physical, and emotional damage that they experienced. If we average the estimates cited earlier in this chapter of the number of students who are the victims of school employee sexual misconduct during K–12 and divide by twelve, we have an estimate of 438,117 students that would experience abuse in the coming year. The cost to the country for those abused in just 2024 will be between $81.1 and $112.4 billion.

Financial Cost to Schools

The number of civil lawsuits against both public and private school districts has increased over time. Companies that insure schools have been aware of the rising costs of settlements and damage awards for victims of school employee sexual misconduct. United Educators (UE) was one of the first, along with The Washington Schools Risk Management Pool (WSRMP), to try to reduce sexual abuse by school employees through training for their members.[25] Both regularly work with member organizations on strategies to prevent sexual abuse. An analysis by WSRMP of both student-to-student and teacher-to-student sexual misconduct claims in 2018 indicated that in

TABLE 3.1 Cost analyses of child sexual abuse

Type of cost	Data from Letourneau et al.				Data from Bouchard et al.	
	Female (2015)	Female (2023)	Male (2015)	Male (2023)	Female & male (2015)	Female & male (2023)
Health and welfare costs ($)						
Child health care costs ($)	14,357	18,453	14,357	18,643	14,357	18,377
Adult health care costs ($)	9,882	12,701	9,882	12,701	9,882	12,649
Child welfare costs ($)	8,333	10,710	8,333	10,710	8,333	10,666
Productivity costs ($)	223,581	286,887	0	0	194,908	250,095
Loss of wages ($)						
Violence/crime costs						
Assault ($)	1,389	1,785	1,389	1,785	1,389	1,778
Robbery ($)	909	1,168	909	1,168	909	1,164
Burglary ($)	113	145	113	145	113	145
Theft >$50 ($)	23	30	23	30	23	29
Other costs						
Special education costs ($)	3,760	4,833	3,760	4,833	3,760	4,813
Suicide deaths ($)	20,387	26,203	20,387	26,203	20,387	26,095
Total cost ($)	292,734	376,251	74,691	96,000	302,270	386,906
Additional costs						
Quality-of-life losses measured (QALY) ($)	41,001	52,699	38,904	50,003	39,953	51,139

Sources: Elizabeth J. Letourneau et al., "The Economic Burden of Child Sexual Abuse in the United States," *Child Abuse & Neglect* 79 (2018): 413–22; Amy E. Bonomi et al., "Health Care Utilization and Costs Associated with Childhood Abuse," *Journal of General and Internal Medicine*, 23, no. 3 (2008): 294–99; Kerry DeVooght, Robert Green, and Tiffany Allen, "Federal, State, and Local Spending to Address Child Abuse and Neglect in SFY 2006," https://www.aspponline.org/docs/sex_abuse_7Child_Trends-2009_02_17_FR_CWFinancePaper.pdf; John Robst, "Childhood Sexual Abuse and the Gender Wage Gap," 99, no. 3 (2008): 549–51; Bernadette D. Proctor, Jessica L. Semega, and Melissa A. Kollar, "Income and Poverty in the United States: 2015," US Department of Commerce, September 2016, https://www.census.gov/library/publications/2016/demo/p60-256.html; Samantha Bouchard et al., "Child Sexual Abuse and Employment Earnings in Adulthood," *American Journal of Preventive Medicine* 65, no. 1 (2023): 83–91; Janet Currie and Erdal Tekin, "Understanding the Cycle," *Journal of Human Resources* 47, no. 2 (2012): 509–49; Lance Lochner and Enrico Moretti, "The Effect of Education on Crime," *American Economic Review* 94, no. 1 (2004): 155–89; Melissa Jonson-Reid et al., "A Prospective Analysis of the Relationship Between Reported Child Maltreatment and Special Education Eligibility," *Child Maltreatment*, 9, no. 4 (2004): 382–94; Arthur J. Reynolds et al., "Age 21 Cost-Benefit Analysis," *Educational Evaluation and Policy Analysis* 24, no. 4 (2002): 267–303; Margaret C. Cutajar et al., "Suicide and Fatal Drug Overdose in Child Sexual Abuse Victims," *Medical Journal of Australia* 192, no. 4 (2010): 184–87; "Fatal Injury and Violence Data," WISQARS Injury Center, https://wisqars.cdc.gov/; Phaedra S. Corso et al., "Health-Related Quality of Life Among Adults Who Experienced Maltreatment During Childhood," *American Journal of Public Health* 98, no. 6 (2008): 1094–100; Linda Ryen and Mikael Svensson, "The Willingness to Pay for a Quality Adjusted Life Year: A Review of the Empirical Literature," Health Economics 24, no. 10 (2015): 1289–301.

484 closed cases over eight academic years between 2010 and 2018, there was a 53 percent increase in claims from the first four years (2010–2014) to the last four years (2014–2018). Average closed case claim settlements went from $172,000 in 2010–2011 to $8.1 million in 2017–2018.[26] Overall, comparing 2010–2014 to 2014–2019, the average total claims were $2.17 million to $22.82 million.[27] While these costs are paid by insurance companies, eventually the costs come back to the school or school district and its taxpayers in increased premiums.

The settlement and damage awards in recent verdicts are high. UE, like other insurers, has raised the definition of what constitutes a large loss. For UE, $250,000 was considered a large loss in 2020, but by the end of 2022, $1 million or more constituted a large loss, "based on a sea change in the volume of losses at higher ed and K–12 schools."[28] Some of the K–12 payments in 2022 included the following:

- $102.5 million to two students in the San Jose Unified School District who were abused by a middle school music teacher
- $52 million to multiple plaintiffs sexually abused by a high school wrestling coach
- $17.5 million to multiple victims in the 1970s–1980s who were abused by an elementary school teacher in the Tonawanda Union Free School District
- $14.7 million to seven students abused by an elementary school teacher when they were nine and ten in the Los Angeles Unified School District
- $13.7 million to ten students abused by a school technology aide between 2014 and 2017
- $10 million to a nine-year-old special needs student molested in 2017 by a bus driver in the Lucia Mar Unified School District in Arroyo Grande, California
- $9 million to students abused by a bus driver in the Clark County School District in Nevada
- $7.5 million to four men who were abused in the late 1970s and early 1980s by a teacher in the San Jose School District when they were in elementary school
- $3.5 million to students abused by a teacher in the 1980s in the Marysville School District in Washington
- $3.4 million to a student track athlete abused by an assistant coach in high school

- $3 million to a student who was abused by a high school coach and instructional assistant in the Seattle Public Schools
- $2 million to a student sexually abused by her Spanish teacher in the San Jose Unified School District in California
- $1 million to a student who was sexually assaulted by a teacher in the Concord School District in New Hampshire; another student was awarded $545,000 in 2020 for abuse by the same teacher

MOVING FORWARD

School employee sexual misconduct harms the children, their families, the families of abusers, members of the school community, the community at large, and even the offenders. The costs to all are high, with the highest costs borne by the student victims, both in the abuse and in the post-traumatic stress that follows.

PART II

Who, What, Where, and How

CHAPTER 4

Abusers

FROM A STUDENT: He was a really great teacher. I can't believe he could have done what they are saying he did. I wouldn't have graduated if he hadn't helped me. And I know lots of other kids that wouldn't have made it without him.

FROM A TEACHER: She's married with three children, for God's sake. And she's old. I just don't see her having sex with high school students. She is not that kind of person. She teaches physics, and she sings in the choir. She coaches girls' volleyball.

It's hard for many people to believe that a teacher would sexually abuse a student. It may be especially hard for fellow teachers and other educators. Most ask the reasonable question, "Who would do a thing like that?"

It is an appropriate question. Who are they? Males? Females? Beginning teachers? Veteran teachers? Substitute teachers? Good teachers? Bad teachers? White teachers? Black teachers? Latina/o teachers? Band directors? Drama club sponsors? Coaches? Counselors? Administrators? Bus drivers? People who are married? Single? People with children? Heterosexual? Homosexual? Church goers? Atheists? Pedophiles? Unethical narcissists?

Yes.

Put away the stereotype of the creepy guy who slinks around corners and forces himself on an unsuspecting student. That's not what school employee sex offenders look like or how they act. But first, what to call them? *Boundary crossers, predators, sexual abusers,* or *exploiters*? As accurate as those labels are, none completely bracket the range of predators, motives, behaviors, and outcomes; there is no single modus operandi (MO). I use the label *abuser* to describe sexual misconduct of students, but it could just as well be *trust breaker, criminal, liar, narcissist,* or *killer of souls.*

To protect children, we must ask, "Protect from whom?" The prevailing thought has been that this requires knowing as much as possible about the demographic characteristics of abusers. I argue that although it is helpful to know the personal descriptors of those who abuse, it isn't the most effective way to prevent the sexual abuse of students. Implementing and enforcing organizational practices are more direct and successful.

The most helpful thing about those demographics is realizing that almost anyone in the school could be an abuser. Therefore, we must look at what employees do and how they interact with students, not just their demographic descriptors. Despite the lack of predictive power of demographic characteristics, knowing a bit about who abuses helps to remind us to be universally watchful and not to count anyone out.

Psychologists, criminal justice officials, and mental health professionals agree that there is no omnibus description of child sexual offenders, and my research supports these conclusions. However, some consistent characteristics set them apart, starting with the understanding that school employees who sexually abuse students are takers, not givers. They are all about what they want, not what the child needs.

James Martin is a Jesuit priest who has written about sexual abuse in the Catholic Church. Martin notes that two traits of a sexual abuser are narcissism and grandiosity. Martin describes the narcissism:

> When an emotionally healthy person accidentally does something offensive to someone and notices another person recoil or senses a feeling of discomfort in the other, the healthy person will stop because he or she respects the needs of others. To take a benign example, if you are speaking to someone at a party and physically move too close, accidentally invading someone's "personal space," you may notice the other person take a step back. If you are healthy, you will say to yourself, "I'm making someone feel uncomfortable." And you will take a step back as well.
>
> When the narcissist, however, experiences another person's recoil or discomfort, he will not take that step back. He will not consider the other's feelings. He may not even notice those feelings. Why? Because, as the saying goes, "It's all about him." The narcissist's needs are paramount. This, in part, helps to explain the tragic tendency of the abuser to continue to abuse even when the other is clearly suffering.[1]

Grandiosity is "often the 'Pied Piper,'" who easily gathers around students, football players, altar boys, or adults. Often a larger-than-life character, he may be an organization's charismatic founder, the successful school president, the beloved teacher, the energetic Scoutmaster, the popular pastor, or the well-respected principal.[2] Children and adolescents gravitate toward him because of his charisma, and more importantly, because of his exalted status, adults may feel more comfortable leaving their children in his care. In my research, the abusers who fit this description are male. Females behave somewhat differently, as will be evident in the descriptions of abuse patterns later in this book.

Abusers of middle and high school students are, more often than not, adults who take sexual advantage of a situation but who may not be exclusively attracted to children or teenagers. These adults tend to be emotionally arrested and operate at a teenage level. They are adults with boundary and judgment problems and are not difficult to identify once others in the school or district learn to recognize them. They are sometimes referred to as opportunistic abusers.

One way to classify abusers is to separate them into two classes—*fixated* (sometimes referred to as preferential) and *opportunistic*. Fixated abusers, in my studies, are more likely to concentrate on elementary and early middle school children. And there seem to be fewer reports of their abuse. This may be because there is less abuse of younger children in schools or because younger children don't know how to report or understand what is being done to them by a teacher. But no matter the motivation of abusers, these offenders can be stopped.

The majority who cross sexual boundaries with students in the data for this book are opportunistic; they are not "programmed" or "predisposed to abuse." Instead, they take advantage of students and an organizational culture of willful blindness—looking away from employee misconduct. They see a student's vulnerability and exploit it—a single-parent home, declining grades, uncertain sexual identity. And they recognize the latitude their schools grant them—ignoring closed-door meetings with selected students, blaming the student victims, refusing to inquire about "plain sight" misconduct. Opportunistic abusers are described in various ways—exploiters, people with impaired judgment, and narcissists. I think of them as members of an organization and how the organization's actions and inactions shape or allow their behavior.

Both fixated (preferential) and opportunistic abusers spend a lot of time around youths, talking with them, going to the same places they go, and trying to blend in. They are often adults who want to be hip or cool and want the children in their organization to think they are part of the youth peer group. Their conversations with youths are often inappropriately personal.

They also know a great deal about the private lives of individual youths, more than would be available to an adult whose interactions were only supervisory or appropriately friendly. These abusers also overshare their personal lives, providing youths with information about themselves that should be private.

For my purposes, these classifications aren't necessary for prevention. Looking at the behaviors of adults, rather than classifications, is more likely to help identify boundary crossing and possible red flags for prevention.

PROFESSIONAL ROLE IN SCHOOL

Several studies have helped identify the roles that abusers hold in schools. The American Association of University Women (AAUW) collected data in 1993 and 2000 on sexual harassment in schools. I analyzed the data from AAUW's national stratified random sample of over 2,064 students in grades 8–11 at one point describing incidents in their school careers.[3] Slightly more than 40 percent of the students' abusers were teachers. The balance came from multiple school titles and functions. It is unclear if any of these abusers were reported to the police.

Billie Jo Grant and colleagues analyzed cases of school employee sexual misconduct reported in US newspapers and archived with Google alerts.[4] Their research (and Grant's continuing monitoring of over 4,600 newspaper reports) has the advantage that the incidents were reported to the police and made public. The most recent update from their research (through May 2023) in table 4.1 indicates that teachers represent the largest group of those who sexually abuse students. Many teachers also serve as coaches, band directors, and advisors to extracurricular activities, giving them additional touch points and opportunities to groom students.

A breakdown of the newspaper reports of teachers indicates that many are in jobs after or before school and have opportunities for time alone with students. Among teachers (who accounted for 87 percent of the reports), a large number were identified through these auxiliary roles: 17 percent were also band directors and coaches; 9 percent were teachers of music/art; 3 percent were exceptional education teachers; 3 percent PE teachers; 2 percent taught electives. The remainder were teachers of the core curriculum.

In looking at these two columns, the reports' differences are striking. In the first column, the incidents come from over two thousand students reporting what was done to them. Very few, if any, of these incidents were reported to administrators or the police. The second table includes 4,226 public reports

TABLE 4.1   Percentage of offenders by school job title

Job title	Percentage reported by students (2000)	Percentage reported in newspapers (2014–2023)
Teacher (substitutes, dual roles)	18	87
Coach (teacher-coaches, volunteers, substitutes, dual roles)	15	12
Substitute teacher	13	7
Bus driver	12	0
Teacher's aide/para educator	11	4
Other employee	10	3
Security guard/resource officer	10	0
Principal, other administrators	6	1
Counselor	5	0

in newspapers over eight years. Newspaper stories focus on a much higher proportion of teachers than the student identification of the abuser (87 percent versus 18 percent) and a lower proportion of administrators (1 percent versus 6 percent). In addition to administrators, students report a higher proportion of abuse by "other staff," such as bus drivers and resource officers. The two sources are close to agreement on the proportion of coaches. Both sources are helpful.

Nearly 40 percent of full-time secondary educators have some coaching responsibility.[5] Among coaches who sexually abuse, male coaches of female teams are highly represented in coach abuse categories. One New Jersey newspaper reported that in five years, sixteen male coaches and one female coach were convicted for sexually abusing students.[6] Many had been abusing students for years. A study in Washington State noted that teachers who coach were "three times more likely to be investigated by the state for sexual misconduct than non-coaching teachers."[7]

Don't imagine that those in charge of schools don't cross the line. Assistant principals, principals, superintendents, and school board members have crossed sexual boundaries with students. For example, four students at Deep Creek Elementary School in Hillsboro, Oregon, charged the principal with sexual abuse between 2005 and 2009. According to the students, he would use the intercom to summon students into his office for "one-on-one" math tutorials. He would then close the blinds, shut the door, and abuse them "steps away from the school's two secretaries."[8]

SEX OF OFFENDER

My research and that of others include information on male and female offenders.[9] My case studies of sexual abuse of students by a school employee who was convicted are essentially studies of male school employee abusers (89 percent).[10] Student reports and analysis of records document that more men than women are the instigators in school employee sexual misconduct cases. The US Department of Education study reported 61 percent male and 39 percent female offenders.[11] The Henschel and Grant study indicates that 67 percent of offenders were male.[12] My case study data set contains fewer female abusers, which I'll discuss more fully in this book's reporting, investigation, and consequences sections.

Female Offenders

There has been an increase in the number of females officially identified as offenders since I began my work, but females are still less likely to be recognized as abusers than males. In 2013, the US Department of Health and Human Services reported that 88 percent of substantiated sexual abuse claims are against male offenders and 9 percent are against females.[13] There is insufficient evidence to determine if the fewer reports are a function of less criminal behavior on the part of women or less reporting of the criminal behavior. A 2017 meta-analysis of seventeen samples from twelve countries published in *Criminal Justice and Behavior* found a similar discrepancy: more abuse by both females and males than reported or investigated.[14] These reports were of all sexual abuse (intra- and extra-familial), not just that in schools.

My studies have focused on schools and cast a wider net of what is identified as sexual abuse (this includes all forms of sexual misconduct, not just physical sexual abuse) and a narrower net in the type of abuse than either of these two studies (sexual misconduct in schools). In the reports of students about their own experiences of school employee sexual misconduct, my 2004 study put the proportion of female offenders at 39 percent. A 2016 meta-analysis published by *Criminal Justice and Behavior* concluded that of all sexual abuse of minors, only 2 percent of reported sex offenders are female.[15]

One reason for these differences may be the types of abuse reported (criminal/physical sexual abuse versus sexual misconduct) or the type of abuser (all people versus school employees). It may also be that female offenders are not reported to administrators or the police as often as male offenders.[16]

The Grant et al. 2017 newspaper study referenced earlier reported that the number of news stories of female abusers over nine years (2014–2023) ranged from a low of 18.18 percent (2015) to a high of 28.64 percent (2014).[17] There was no consistent pattern. Overall, 23.3 percent reported female abusers and 76.6 percent reported male abusers. This proportion is puzzling since it is more than twice the proportion reported by students. It begs the question of what newspapers choose to publish and why.

Forty years ago, when I started this research, many considered that sex from an adult female to a minor (male) student, if not a "good" thing, was at least not harmful. We knew then and know now that this isn't true. However, there was a stereotype that adolescent boys only want sex. Thus, sex from a teacher couldn't be harmful. The stereotype excused the abuser and explained the disinterest of schools in stopping inappropriate and illegal behavior between adult females and male students. The gendered language of sexual violence—predators, hunters, violators—uses "active, aggressive, and traditionally masculine words that are consequently not readily culturally applicable to women."[18] Young noted that the consequence of these descriptions resulted in victims' inability to describe what happened to them with female school employees as sexual abuse.

Mary Kay Letourneau was perhaps the most famous case that went to trial and ended with a prison sentence for sexual intercourse with her sixth-grade student. She became a joke on late-night TV, and the public discussion, by and large, failed to identify harm to the minor male student. But she also cast the female abuser as troubled and needy.

Male Offenders

The overrepresentation of men as abusers in schools is significant. To look only at the percentages of sex of abusers is to fail to consider the disproportions by sex in teaching and other school roles. There are fewer males among the ranks of teachers, yet there are more male teachers among the ranks of abusers; they are overrepresented. Among employees, males are 25 percent of professional educators and are responsible for over 60 percent of all educator sexual misconduct. Females are 75 percent of the profession and are responsible for less than 40 percent of sexual misconduct.[19] Males are five times more likely than females to sexually abuse students. In other words, one-fourth of the school's professional force accounts for 60 percent of the sexual abuse of students. In my case studies of abuse of elementary school children, all offenders have been males. Females are more likely to abuse high school boys.

Same-Sex Offenders

While the assigned sex identification of offenders is recorded, the sexual orientation of offenders is unavailable in any of the relevant datasets. Even if it were recorded, self-identified sexual orientation is not the same as sexual behavior. For instance, I examined 225 cases of educator physical sexual misconduct in New York.[20] Of the one-quarter (24 percent) of the males who had same-sex encounters with students, *all* described themselves as heterosexual, with most living in married or heterosexual relationships.[21] In my case studies of school sexual misconduct, the majority of the males who targeted males were married to or living with a female. Because some individual predators may victimize both sexes, the variance in behavior patterns can be better described on a *scale* from exclusively same-sex targets to exclusively other-sex targets.

Larissa Christensen and Andrea Darling found gender differences in the patterns of teachers who sexually abused students. Male teachers were older, perpetrated more severe and protracted abuse, and received more previous warnings of boundary-crossing behavior than females.[22] Said differently, school administrators were more tolerant of male teachers' abuse than that of female teachers. Men got warned; women got terminated.

Louise Rooney examined the relationship of personal conceptions of masculinity to the motivations of male child sexual abusers. In her studies, the males had distinct gender themes of powerlessness, entitlement, risk-taking, and rigid thinking. Powerless male abusers had nostalgic views of childhood, experiences of trauma or abuse, inability to seek help, and experiences of humiliation or rejection. All of these were experienced or described by males as masculine failures. Those who embraced an entitlement worldview were resentful that they weren't receiving the male privilege to which they were entitled. Risk-takers came from a foundation of boredom, and rigid thinkers and displayed inconsistent or illogical cognitive patterns, poor boundary settings, and inflexible or unattainable religious ideals. Rooney concludes that "men's offenses against children can be interpreted as over-compensatory behavior occurring with the spectrum of normative masculinities."[23]

EXCUSES, EXCUSES, EXCUSES

Mollee Smith has studied male sex offenders and "distorted attitudes and beliefs, or rationalizations, that minimize the severity of their offending."[24] Offenders use justifications and excuses. Justifications are defenses such as "I didn't do any harm; this was consensual," "I helped [the victim] have a better life through tutoring and support," "She came on to me," "She wanted it," "I wouldn't have touched her if she had said no." Some abusers admit their actions and then try to justify their claim that there was nothing wrong with what they did and that they behaved appropriately. Those who use excuses and realize what they did was wrong counter by saying it was an accident, they were under the influence of drugs or alcohol, they experienced emotional deregulation such as depression, they had experienced a disruption of family circumstances such as a divorce, or they were a victim of sexual abuse as a child.

Women, but not men, have reported being overpowered by a male student.[25] Women are also more likely than men to report the abuse as a "relationship" and justify it by saying they had romantic feelings for their target. Like men, they blame the victim for flirting, pursuing, or instigating the sexual interaction.

BECOMING AN ABUSER

It is commonly believed that being abused as a child leads to the child becoming an adult abuser of children, particularly male abusers. Some adult male abusers claim their childhood victimization as explaining their perpetration of the same crime on their victims once they become adults. The childhood experience does not excuse adult crime.

There is a difference between female survivors of childhood sexual abuse and male survivors. More females (20 percent of girls) than males (5 percent of boys) are sexually abused as children.[26] Yet, according to the National Sexual Violence Resource Center, 96 percent of people who sexually abuse children are male.[27] It seems unlikely that 5 percent of those harmed as a child would account for 96 percent of abusers.

Jan Hindman and James Peters have examined the adult consequences of childhood sexual abuse. Hindman and Peters debunk the myth of abused-as-abuser for males.[28] They studied convicted adult offenders who had entered Hindman's treatment center in Oregon over eight years. In one study, sex offenders were asked to recount their sexual histories. Some were told that a polygraph would assess the truth of their accounts. Others did not have a polygraph recording. With the polygraph, 29 percent of the (convicted) offenders said they had been abused as children; without it, 57 percent claimed to have been abused as children. Because nearly all of the studies that explore the relationship between being an abuser and having been abused as a child are studies of incarcerated or soon-to-be incarcerated people, this link is believed to be exaggerated to plea bargain a lighter sentence. The Hindman and Peters study suggests that childhood abuse claims are exaggerated and probably exploited.

Additionally, when a polygraph was present, these convicted offenders described committing *nine times* more cases of sexual abuse than when no polygraph was used.

While evidence indicates that adult abusers were not necessarily abused as children, there is an additional question. When did the adult abusers begin their career of abuse? Were they children abusing other children? Hindman and Peters also explored whether the convicted adult offenders abused other children while they were children. With the polygraph, 71 percent admitted to abusing other children when they were still a child. Without the polygraph, only 21 percent said they had. These studies shed light on the histories of sexual abusers. Males who sexually abuse children are likely to have become abusers when they were still children or young adults.

Does sex abuse begin while the abuser is still a child? Hindman and Peters indicate that it sometimes does. While few studies of school-age abusers exist in the literature, those that do suggest that the problem is more widespread than we have believed and supported the Hindman findings. For instance, the Kempe National Center for Prevention and Treatment of Child Abuse and Neglect at the University of Colorado Health Science Center in Denver maintains a national database from eight hundred programs in the US that treat adolescent sex offenders. At the center, Gail Ryan has analyzed the cases of 1,600 young sex abusers and found that 25 percent said they began sexually abusing other children before the age of twelve. She found that in reports of sexual abuse of children, over 50 percent of attacks on boys and between 20–30 percent of attacks on girls are by other, usually older, children.

In the end, the most practical advice for prevention in schools is not to worry about how one becomes an abuser, but rather to look at the behaviors of the adults. If they are crossing boundaries, there is a problem to be dealt with.

ABUSER MO

Predators in elementary schools are often considered outstanding teachers, not only within the school but also in outside organizations. For instance, one predator in an elementary school in Maryland was described as a "gregarious teacher" beloved by children and parents. The principal described him as "everybody's favorite" until he was arrested for sexual abuse of elementary students.

Outstanding Teacher

Many of these local "heroes" win teaching awards. In Salt Lake City, a first-grade teacher who won the Huntsman Award for Excellence in Education and a $10,000 grant was lauded as "among the best in Utah." He was really a teacher who had been putting his hands into the pants of his female students, sexually abusing at least fifteen first-grade girls. Other students saw him reaching inside the girls' pants and touching them, and finally, one student told his parents, who alerted the police. This teacher spent at least ten hours a week tutoring students at the local library and rewarded increases in reading levels with presents that he delivered to their homes. Parents described him as generous and motivating. One parent, however, reported that her daughter often came home from school crying. The mother said she assumed her daughter had just had a bad day. After learning of the sexual abuse, she advised other parents, "If they come home from school upset, don't say, 'they had a bad day,' find out why. Get to the bottom of it."[29]

The principal also failed to assess the severity of the situation. A third party told the principal that this teacher had inappropriately touched a student. Rather than making a report to the Utah Division of Child and Family Services or the police, as required by law, the principal did her investigation and decided there was no reason to report. Eight months later, a second report was filed, and the teacher was arrested. In those eight months, the award-winning teacher sexually abused at least sixteen first-grade girls.

When the abuser is a beloved educator, celebrated for excellence and caring, parents and some students are disadvantaged. If they see something suspicious, how do they reconcile that with the teacher's reputation? And, even after allegations, investigations, indictments, and in many instances, criminal or civil trials, how do they process the discrepancy between reputation and reality? In many cases, the teacher is so beloved that parents and students harass the victim or victims. In one high school, teachers put jars on their desks to collect money for a teacher charged with sexual abuse and asked students to contribute to his defense fund. The abuse victims were in these classrooms, watching their peers donate money to defend a man who had sexually abused them. Even when he pleaded guilty to the abuse, many community members, students, and parents maintained that he was innocent but had pleaded guilty to spare his family a trial.

At another school, staff and students wore armbands to support the accused teacher, who was later sentenced to prison, daily reminding victims that keeping this popular teacher was more important than helping his victims.

Mentor

Many targeted students yearn for a robust adult connection and positive validation. A mentor offers what they need. Of course, most mentors are not abusers. But abusers often pose as mentors. Offenders gain students' trust by providing a sense of belonging, approval, support, and affection. All exploit the needs of children to be loved, respected, and supported by adults. Often, the sexual abuser uses their powerful position and a child's need for attention to begin a sexual, predatory relationship. In reporting his abuse by his sixth-grade teacher, one student said, "I needed extra help with schoolwork. He offered to provide it. He invited me to his house. He invited me to sleep over . . . I used to call him Uncle Bob. He was like a big brother, an uncle, a father."[30]

Sixteen-year-old Sarah Hitchcock was a top student who played first-chair flute. When she was preparing for the All-State Music Festival, her band director, Harold Meyers, offered extra help. During the three months of "extra help," they were alone four nights a week. Sarah thought Mr. Meyers was different from the other teachers, younger and more like her. And Meyers told Sarah that she was different than other students, more mature, not like a sixteen-year-old. Although pretty and popular, Sarah had never had a boyfriend, and she battled with her parents over their disapproval of dating. She talked with Mr. Meyers about her anxieties, and he responded, "When I was your age, I was timid. I could never have talked to a girl as beautiful and talented as you." Sarah laughed and said she didn't believe him, since he was one of the most popular teachers in the school. After the All-State competition, Sarah continued to drop by Mr. Meyers's office after school, sometimes playing duets with him. Occasionally, Mr. Meyers would stand behind her and correct her posture and hand position, eventually moving his hands down the front of her blouse and touching her breasts.

Sarah told her best friend, Emily, that this scared and excited her. She had never felt this way before and certainly had never been touched sexually by a man. The touching led to sexual intercourse at school, Mr. Meyers's apartment, and in his car. Sarah told the same friend, Emily, that she was in love with Mr. Meyers and hoped to marry him when she graduated. Emily told her she should not be having sex with a teacher, but Sarah laughed and said, "It's okay. I'm old enough to decide for myself what is right. And this is very right."

Substitute Parent and Family

Sexual abusers often choose children who are isolated or increase the isolation of those who aren't. They look for students who are without or are estranged from parental care and affection. Once abusers target those students, they cast themselves as a "father figure" or a trusted family member who cares as much or more about them as the target's parents. "You are like a daughter to me." "I think of myself as your uncle or big brother."

An account of a student who tried to commit suicide seven months after her teacher started sexually abusing her demonstrates the conflict that many targets experience. In this case, the student lived in an alcoholic family, where she had been physically and emotionally abused for years. When her teacher began encouraging, paying attention to, and valuing her, the student understandably felt cared for. Unfortunately, with a sexual abuser, students receive that attention at a high price.

> The mother figure who showed me kindness, attention, and caring was also getting her sexual needs met by using me. It just made no sense to me. I knew that I couldn't live without the good stuff in life that I was finally experiencing, and I couldn't live with the sexual encounters. . . . That April day that I tried to end my life was the most freedom I had ever known. All these months, I was enjoying the good things Miss Elizabeth was saying, doing, and giving me, but the sexual experiences created so much confusion, pain, tears, and fears. I felt so trapped. Here was this person providing so many of the good things in life to me, on the one hand, and then engaging me in sexual activities with her. Why was this happening to me?

Some abusers prey on family tragedy. One boy, who I'll call Martin, was a good student up to the fourth grade when his father committed suicide. In addition to being a strong student, he was well-liked, with lots of friends and activities. His father's suicide hit him hard. In the fifth and sixth grades, he became depressed, anxious, and isolated; he developed stomach problems; his school performance dropped; he was diagnosed with attention-deficit disorder; and he began to fight with his sister.

His mother, Carolann, was worried about these changes that had turned Martin into a marginal student with psychological and physical manifestations. She wanted her son "back."

Carolann learned of a school that specialized in serving children with conditions like her son's and enrolled him beginning in seventh grade. This was a school with small class sizes and attentive teachers. Martin attended this school his entire seventh- and eighth-grade years and was a well-liked, athletic, and high-achieving student. Carolann was relieved that the cycle of dysfunction which had triggered a change in Martin had ended.

Mark Robbins was the principal of Martin's new school. He was very hands-on with the students and developed strong relationships with them and their parents. He greeted the students every morning when they were dropped off at the school. He befriended Martin and became a mentor/surrogate "father" to him, routinely taking Martin to recreational activities intended to create bonding experiences between fathers and their children. Many of these activities were part of the "Dad's Club," which was started by Mr. Robbins as a way for male students to have closer relationships with their fathers or father figures.

Carolann said that Mr. Robbins and Martin became close over time: "Whenever Martin would have an issue, Mr. Robbins would reach out to me. It was almost like Mr. Robbins was trying to become Martin's dad or grandpa." The principal occasionally made meals for the family and repaired things around the house. Carolann's work included some late nights and some out-of-town travel. Robbins offered to babysit Martin and his sister.

While Martin was in seventh grade, Anthony Robbins began improperly touching Martin. While Martin was doing schoolwork, Mr. Robbins "would, like, move his chair around the desk right up next to me and start rubbing my thigh, my upper thigh; sometimes he would get close to my underwear but mostly rub on my thigh." Martin said this happened often: "Sometimes in the morning, sometimes in the afternoon, sometimes after school, sometimes later in the day . . . in his office with the door closed when I was supposed to be doing homework." By the time Martin entered eighth grade, Anthony Robbins had developed a bond with Martin and gained the complete trust of the boy's mother and sister. While babysitting the children during spring break, Robbins climbed into bed with Martin and rubbed his penis. After that, Martin reported, "Mr. Robbins would wait for me to get to school and then take me into his office, tell me to sit down, and rub my leg under my shorts."

Sometimes, the family metaphor means creating a club or group the abuser calls his family. Providing a group identity is powerful, especially if the leader is a beloved or inspiring teacher or coach. For instance, in an infamous case, the teacher used the drama club to isolate students from families and the rest of the school context. Students spent "long hours working on each production, and it soon became the major focus in their lives."[31] Isolating children from families and friends by providing membership in an activity that takes much of the child's time allows the offender to substitute the new group as the emotional "family" for the child. Similarly, the highly respected high school drama teacher would keep students at rehearsal late into the night and refuse to let parents into the rehearsals.

Typical of this strategy is this description by a superintendent of a music teacher who had sexually abused students for years. This teacher created an emotionally crippling, physically harmful substitute family for the music group:

> As we began to investigate, more and more kids came forward. What we began to see is that he [the abuser] created a sense of family in the music department. The department took care of their own problems; problems weren't supposed to go outside the family. He had befriended kids. It was difficult to deal with kids who had experienced him as a teacher. Their sense of loyalty, of family, was strong.[32]

Ethical Leader

Several school employees who sexually abuse students serve two roles, either in school or outside, that present them as honest and moral leaders: Sunday school teachers/church youth leaders and coaches. In this capacity, they present themselves as ethical and moral leaders working to develop children and adolescents into sound, honest, and ethically or religiously guided adults.

Photographer

A common tactic that allows the abuser to get close to students is to photograph them for supposedly educational purposes. There are many ways that this happens. The case below is one example.

Mr. Harrington was an elementary school teacher who was a lot of fun. In his class, students dressed up, put on plays, and did theatrics as part of their learning. Mr. Harrington would video the students in these activities, asking them to pose in funny ways. One day, a custodian came across hundreds of photographs of the students in these poses. Mr. Harrington had positioned the camera to look up the girls' skirts and focus on breasts, buttocks, and other body parts. While the students were not undressed, they often wore loose costumes that showed different body parts. In the guise of theater for learning, Mr. Harrington had pictures of underwear, crotches, breasts, low pants with buttocks showing, and other focused images of elementary children. Harrington used his facility with digital photography to photoshop the students into pornographic situations, which he posted on the internet.

Lover

We tend to think of misconduct as involving direct coercion. And sometimes it does. But at the upper middle and high school level, it often requires grooming, flirting, manipulation, and an experience of attraction and even love for the victim. Female and male students sometimes get crushes on their teachers, something most teachers are warned against. The typical advice to teachers, particularly young male teachers, is not to be alone with a female student because they, the teacher, might be falsely accused of sexual harassment or abuse.

It is not at all uncommon to hear teachers and administrators in the staff room talking about how provocatively high school girls dress: "They look like prostitutes," "I feel sorry for the poor male teachers having to be in a classroom with girls who are barely covered up," "If you saw the students I teach, you would have a hard time keeping it in your pants." The focus on how female students dress and connecting this with a temptress myth results in the story of the young male high school teacher lured into sex by a promiscuous high school student.[33] The focus on the female ignores the responsibility and agency of the male teacher and ends up with the community sympathizing with the male teacher and condemning the female student.

The reality is different. While there are students with crushes, it is more likely that the adult has cultivated them through flirtatious words and actions, all part of a grooming process. This grooming is often aimed at female students by adult male employees and looks much like the romances in movies, TV, and novels. The same skills and behaviors used to romance a legitimate target for love and sex are used with students. The text is love; the subtext is sex. And it is all illegitimate romance.

A typical pattern for male adult to female student sexual misconduct begins like any peer attraction would begin, except in these cases, it is almost always the adult who makes the first move: flirting, finding a way to "bump" into each other, inviting the student for a cup of coffee, meeting after class, sending text messages, sitting and talking for hours. The difference is that this is not a peer relationship; it is an adult professional crossing boundaries with a student, no matter who made the first move. Both actors respond as if they are equals, peers in a relationship. They aren't. The teacher is the adult. The student is not. The teacher has authority and power; the student has neither.

Female employees who target students for love often believe their own narrative. Mindy was an art teacher, wife, and mother of two who "fell in love" with one of her male high school students. She believed she had found her "soulmate" in Kevin. They met daily for lunch, coffee, and soon, sex— sometimes in the school, sometimes in Mindy or Kevin's car, sometimes at a motel, and sometimes at Mindy's home. Mindy and Kevin talked about marriage and children. Kevin didn't say much in response except that he cared about her. When Mindy told her husband she was leaving him for Kevin, the husband called Kevin's parents. They talked to Kevin, who admitted having sex with Mindy but was adamant that he wasn't marrying her.

Same-sex targeting differs between males and females. In all of the cases that I have studied, male same-sex abusers are focused first on sex and then maybe on an emotional connection. Female same-sex abusers are focused first on emotional connection and then on sex.

A Girl Just Wants to Have Fun

Not all female abusers are looking for an emotional connection. Some female employees target high school boys just for sex, with no strings attached. Other students report that these teachers use the classroom to attract the interest of male students: "She sits in her desk with her skirt pulled up and her legs crossed," "She leans over the boys to look at their work in a very low-cut blouse, and you can see everything," "She flirts with the boys in a very sexual way." These student comments usually describe a young, attractive female teacher who uses flirtation as both a teaching technique and a signal that she is interested in sex.

SUMMARY

Although abusers come in different sizes, shapes, and skin tones, there is one thing they all have in common. They care more about their pleasure than they do about the welfare of students. They all satisfy their needs at the expense of the children they target.

This chapter has described the characteristics of abusers, but that information has limits. Saying that the average abuser is thirty-seven years old doesn't mean that all thirty-seven-year-olds are abusers or that we should be concerned only with thirty-seven-year-olds. The same applies to coaches, drama teachers, and bus drivers. If offenders come in all types and look like you and me, how can we possibly stop them?

My research leads me to conclude that the best way to stop abusers is not to focus on abuser demographic characteristics but, rather, for organizations that serve children to become places where adult behaviors that are red flags are recognized, reported, investigated, and stopped. Focusing on organizational safety and responsibility provides the most effective prevention. For offenders and for identifying offenders, it is all about behavior. Guidelines are helpful to school people in governing themselves and to parents in knowing what is appropriate and what is troublesome. Those are detailed in part III of this book: "Standard of Care for Preventing School Employee Sexual Misconduct."

CHAPTER 5

Victims, Targets, Survivors

There are many ways to identify the student at the end of the offender's gaze. Traditionally, these children have been labeled victims. And they are. Through no fault of their own, they have been abused and exploited and left with the scars of betrayal, which can last a lifetime. Some become survivors. Those who can, move forward. They repair and heal some of the harm done to them and function successfully in academics, employment, and relationships.

Not all abused children carry the burden of victimization. Not all abused children survive. Some commit suicide. Others turn to self-harming behavior to deal with the shame they tragically and wrongly assign to themselves: abusing alcohol, overdosing on drugs, cutting, eating to stop the pain, and many other forms of self-abuse. These victims are still in society. They may or may not have families and jobs, but they are alive and coping to the best of their ability. All were targets of an offender. Therefore, I have often used the word *target* to describe students who have been abused and exploited by a school employee. To be "named" a target is also a reminder that someone other than the student is responsible for the abuse.

DEMOGRAPHICS

Students in all kinds of schools are sexually abused by adults who are employed in schools. They are targeted for contact and noncontact sexual abuse. At all ages, there are children whose breasts, buttocks, and genitals are touched by teachers, who are kissed and forced to have sexual intercourse, who are bullied (both emotionally and physically) into touching a teacher's penis, who are shown pornographic photographs, and who are made to listen to sexual slurs and stories. Those who are abused come from all grades: 38 percent of reported adult abusers target elementary students, 56 percent abuse middle or high school students, and 6 percent abuse students through-out the K–12 grades.[1]

A 2023 study by Jeglic et al. confirmed that abusers may be careful in selecting targets.[2] Comparing those who had been sexually abused with those who hadn't, victims were more likely (in order of frequency) to feel unwanted and unloved, to have parents who weren't available or weren't a resource, to have been unsupervised, and to have been "troubled." To a lesser extent, those who experienced child sexual abuse were lonely, isolated, and had low self-esteem. There were no significant differences between those living in a single-parent home and those in a two-parent home.

We know more about offenders than targets, although the patterns described in a later chapter provide insights into both. For reasons discussed previously, very few studies map a reliable and generalizable portrait of school employees' targets.

Gender

Billie-Jo Grant, who analyzed newspaper accounts from 2014, reported that 56 percent of those targeted were female and that victims ranged in age from five to eighteen, with an average age of nearly fifteen years old.[3] I analyzed the characteristics of over 4,000 respondents who indicated they had been a target of some type of sexual misconduct by a school employee. More females (55 percent) were targets than males (44 percent), corroborating Grant's finding, although the predominance of females is less than some observers expect.[4] Earlier studies of small and geographically contained populations found higher proportions of females, as high as 76 percent in the Hendrie study.[5]

Gender and Race

A higher proportion of students of color than white students are targeted. A larger proportion of students who identify as Black, LatinX, or Native American report sexual misconduct directed to them than do White and Asian students. While these differences aren't large, they describe the additional risk students of color face in schools.

In my 2004 analysis, Black females were 11 percent of the sample but 15 of those who reported being targeted; Black males were 9 percent of the sample but 10 percent of those targeted. The same pattern applies to Latina students (7 percent of the sample but 11 percent of those targeted). Latino students were nearly equally represented in each group (5.2 percent), and Native American students were 0.4 and 0.5 percent of the sample but 2 percent of those targeted.

White females were 31 percent of the sample studied but 27 percent of targets, and White males were 28 percent of the sample studied but 25 percent of those who reported being targeted by a school employee. Asian males were 1.6 percent of the sample and 0 percent of those who reported being targeted, and Asian females were 1 percent of the sample and 0.5 percent of those targeted. Thus, for White and Asian students, the proportion of those targeted is smaller than their proportion in the sample. The abusers are selecting targets that they believe are more vulnerable, less likely to report, and less likely to be believed if they do report.

Sexual Minorities–Same-Sex Abuse

A study of 2,205 students by Smith, Johns, and Raj on sexual harassment of sexual minorities in schools indicated that sexual minority females and males reported "a higher prevalence of sexual harassment and assault than their straight peers," whether by other classmates or adults.[6] Over half (54.7 percent) of sexual minority females experienced harassment or assault in high school, compared to 25.7 percent of nonsexual minority females, 25.6 percent of sexual minority males, and 9.9 percent of non–sexual minority males. Sexual minority students are at least twice as likely than others to be targeted.

Female Abuse of Males

Males, in general, and Black males, in particular, when targeted by an adult female, are often dismissed as nonvictims. A cultural view is that they have not been harmed but, instead, given a gift of free sex. The teacher's crime is explained away as "victimless." Society does not take female-to-male sexual misconduct as seriously as male-to-female sexual misconduct.

VULNERABLE STUDENTS

Students with Disabilities

There are scant US data on the prevalence of school employee sexual abuse of students with disabilities. Studies do indicate that students with disabilities are more likely to be maltreated than students without disabilities.[7] While helpful, these data are not broken down by the role of the offender, so there is no way to determine how many of these reported cases are examples of educator sexual misconduct. Although not a US study, Gallagher's UK (2000) examination of reported incidents in institutional settings, which included schools, found that students with special needs were targets in 17 percent of the cases.[8]

Mary Lou Bensy, who worked with me during her PhD research, examined patterns of school employee sexual abuse of students with disabilities in her dissertation.[9] Using an open-source website formatted to reach a sample of parents, advocates, and students, she received 352 responses to her survey, providing information on student victims in forty-one states. Male respondents (53.4 percent) were slightly more represented than females (46.6 percent). Children between six and thirteen were the targets in 52.6 percent of the cases. More than half of the abused students (55.1 percent) were classified with significant disability and support needs (e.g., autism, intellectual disabilities, multiple disabilities). These classifications require high levels of adult support, and the educator or aide is likely to be with the student more continuously than the typical student. The more opportunities for the student to be segregated from others (e.g., self-contained classrooms, pull-outs for special services with a provider), the more likely the student was to have been abused. Three-quarters of the respondents reported multiple incidents of sexual abuse. Thirty percent of the abusers were identified as teaching personnel, followed by other service providers.

Buses are one of the environments where students with disabilities are at risk. The University of Alberta Abuse and Disability Project (1992) documented that 7 percent of the sexual abuse of disabled children came from bus drivers, an important finding since children with disabilities are often transported off-site for services.[10] And since transportation is often contracted outside the school or district, there can be gaps in supervision.

Small buses carrying only one unsupervised adult and students with disabilities with different schedules are not uncommon in school districts. Chloe Mendez was one of these students who was targeted by Phillip Black, a man who lost his driver's license once for driving while intoxicated. The driver's license he lost was one where he had changed his date of birth with the Department of Motor Vehicles. When he applied for the bus driver job with a large city school district, Mr. Black used his actual birth date. A background check was done using the actual birthdate, not the false birth date he had been using when he was arrested for driving while intoxicated, and Mr. Black's ruse allowed him to be hired.

For at least twenty years before Mr. Black sexually abused Chloe, there were documented complaints of his physical abuse of disabled students. In one case, Mr. Black beat up an autistic child. When the district opened an investigation of the complaint by the child's mother, Mr. Black went to the pick-up location of each of his students and demanded to know "who told on him," threatening the students with harm. In another confirmed complaint, Mr. Black hit a student on his bus. Despite documentation that these complaints were accurate, Mr. Black was not suspended or disciplined and continued to drive a bus for special needs students in the school district.

Along with all the other confirmed complaints, the sexual abuse of a disabled female student was also documented in Mr. Black's personnel file. He was suspended for four months but then allowed to transport students again.

Eight years later, Margarita Mendez put her three-year-old daughter Chloe on the school bus for a special-needs district-wide preschool and went to work. Due to a car accident that stopped traffic, Margarita could not be home at 1:50 p.m. when Chloe was to be dropped off. She called the school and was told that Chloe would be kept on the bus, returned to school, and Margarita could pick her up there.

When the bus arrived at the school at 3:00 p.m., Margarita was already there. She couldn't understand why the bus was so late since Chloe was the last drop-off on the route, which should have happened at 1:50 p.m. Margarita knew it didn't take an hour and ten minutes to get back to the school.

When Chloe got off the bus, she was crying. Margarita asked her if someone had hurt her, and Chloe pointed to her vagina, confirming that Mr. Black had touched her twice. She also told her mother that he had taken her clothes off and slapped her two times. Her cheeks were pink. Her mother immediately called the police.

Chloe told investigators that Mr. Black took her shorts off, put them in her backpack, and touched her under her panties. She said she saw his "pee-pee" because his underpants and pants were down but not off, and his penis was "up." Chloe said she wasn't made to do anything to his penis. She was scared and tried to remove her shorts from her backpack and cover herself. Mr. Black became angry and slapped her hard on the face with his hand and continued to touch her.

When Chloe was bathed that night, she cried and said it hurt a lot because the bus driver had put his hand in, and her private parts were very red. The next day, Chloe started wetting her pants at school and home.

In the investigation by the police, a new criminal history was done, using both of Mr. Black's birth dates. This background check found that Mr. Black had been arrested multiple times, including arrests for a lewd act with a child and rape by force. They also found the complaint in his school file documenting his sexual assault of a minor, disabled child.

Although the police concluded there was probable cause that Chloe had been sexually abused, the district attorney did not take the case to trial, saying that the testimony of a three-year-old disabled girl couldn't be trusted.

Academic Vulnerability

Vulnerable students are most students. However, abusers often target students who need extra academic help. Not because they want to provide useful instruction but because the adult can use the student's academic vulnerability to be alone with the student, supposedly tutoring and helping.

Betsy Burns had never been a strong student but was especially weak in science and math. When Betsy started at Alma May High School, she was assigned to Mr. Calvinage's biology class. From the start, Mr. Calvinage started paying a lot of attention to Betsy. He singled her out by making fun of her intelligence and hurling insults. Betsy didn't understand why he was doing that and began to sink in her seat so Mr. Calvinage wouldn't notice her. Betsy realized that Mr. Calvinage paid more attention to her when she wore short skirts or tops that showed her midriff, so she decided she needed to dress differently to keep Mr. Calvinage from picking on her. By October, she wore baggy pants and at least two layers of oversized shirts or sweatshirts.

In early October, Betsy came home from school angry. She slammed her backpack on the kitchen table and screamed, "I can't take this." Her mother was startled. This was not the way Betsy usually behaved. When her mother asked what was wrong, Betsy said, "Mr. Calvinage is always staring at me and saying mean remarks about my learning in class. Yesterday, he said I was dumb, and everyone else in the class was smarter than me. He said this in front of the whole class. Today, he said my hair is gross, and I don't know how to dress. I started wearing big clothes so he wouldn't look at me, and now he says I don't know how to dress. I can't stand him."

Betsy's mother offered to go to the school and talk to the principal, but Betsy pleaded with her not to do it because it would worsen things. "I'll figure it out," she told her mother. Betsy tried keeping Mr. Calvinage's attention off of her for the next three months.

After the winter break, Betsy asked her mother to come to the school with her and ask the counselor to take her out of Mr. Calvinage's class and put her into another biology section. It wasn't just because Mr. Calvinage picked on her that Betsy wanted to transfer sections. She told the counselor, "He's just not a good teacher, and I have trouble understanding what he is trying to explain. Anyway, he isn't really teaching. Most of the time, he plays a game on his phone." The counselor denied Betsy's request for a transfer because the other classes were at a different pace, and the counselor didn't think Betsy could keep up.

Betsy and one of her friends discussed Mr. Calvinage's class a lot and concluded that he graded based on how students treated him rather than the effort they put into the class. They noticed that students, especially girls, who complimented or flirted with Mr. Calvinage fared better in his class. Betsy knew she wasn't the only girl that Mr. Calvinage stared at. After Mr. Calvinage was arrested, one of the boys in the class told the police, "It was common knowledge that he flirted with the girls. He hugged and touched them. He looked at their body parts, like their cleavage and rear end."

Mr. Calvinage had often offered to tutor Betsy, usually after he had made fun of her for not knowing an answer to a question in class. Betsy had resisted because she didn't like Mr. Calvinage. After being denied her transfer in January, Betsy went to Mr. Calvinage's classroom after school for tutoring since she had run out of other options. She did not want to fail this class.

From then on, she went for tutoring twice or thrice a week. Sometimes, it was just her alone in the classroom with Mr. Calvinage; sometimes, other students were in the room. Mr. Calvinage kept food in his room, stashed in different places. Sometimes, he sold the food to students and sometimes gave it away. Mr. Calvinage often gave Betsy food or snacks. Once the tutoring started, Betsy realized that even though Mr. Calvinage was mean to her during class, he was nice when they were alone. He talked to her and seemed interested in her life. Betsy's grades improved; sometimes, she even looked forward to the after-school tutoring. In April, Mr. Calvinage gave Betsy a watch ring for her birthday.

At the end of the school year, Mr. Calvinage gave Betsy his cell phone number, and they began texting. Betsy said, "He would give certain girls his phone number to contact him about tutoring or a question on the homework or other stuff. He only gave his number to girls."

During the summer, Betsy and Mr. Calvinage began texting daily. The content became more personal as the summer wore on. Mr. Calvinage texted Betsy that he "wanted to have sex with another student, but that she already had a boyfriend." He began to text Betsy about how lonely he was and what a good boyfriend he would be. In one text, he said he wanted to kiss Betsy. In another, he told her what kind of sexual things he had done with previous girlfriends and said he wanted to do those with her. He told Betsy that they should have sex because the babies would come out cute.

Mr. Calvinage began asking Betsy to text pictures of her breasts. Betsy didn't want to do it, but he just kept asking, and she finally gave in and sent a couple of pictures of her breasts. Mr. Calvinage texted back that they were beautiful and asked for more. Mr. Calvinage asked Betsy to pose naked and texted her, "Let's fuck." Betsy did not reply to either text, so Mr. Calvinage offered to be "friends with benefits."

At the end of the summer, right before school started, Mr. Calvinage texted her that he would be her chemistry teacher. When school started in the fall, the text messages between Betsy and Mr. Calvinage continued. By text, Mr. Calvinage invited Betsy "to the motel or to hang out" or to meet him "outside of school." He encouraged Betsy to stay after school and told her if she did, he would "find a place for [them] to hang out or to stay."

Betsy said that Mr. Calvinage "would try to touch my thighs, and he tried to kiss me during tutoring." As tutoring continued, Mr. Calvinage told Betsy she was special and thought he was falling in love with her. Betsy resisted but was flattered by the attention and liked that an adult thought she was pretty. At the end of a tutoring session, Mr. Calvinage put his hands around Betsy's waist and pulled her pants down. He began to kiss her, and she kissed him back. Soon, they were touching each other at every tutoring session.

Mr. Calvinage began pressuring Betsy to meet him outside of school. One Thursday night, Mr. Calvinage picked Betsy up at the 99 Cent Store and drove Betsy to his home. They started watching movies, and Mr. Calvinage told her he wouldn't take her home until she went upstairs with him. She finally climbed the stairs and found Mr. Calvinage in bed. She stated, "I climbed on the bed, and Mr. Calvinage started kissing me and touching my breasts. He told me to touch his penis, and he put his fingers in me. Then he told me to suck it."

Mr. Calvinage continued to ask Betsy to hang out with him. The next week, she met him at the 99 Cent Store again, drove to his house, and went straight to the bedroom. "Mr. Calvinage took off all his clothes and then told me to take mine off. I did. He got on top of me, put his thing in me, and moved around. Then he took it out and put it in my mouth. I didn't like that and asked him to take me home," Betsy recalled.

Mr. Calvinage drove her close to her home and told her not to tell anyone what happened. Later on, Betsy told the police that she was afraid of him. She said, "He told me once that he didn't let anyone get away and that he had been in the Marines and knew how to hurt people."

She also had another reason: "He kept failing me in class." Mr. Calvinage never directly told Betsy that sex with him would help her grade, but he demonstrated that if she were nice to him, it would help her grade. She said, "One day, I stayed after school to make up a test. I was nice to him, and he changed the test for me and gave me the answer so I'd pass." Betsy also thought that if she went with him to his house, "he would quit being mean to me in class in front of everybody."

After taking Betsy to his house and having sex a handful of times, Mr. Calvinage told her he didn't want to see her after class anymore. She stated, "He started avoiding me, and I realized he had used me." After that, Betsy started staying home from school because she didn't want to see him.

Betsy's mother knew something was wrong but didn't know what, and Betsy wouldn't tell her. Soon, Betsy began cutting herself, first on her thighs and then on her stomach. One morning, her mother walked into the bathroom, not knowing that Betsy was already there. When she saw the cuts on Betsy's body, she began to cry and begged Betsy to tell her what had happened. Betsy would not say anything, so her mother made an appointment with a therapist, and Betsy began seeing the therapist twice a week. Finally, Betsy told the therapist what had happened. The therapist contacted the police, and Mr. Calvinage was arrested.

But the victimization wasn't over for Betsy. When she returned to school, everyone knew that she and Mr. Calvinage had sex. Other students whispered behind her back, boys made fun of her when she walked by, and girls wrote nasty things on the bathroom walls about what she and Mr. Calvinage had done.

Betsy changed schools at the end of that year and has been in therapy since. She is getting stronger, but the damage to her self-esteem and her ability to succeed in school is great. Three years later, Betsy was still in therapy and thinking about killing herself.[11]

Vulnerable Home Life

Many target children are vulnerable because they are living in dysfunctional homes. This might be because the parents aren't always at home: they might need to work extra jobs to provide for the family, or one parent works at a distant job and comes home for the weekend or every other month. A member of the family might be struggling with mental health or substance abuse issues, which require the adults' energy to focus mostly on that child and not the other children. Or the parent could be struggling with disruptions such as divorce, physical abuse, and depression. These are common family issues, but sexual predators identify them and exploit them by targeting the student who is living in an unstable situation and by providing attention, gifts, and some stability.

Andrew Lange began attending third grade at Jeramiah Elementary School when he was nine. Andrew had an individualized education program (IEP) in his previous school addressing his specific needs and was transferred to Jeremiah Elementary School because of those needs. At the time, Andrew Lange and his siblings lived with his grandmother, who had legal custody of the children because his mother, Dolores Lange, had been incarcerated. After her release, Dolores moved in with her mother (Andrew's grandmother) and her children and lived there for about nine months until she moved in with her boyfriend. Dolores's mother would not give Dolores custody of the children, and the children remained with their grandmother.

Henry Chosen was a custodian at Jeramiah Elementary School. Andrew got to know Mr. Chosen by helping him pick up trash after school. Andrew was let out of class once a day by his teacher to help Mr. Chosen. Mr. Chosen said that all the teachers on the "top" floor knew that Andrew Lange was out of class, helping him. Mr. Chosen was under the impression that at least two teachers were supportive of his time spent with Andrew Lange. According to Mr. Chosen, no school employee ever questioned him about spending time with Andrew.

Mr. Chosen would pay Andrew to help with trash collection and disposal. Sometime around the middle of the school year, Mr. Chosen started sexually touching Andrew. The first incident was in the custodian's office. Mr. Chosen reached into Andrew's pants and rubbed Andrew's penis. Soon after, Henry Chosen performed oral sex on Andrew in the stock room. At some point, Mr. Chosen began giving Andrew a ride to and from school, and Andrew would be in Mr. Chosen's office before and after school. The principal and two assistant principals knew where Andrew was before and after school. Mr. Chosen kept the door to his office closed on instruction from the principals because, he said, "of the chemicals."

After about a year of this arrangement, Mr. Chosen asked Andrew's grandmother if Andrew could stay with him at his home, which he shared with his wife. Andrew said his grandmother did not ask questions and allowed him to move in with Mr. Chosen. Andrew lived with Mr. Chosen on and off for a significant portion of the next two school years, even though Mr. Chosen did not have legal custody of Andrew. During the first year, Mr. Chosen lived with his wife, but at the end of the year moved in with his sister because his wife was divorcing him.

Andrew went with him. Mr. Chosen would bring Andrew to school, and the teachers and administrators would see him drop Andrew off. Before living with Mr. Chosen, Andrew took the bus to school.

The sexual abuse continued regularly for the next two years on school property, at Mr. Chosen's home, in his vehicle, and in other places. After Mr. Chosen was arrested, Andrew reported that Mr. Chosen had touched his private parts every day, multiple times per day. Andrew also reported that Mr. Chosen touched his "privates" and "butt" every night and threatened to kill Andrew's mother if Andrew told anyone. Andrew also disclosed that Mr. Chosen touched him daily at school in the janitor's closet, in the cafeteria, in the boiler room, and in the stock room, where Andrew was forced to give Mr. Chosen oral sex. Andrew said, "I told him I didn't want to do that, but he made me anyway." At the end of each day, Henry Chosen would buy Andrew a Mountain Dew on the way home from school.

During the summer and on non–school days, Andrew went with Mr. Chosen to school while Mr. Chosen did his custodial work. Sometimes, they would go to Mr. Chosen's parents' farm on weekends. Mr. Chosen bought Andrew food, clothing, and expensive gifts; hugged and touched him in the cafeteria; took Andrew on out-of-state trips; removed Andrew from teacher's classes periodically, sometimes for extended periods; spent many hours of unsupervised time with Andrew in secluded and remote areas of the school building; and took Andrew to afterschool athletic activities and other non-school-related activities. Henry Chosen showered Andrew with gifts, including but not limited to games, an Xbox, nerf guns, clothes, a red bike, money, and a yearbook in which Mr. Chosen wrote to Andrew, "You're my little angel."

Each activity was witnessed by some combination of individuals, including various Jeramiah Elementary School teachers, staff, and administrators. According to Mr. Chosen, teachers saw him with Andrew when he went on little trips. Mr. Chosen also paid the fees for Andrew to be able to play sports and stated that the coaches and Andrew's homeroom teacher knew he paid.

Mr. Chosen and Andrew slept in the same room alone every night, both when Mr. Chosen lived with his wife and when he lived with his sister. When Mr. Chosen and his wife were getting divorced, she reported Mr. Chosen's behavior with Andrew to the Department of Social Services (DSS). During the interview, Andrew reported that Mr. Chosen was good to him, and Henry Chosen told interviewers that he cared for Andrew, who was like a son to him. DSS found the complaint unsubstantiated and closed the case.

DSS notified the principal of Jeremiah Elementary School of the complaint against their employee, Mr. Chosen. However, the school did not conduct any internal investigation or monitor Chosen in any way.

Andrew moved to the middle school the next year and no longer saw Mr. Chosen. However, later that same year, a first-grade student at Jerimiah Elementary School told his parents that the janitor fondled his genitals in the custodian's office. The following day, the boy's stepfather reported the incident to the principal, who contacted DSS and interviewed Mr. Chosen. The school district allowed Mr. Chosen to work until the end of the day and then placed him on paid administrative leave.

During an interview with the Sheriff's Office and DSS, Mr. Chosen admitted sexually assaulting Andrew Lange at school and Chosen's home. He also admitted to sexually assaulting the seven-year-old boy who reported the incident to his parents. Mr. Chosen was arrested, and in the continued investigation of his crimes, he ultimately confessed to the serial sexual abuse of up to forty-eight boys.

The sheriff's investigation into the allegations of sexual abuse by Henry Chosen revealed that the district's administrators, teachers, and staff were aware of the inappropriate relationship between Henry Chosen and Andrew Lange and that they regularly witnessed and were aware of many behaviors and activities that should have triggered a child sexual abuse report and sexual abuse investigation against Henry Chosen soon after Henry Chosen and Andrew Lange became acquainted with each other.

ATHLETIC AND EXTRACURRICULAR ACCESS

In the cases I have studied where another male abuses a male, the abuse most often occurs from a coach to an athlete. This also happens to female athletes with male and female coaches. Coaching allows individuals to abuse their authority and role by manipulating and controlling student-athletes—favoritism, divisiveness, and reward cycles that the coach determines. Coaches control critical aspects of the athletic and even postsecondary careers of student-athletes. They reward behavior and they provide access to status and visibility. This privilege and power can increase the vulnerability of student-athletes.

STUDENT-ATHLETES ARE VULNERABLE TO THOSE ADULTS WHO
COACH THEM:
- Athletic accomplishment is celebrated in the culture of adolescents and schools.
- Athletic accomplishment is celebrated in many families and many communities.
- Athletic accomplishment can create access to postsecondary schooling and careers.
- Coaches determine who is cut from a team and who remains.
- Coaches determine who plays at what level of visibility—varsity, "first team," "starter," etc.
- The essence of coaching is to make judgments about performance. Student-athletes understand their dependence on coaches' judgment.
- Teamwork requires subordination of individual judgments to group well-being, and suspending individual judgment to trust the coach increases vulnerability.
- High performance often requires extraordinary effort and exertion, and the students trust the coaches to keep them safe.
- Coaches have access to student-athletes when they are especially vulnerable—when they lose games, win games, get injured, etc.

- Coaches are often subjective in recognizing performance or its absence and rewarding it or not.
- Coaches often have access to student-athletes in remote, noninterruptible settings, for example, after school or on detached playing fields.
- Coaches often have access to student-athletes when few, if any, other adults or educators are present, such as in locker rooms and during after-hours practices.
- Associations that support interscholastic sports emphasize the special role and the particular influence that coaches have over impressionable young people.

The net effect of those many characteristics peculiar to coaching and the structure of secondary school sports increases (1) the access and influence that coaches have over student-athletes and (2) the vulnerability to and risk from coaches to students. Often, the team members can recognize harassment and manipulation. They complain to each other, talk to their parents (some of whom may share their suspicions), put up defenses against it, and try to distance themselves from the harassing coach. While the student-athletes often discern grooming and harassment, those observations and conclusions are not often as widely understood by the school's administration or faculty—especially if the coach has a winning record and is a "local hero."

Athlete vulnerability to a coach's grooming and abuse is not uncommon, and for all the reasons that coaches have access, and athletes are vulnerable, so, too, are music directors, drama coaches, and others who work with students after school in extracurricular activities.

Nearly fifty years ago, when I was a student in a small Iowa high school, we had a teacher that students described as odd, weird, and creepy. He was also the faculty sponsor for the yearbook. I was recently talking with my high school best friend, the editor of our high school yearbook. She shared that this teacher took yearbook pictures and instructed the student photographers to take pictures of girls in odd poses and position the camera at unusual angles. For instance, a shot of a cheerleader doing a spread leg jump would be taken from the ground, looking up under her skirt.

While many students and faculty saw the pictures, only one student editor, my best friend, recognized their likely implications. She told her mother, a member of the school board, that the pictures were creepy. Looking back on this incident, my friend believes her mother somehow acted on the information, although at the time, she didn't think much more about it. The teacher left at the end of the school year. Nothing was ever discussed with students.

In the cases I have studied, several yearbook-sponsor teachers, as well as music and drama teachers, are reported to have crossed boundaries. These positions provide access to students after school hours, access to cameras and photo shoots, and access to students alone, all while working on the activities that are important to students and that often go late into the evening.

A more recent version of school yearbook director misconduct is Timothy Herricks, a forty-eight-year-old mathematics, science, and fine arts teacher and yearbook design teacher in a middle school. Teachers and students alike remarked that he was never without his tablet or phone, taking pictures and recording events.

He set up his classroom with all the girls in the front and the boys in the back rows. Female students complained to administrators that he was favoring girls and treating boys unfairly. Not only were the girls segregated and placed up-front in the classroom, but Mr. Herricks also selected six to ten girls to be "special assistants" to come to his classroom to help with "special" teacher tasks and to spend lunch in the classroom with Mr. Herricks, eating together.

The selected female students at first thought this attention was an honor. One student stated, "I felt special to be chosen to help with teaching jobs." Another student said, "Being one of a few invited to have lunch with my friends and Mr. Herricks made me feel smart."

These female students didn't know that Mr. Herricks was also "up-skirting" them as they sat in the classroom and performed "educational support" tasks during lunch. Up-skirting is the act of secretly recording or photographing underneath a female's dress or skirt.

Janella, for instance, reported that she had come to school wearing "short shorts" and that her desk was in the front row. Unbeknownst to her, Mr. Herricks was using a selfie stick on his cell phone, under his desk, with the camera pointed at her legs and shorts as she sat with her legs spread. He was videoing Janella's legs and crotch.

Mr. Herricks required all students in the class to take breaks from math and stretch. During those stretches, Mr. Herricks held his cell phone under the girls' dresses while they were stretching and looking the other way. At one point, another student described that the cell phone was "so far under [her classmate's] dress that I could no longer see it." When the classmate sat down, that action knocked the phone out of Mr. Herrick's hand. The targeted girl was puzzled about why he had dropped his phone.

Another student, Zepher, described seeing Mr. Herricks approach one of the girls in the front row who had dropped a pencil on the floor and was bent over to retrieve it. In camera mode, Mr. Herricks was holding his cell phone under her desk. Zepher could see a zoomed-in image of her classmate's legs and underpants on Herrick's phone.

When the selected female students came to lunch to both eat and help Mr. Herricks, they were often asked to climb a stepstool and tape assignments and papers to the wall. At those times, Mr. Herricks was behind them with his tablet or phone, taking pictures and recording videos.

Picture-taking also occurred on the playground. One student stated, "I got pulled over by the tether ball pole by a friend and told that Mr. Herricks had his phone out. I was wearing a dress (with undershorts), and he was taking a video or picture of me. At first, I didn't really believe it but the next day I saw him do it to someone else and I saw his phone, which was a picture of Jennie. I saw him do it to Jennie. So, I knew he did it to me."

Another female student reported that one of her friends told her that at recess, "He had taken pictures of in between my legs!' I didn't know how to feel. I didn't believe her until the next day in class. I told her to watch to see if he took a picture when I went to his desk to ask him the answer to a math problem. I looked over at her, and she said he was! I was shocked!!! I felt uncomfortable."

Students and teachers observed his habit of always carrying a device but "didn't think anything of it." They did think it unusual that Mr. Herricks hosted selected female students during lunch behind closed doors while no other teachers in the school allowed students in their classrooms during lunchtime. However, no one said anything to him or each other. Adults recalled that Mr. Herricks carried his "iPad with him everywhere," holding it under a table and "checking it frequently."

Mr. Herricks had special apps on his phone that allowed him to take pictures without showing them on the phone. He also had lights on his desk that he pointed toward the students to get clearer shots.

Mr. Herricks sent the pictures and videos he took of female students on his school email account to his private email account. He then downloaded them and modified the pictures, superimposing images of female genitalia on some of his victims. He photoshopped the pictures to show him having oral and vaginal sex with these middle school girls. Police recovered hundreds of pictures and videos of students as well as photoshopped images of the girls in sexual activities.

SUMMARY

Targets are children that an offender identifies as vulnerable to abuse. Because of a disability or inability of the parents to speak English, an unstable home life, academic weakness, or sports and academic needs, the target's vulnerabilities are picked up by the offender, who uses them to gain access to the child.

All children have some need or disability or history that can be exploited by an adult who wants to harm that child. Adults who work in schools are given opportunities to know the child, talk with him or her, and learn about the child's needs. No child is safe from a predator if the school falls down on the job.

The employee's abuses are often in "plain sight." They are often coupled with teachers' work or assignments such as advising, cocurricular projects, coaching, or music. Other educators see the activity but don't notice unusual or additional components. If they do not know the signs of abuse—either in the abused or in the abuser—they do not know what they are seeing. In subsequent sections, I will turn to the difference between good teaching and exploitation, between expected and questionable action that should trigger suspicion or reasonable belief.

CHAPTER 6

Patterns

C hild sexual abuse is a process, not an event. Only in rare circumstances does school employee sexual misconduct occur "out of the blue." In every case I have studied, the school's culture provides an environment that tolerates, permits, and supports boundary crossing. This normalizes potentially dangerous action, which becomes grooming and results in the sexual abuse of a student, shattering the student's life and leading to long-term psychological and physical problems.

Grooming, according to the Rape, Abuse, and Incest National Network (RAINN), consists of "manipulative behaviors that the abuser uses to gain access to a potential victim, coerce them to agree to the abuse, and reduce the risk of being caught." Those activities include victim selection based on perceived vulnerability; trust development through gifts, attention, and sharing secrets; desensitization to touch in ways that seem harmless; and discussion of sexual or sensitive topics.[1]

SCHOOL CULTURE CAN FACILITATE MISCONDUCT

Every organization has a culture, a set of assumptions, attitudes, and practices that influence how its members act. The culture of UPS drivers differs from that of lawyers in a litigation practice. A fashion design house and a McDonald's franchise have different cultures. Although both health care and education are "people-serving," their cultures differ. The culture of too many schools is one of "willful ignorance" toward the possibility and even the reality of employee sexual misconduct. But why? People who go into public schooling know it is challenging and do it anyway because of the rewards of helping children. Teaching has been described as overdemanding and under-rewarding, at least financially, a combination that leads to solidarity among the faculty. Many principals conclude that their job is to protect the faculty from the parents and the students. Many superintendents conclude that teacher organizations control their contract renewal.

The culture of schooling has many consequences. One consequence is that some schools are run to benefit teachers more than students. The culture encourages mutual support among employees, which is understandable but sometimes uncritically dysfunctional. Teachers want to respect their colleagues, they want to protect their colleagues, and they don't want to "interfere." In most circumstances, those attitudes advance the work of teaching and learning. But sexual misconduct is not "most circumstances": it is extreme, and the ordinary culture of schooling, the regular business of schooling, is not a sufficient deterrent to crossing boundaries, grooming, and abuse.

CROSSING BOUNDARIES

All sexual misconduct in schools begins with an adult crossing a boundary with a student. Sometimes, this starts without the intent to abuse. Other violations are purposeful to develop a sexual bond with the student. Either way, boundary crossing is where bystanders are most likely to see red flags that call for action.

This is the stage at which intervention is most likely to deter the clueless, privileged, or would-be abuser and prevent the sexual abuse. In some cases, timely and pointed interventions derail the conversion of the boundary crosser from a teacher to an abuser.

Standard advice to new male high school teachers (female teachers rarely receive this advice) is, "Don't be alone with a student. She might accuse you of sexual misconduct, and you don't want that. This is for your protection." This counsel focuses only on harm to the teacher; without considering the student, it is incomplete.

Better advice would be, "Don't be alone with a student. That might encourage an intimacy that would lead you to behaviors that harm students and are criminal." Adding a warning about the possibility of false accusations is rarely valid. The more complete advice emphasizes the consequences of the teacher's actions for both the student and the teacher and underscores the teacher's responsibility to maintain boundaries.

Some adults are predisposed to be sexually attracted to children and adolescents. Others aren't, but they become drawn through experiences they initiate that foster intimacy. Boundary crossing is the first step for both groups.

When predators and potential predators get away with crossing boundaries, the behavior is normalized by colleagues, students, and parents. This boundary crossing is the prequel to grooming and sexual abuse of a student. These boundary crossings are often identified as red flags. Boundary crossers are enabled by schools that don't (1) have codes of conduct that specify acceptable and unacceptable adult-to-student behaviors, (2) teach adults and students about what is acceptable adult-to-student behavior, (3) fail to train student and adult bystanders on red flags for reporting, and (4) fail to ensure compliance with the code of conduct.

Boundary violations in the public eye—for example, on public social media forums or in full classrooms—are often defined by their subtlety. The tactic is a succession of acts that make children feel that these violations are "normal" or on par for the course. Districts appoint teachers to have authority over children, stressing that the teacher should be "obeyed." Without appropriate training, the culture of the school conditions children to accept the teacher's direction. Teaching about "stranger danger" is correct, but it does not protect against another potential danger—the misconduct of school employees. Students experience teachers, as they should, as people who are there to help. But the additional reality is that some teachers are a threat.

Hugs are often used to normalize crossing boundaries. For example, a teacher in an elementary school who hugs students in the hallway and "when we would come in from recess" may broadcast an image of friendliness when the intent is to normalize inappropriate touching of children. The teachers who do this often portray hugging as giving extra support for students, "letting them know we care," a rationalization accepted by students, colleagues, administrators, and parents. In middle and high school, hugs are normalized as praise or reward but can be a practice that can camouflage sexual touch as caring.

In one school, Jayne, an eighth-grade student, noted that a male teacher would stand behind students ostensibly to examine their work. She stated, ". . . he [the teacher] made me uncomfortable and . . . he would rub his penis against my back while touching my shoulders." Because the teacher acted as if nothing was happening, the student thought maybe the teacher didn't realize what she was experiencing. She continued, "I decided that it was innocent, even if it felt weird. . . . I just tried to move forward in my seat so he couldn't rub me." She gave the teacher what he didn't deserve—the benefit of the doubt. Instead of reporting, she accepted behavior that she felt was borderline sexual.

Sometimes, the normalized boundary crossing blinds bystander employees to the reality of the violation. School employees may give student victims rides to and from school or other locations and are often seen by adults and students leaving the school. And yet, this misconduct goes unreported, even though it is explicitly prohibited in most schools.[2] When questioned about these actions, students report, "I just assumed it was okay. No one ever said I couldn't ride in her car." If the school staff noticed the rides, they thought, ". . . doing a favor."

Adult conversations with students—often in the classroom or to groups of students during lunch or other non-class times—include sexual topics; personal disclosure of the harasser's sexual problems, preferences, and activity; and questions to students about their sexual lives. When the adult presents these discussions as unexceptional, they flatter the student with a "grown-up" conversation and normalize sexual talk. These behaviors often go uninterrupted or only lightly reprimanded by other employees who overhear the boundary-crossing conversations. "He told us about his first sexual experience when he was our age and then about what he does now and how it is different," one student reported.

Normalizing also occurs when the adult takes on student-like behaviors, acting as a peer. This is often presented as romance, leading other students to believe (overtly or covertly) that it is okay for adults working in the school to date a student. Bystander students, as a result, see sexualized behavior between the adult and, in most cases, a high school student and explain it as "normal" romantic behavior: "They are dating. . . . They are boyfriend and girlfriend. . . . [the predator] didn't molest [the victim]; they were just making out. . . . If they weren't allowed to date, the administration would have stopped it."

Preventing sexual misconduct and abuse directed toward students requires adult bystanders and other students to understand the *red flags* of grooming. Students make sense of these boundary crossings from their frame of reference, and a student's worldview seldom extends to violations of district policy or state law. The student's failure to recognize the harm comes from the staff's failure to teach the policies regulating adult-student interactions (if they exist), and the culture of the school encourages everyone to look the other way rather than teaching what the appropriate teacher-student bound-aries are and what to do if they see them being violated.

GROOMING

Those who cross boundaries with sexualized intent or who develop sexual-ized intent because of the boundary crossing use these boundary crossings to build trust with student targets, colleagues, and parents. The adult needs the student to trust their actions and thus deploys a series of escalating non-physical behaviors that lead to physical sexual misconduct.

The purpose is to create an environment where the adult's sexual gratifi-cation can be unnoticed. This trust-building is referred to as *grooming*.[3] It is a beginning stage and focuses on emotional manipulation.[4] Understanding the difference between good teaching and sexual grooming is nuanced and critical.

Jim Tanner and Stephen Brake developed a framework for understanding the grooming process.[5] They distinguish between grooming the environment and grooming the individual. Schools are intimate and interconnected work-places. Teachers and children are together 6 hours a day, 5 days a week, and 180 days a year. The school environment is a partly private, partly public workplace. Teachers talk to each other, students talk to each other, students talk to teachers, and 5,400 hours a year in a shared and confined space fos-ters communication. Maximizing access to vulnerable children and minimiz-ing the chance of detection requires that offending employees manage that environment, and one way to do that is to be a "model teacher," a "teacher of the year."

ENVIRONMENTAL GROOMING

Typically, the offender grooms the work and community environment first, then grooms potential victims, the actual victim, and in many cases, the victim's family. Before physical sexual abuse of the potential target, the envi-ronmental groomer seeks to be admired by colleagues, recognized in the community as a productive and valuable member, and appreciated by parents as someone helpful to their children's success. To achieve this goal, abusers engage in environmental grooming: helping the family, helping colleagues, gaining attention for supporting students, and being popular. Environmental grooming requires charm, outreach, and self-promotion. The complication is that many offenders perform those services and earn those reputations. The tragedy is that offenders do more than provide good teaching. The challenge is for faculty colleagues, building administrators, and families to recognize both components–the service and the damage.

Families/Parents

In many cases I have studied, the abuser provided families extra services, and the parents responded with gratitude and trust. In a pattern I saw repeated across schools, a male teacher contacted a mother in a one-parent household, expressing concern about her son's academic work. The teacher usually praised the boy as bright but as a student who needed extra guidance to get on track. The teacher then offered to tutor the boy. The teacher would inject himself into the family, offering to bring the boy (and often siblings) home from school, provide little extras to the household—food, movies, toys—and become a confidant to the single mother. The mother described the experience as a dream come true. Worried about the effects of raising a male child in a fatherless home, she felt grateful that "the teacher all the parents hoped their child would get" was helping her son learn and providing her son with a positive role model. Grooming the mother was an essential step to abusing the child.

Colleagues

Colleagues, too, have to be managed. After a teacher had been arrested or convicted, colleagues reported how surprised they were. The following were typical comments colleagues made: "He was always so helpful, offering to take care of things after school so that I could get home to my kids." "I just couldn't believe it. He was the nicest person. Always there to help and focused on the well-being of students." "He was the teacher of the year in our school district." "He was always available to help with a student or go the extra mile." "I don't care what they say. I know this man, and he didn't do what he was accused of."

It is common for an abuser to be a member of several school committees, to be appointed to additional co-curricular roles, to show up early, and to stay late.

Their personnel files are filled with accolades. The more valued the abuser is as an organizational citizen, the less likely he is to be suspected or supervised. In the cases I studied, this profile always described a male employee.

Environmental and individual grooming can occur simultaneously, but commonly, the offender has established themselves as a highly regarded education or coaching professional. This is truer for male abusers than for females. Environmental grooming is part of how abusers manipulate colleagues into believing grooming acts toward students are only helping and supporting students. Not every abuser grooms the environment, but those with a history of abuse almost always do. It is how the school culture enables their abuse.

Grooming the Target

Grooming is rarely violent, such as pulling a student into a stairwell or pushing a girl into a supply closet. That comes later. Instead, it consists of actions that bond the target to the offender, such as time spent together, secrets, gifts, privileges, and special attention. The process presents the offender to the child as kind, gentle, understanding, caring, generous, charming, and accessible. The offender's goal is to be desirable, needed, and wanted by the child. As the child is progressively drawn to this "special" bond, the offender assures the child that the relationship is "normal," often by telling the target that they are more mature than other students, smarter, or extra-special. The more an offender can minimize the nature of the offense and shape it into an acceptable relationship—counselor, teacher who cares, friend, father figure, peer—the more the student is led to believe that what the adult is doing is acceptable.

Generally, the offender uses threatening methods only when the student tries to stop the predator after the grooming period and well into physical or emotional sexual misconduct. At this point, offenders use guilt, threats, and fear to keep the student quiet and involved.

The goal is trust and compliance from the child, which abusers willfully misinterpret as consent. Minors are not legally able to consent to illegal acts. Children aren't legally or emotionally able to agree—this is not an equal interaction—therefore, compliance is used by the offender as a stand-in for consent, drawing the child into a belief system that the child has control or power when that is not the case. The bystander version of this misinterpretation is "Well, she came on to him," or "She was asking for it." Not only does that blame the victim, but it also excuses and enables the predator.

Kenneth Lanning, retired supervisory special agent from the FBI and a seminal researcher of criminal sexual behavior since the 1970s, describes grooming as "specific nonviolent techniques used by some child molesters to gain access to and control of their child victims." Lanning writes that grooming is "patterned behavior designed to create opportunities for sexual assault, minimize victim resistance or withdrawal, and reduce disclosure or belief."[6]

Boundary-crossing and grooming behaviors and patterns are red flags, signaling that something isn't quite right and that attention, monitoring, and supervision are needed. These are the patterns that bystanders and families should be alert to.

IS IT GROOMING OR JUST EDUCATOR PROSOCIAL BEHAVIOR?

A 2023 study by Jeglic, Winters, and Johnson examined the difference between grooming and "innocent" or ordinary prosocial actions by a trusted other.[7] They compared a group of individuals over eighteen recruited to an online survey-taking website. Of those who completed the survey, 45 percent had experienced sexual abuse before age eighteen and 55 percent had not.

The authors compared the respondents' experiences as reported on the Sexual Grooming Scale that they had developed.[8] In every category, the red flag behaviors were statistically significantly more likely to have been directed at those who were abused versus those who weren't.

They grouped the red-flag behaviors listed in table 6.1 into levels of risk. Those who had been sexually abused as children were more likely to have experienced these behaviors than those who hadn't been sexually abused.

While many of these behaviors are not unusual, they become red flags when an adult in a school continues to exhibit the behavior toward a specific child. This study is critical because it confirms that "if you see a boundary crossing, report it." Bystanders often overlook or don't report red flags because they imagine the behaviors are just ordinary prosocial, helping behaviors, even if they would never exhibit such behaviors themselves. Jeglic et al.'s findings provide strong evidence that some of those behaviors may indicate that a child is at risk for sexual abuse.

Gaining Access and Isolating

Most employee-to-student sexual misconduct in educational organizations involves "preparing" the student for the misconduct so that the student trusts the employee. As discussed above, the misconduct rarely begins with unwanted sexual touching, although that occurs later. For example, coaches isolate selected students by recommending that they drop extracurricular activities other than the coach's sport. Teachers offer extra help but only one-to-one, after school and behind closed doors. Abusers criticize their targets for having boyfriends or girlfriends.

Those who target children use isolation techniques such as separating the child from family and peers, manipulating a family to allow that separation,

TABLE 6.1   Risk level of red flag behaviors

Enhanced risk	Moderate risk	High risk
1.68–3.46 times more likely to be experienced by abused students than nonabused students	3.47–6.7 times more likely to be experienced by abused students than nonabused students	At least 6.71 times more likely to be experienced by abused students than nonabused students
Engages in activities alone with a child that exclude adults	Asks questions about child's sexual experiences and relationships	Increases sexualized touching
Engages in childlike activities with the child	Uses inappropriate sexual language or tells "dirty" jokes around the child	Engages in frequent seemingly innocent or nonsexual touching
Gives child lots of attention	Teaches the child sexual education (when not their teaching assignment)	Exposes naked body to child
Spends lots of time with child or communicates often with child	Provides the child with drugs or alcohol	Watches child undressing or while naked
Shows child love and affection	Gets close to the child's family to gain access	Shows child pornography: magazines, images, or videos
Shows favoritism and tells the child they have a special relationship	Gives the child rewards or privileges others don't get	Tells the child about past sexual experiences
Takes child on overnight stays or outings		Separates or isolates child from family
Gives child rewards or privileges		

Source: Elizabeth L. Jeglic, Georgia M. Winters, and Benjamin N. Johnson, "Identification of Red Flag Child Sexual Grooming Behaviors," *Child Abuse & Neglect* 136 (February 2023): 105998, https://www.sciencedirect.com/science/article/pii/S0145213422005324.

engaging the child in activities without other children or adults, and taking the child on outings, including overnight stays. Jeglic et al. found that children who experienced sexual abuse by a trusted other outside the home were nearly thirty-three times more likely than those who didn't to have been separated from their peers and family using various tactics.

It is said that grooming occurs in public and sexual abuse in isolation. For the most part, that is true. But grooming can also occur in isolation.

Isolation is not only a tactic to keep actions hidden. It is also a strategy to remove the target from friends and family, leaving the employer-abuser as the only person the student can confide in.

Isolation is a red flag that can go unnoticed if it is seen as "helpful" or "beneficial." Isolation gives the abuser access to the target without suspicion or detection from those in other environments. This can take many forms, such as having individual coaching sessions, private tutoring, or one-on-one help after school in a classroom. It's not just about being in a personal space but also about spending time with a child and keeping that child away from friends and family, both physically and emotionally, such as convincing the student that her friends don't like her or that her parents are not fair.

In one school, a teacher, Mr. Park, offered to tutor a student, Marcie. This gave him access to her without other students present and behind closed doors. Mr. Park began pressuring Marcie to meet him outside of school. Marcie said, "If I found a way to make it happen, he would find a place." Mr. Park picked up Marcie at the 99 Cent Store, and they went to his house, where he sexually assaulted her. Park had begun by tutoring Marcie, which decreased her time with friends and family. Park told Marcie her "parents didn't understand me and aren't good parents." He discouraged her friendships, commenting, "You are more mature than them. They are a waste of your time." This eventually allowed Mr. Park to isolate her in his home. Isolation almost always leads to sexual abuse since it is generally invisible to others.

The exception is isolation at school, where it is possible to notice when an adult isolates a student. Administrators must monitor, observe, and supervise school spaces during, before, and after school hours.

When Jill, a student with special needs, didn't return to the classroom promptly, her teacher went to look for her and found her with the male classroom aide. They were both stepping out of a dark, recessed area next to an empty classroom. The male aide told Jill's teacher that Jill was afraid to go to the restroom alone and that he had accompanied her. The aide would watch Jill in the classroom, looking for ways to isolate her in the building that could be explained as "helping." Jill's teacher noticed that whenever Jill left the classroom, the aide left soon after with a variety of excuses. The teacher also noticed that the aide and Jill returned to the classroom simultaneously whenever this happened. And yet, Jill's teacher didn't report these behaviors. She claimed, "I just thought he was overly protective of her."

Sarah, a middle school student, described how her social studies teacher would ask her to stay after class. She had a study period after his class, so he would send a note to her study period class teacher that he was working with her on a project. The teacher started slowly, "maybe once a week," and then "soon he was asking me to stay after every class. We talked about history, current events, and my life. He asked many questions about what I did and if I had a boyfriend. He told me I wasn't like other students. I was more mature, more like an adult than a middle schooler. I was flattered." The student described how these activities and the teacher's focus caused her to separate from her friends. Instead of being with them after school, Sarah was with her social studies teacher. She felt she couldn't tell her friends or her family what was happening, which isolated her from friends and family.

Mary shared that she liked the special attention she received from Mr. Novack. Mary stated:

He gave me A's on my tests and homework even when I didn't finish or turn them in. He let me leave study hall and come to his class, where he had candy and soda. He often brought lunch from Taco Bell or Burger King, and we ate together. Novack gave me presents and was nice to me. He was funny. I didn't realize at the time the toll all this took. I stopped spending time with my friends, became isolated, and didn't know what was happening with the other kids in school. I worried about getting caught and the shame and ridicule I would experience.

Isolation is often place-related. Andrew recalled that in high school, his "shop" teacher would take selected boys to his cabin on a lake for weekends to hunt, fish, swim, and hang out. These were regular outings. Andrew asked his parents if he could go, and they agreed if the other boys were going. His teacher, Mr. Prescott, was well liked, respected, and known for looking after boys who were not on the "academic" track. The first trip was low-key, with a few boys fishing and sitting around the fire talking. Each boy had his own bedroom. Mr. Prescott added alcohol to the next trip, and the kids were flattered to be treated like adults. Mr. Prescott would always sit next to Andrew or take him in the boat to a secluded fishing spot on the lake. Soon, Mr. Prescott was slipping into bed with Andrew to talk. And then touching.

Many of the students in the cases I studied report that a teacher separated them from their parents by criticizing the parents, manipulating the inevitable tension between adolescents and parents. One student said, "Mr. Dancer felt that my parents' religious beliefs and expectations about my religious involvement were hampering my growth. He encouraged me to leave the church, which I did. . . . Dancer kept telling me that my parents didn't understand me and weren't being fair to me. Of course, I agreed with him. The more Dancer reinforced my parents' unfairness, the more angry I became at my parents."

For some students, isolation has meant moving out of their homes and moving in with the teacher and the teacher's spouse. In none of these situations was the school notified of the student's change in living arrangements. One student stated, "I moved in with Mr. Bracken and his wife. This meant that he had more access to me at all times of the day. I didn't mind. I thought we were in love."

Isolation makes the child more reliant on the abuser. Sometimes, the reliance is academic, such as trading grades for time: "I didn't have to do my homework. He would give me a grade as long as I spent time with him. But it also meant I didn't see my friends as much." Reliance and isolation are when a school employee tutors and teaches a student but withholds that learning if the student doesn't comply with increased intimacy. In one case, an expelled student was being homeschooled and wanted to be readmitted to the high school. When he voiced that he wanted to return to a brick-and-mortar school, the homeschooling teacher proposed trading unearned good grades from the teacher for sexual participation from the student. When the school refused his request to return, he felt he had no choice but to accept the homeschool teacher's terms.

Gifts and money offer students things they don't have and increase their reliance on the adult. Often, the gifts are cell phones and burner cell phones, used for private communication, and iPads that provide easy access to the student. Other times, students are given trendy clothes and accessories.

Mr. Toledo targeted a female student for sexual activity and began a full-on "courtship," buying her gifts and providing her with things she wouldn't otherwise have. One day, for instance, he texted her and told her he put a "surprise in her locker." When Sophie went to her locker, she found a pink iPad Mini. And she was delighted and excited to have it. When she took it home, her mother questioned her about it. Sophie told her mother that Mr. Toledo had loaned it to her, and others also received loans. Sophie felt special when she got this gift. And it made her like Mr. Toledo even more. Mr. Toledo counted on that. He knew that an expensive and lavish gift would escalate his access to Sophie and make it less likely that Sophie would rebuff his subsequent advances. So important was this gift and bond to Sophie that she lied to her mother.

Gift-giving to girls is not uncommon, but depending on the gift, it may raise concerns from parents. Parents aren't aware of food and candy and privilege handouts to their child from an adult employee in the school, but they are likely to notice "things" that get brought home. Thus, these need to be cloaked as being for school purposes.

Mr. Lester targeted Marianna and began giving her extra school supplies. When she brought these home, her mother noted them but assumed they were part of the school package. Even when she realized that they weren't given to all children, Marianna's mother treated the supplies as a way the teacher acknowledged their tight finances and was helping her child succeed in school.

However, when Marianna came home with a new purse given to her by Mr. Lester, her mother knew immediately that this was an inappropriate gift. This realization came too late to stop Mr. Lester from having sex with her daughter.

Typically, parents and administrators would not question the school supplies given to a student whose family could not afford them. And yet, they can serve the same purpose as the gift of the purse: gaining a child's trust while crossing boundaries and manipulating a child's affection. The solution is not to stop providing school supplies but to make it a school responsibility, not a teacher's decision.

If teachers provide food and candy to some students but not others, an environment conducive to boundary crossing is established. A targeted student is often invited to have lunch alone with the teacher in the classroom. These violations are carefully planned transgressions that scale in boldness relative to how often the predator can get away with the behavior in the presence of bystanders.

Trust Development

Jeglic et al. found that attributes and conditions to build trust were experienced more often in those who were sexually abused than those who weren't and included (in order of frequency): (1) affectionate and loving behavior, (2) attention to the child's needs and feelings, (3) the abuser's authority and reputation, (4) rewards and privileges, (5) creating alone time, (6) providing drugs or alcohol, and for younger students, (7) engaging in childlike behaviors and games.

Personal social media is a standard vehicle for bonding and grooming. Although districts forbid the illicit use of school-supplied social media and most require everyone to use school platforms, harassers use platforms that the school does not monitor and are seldom caught and stopped. Contacting a student using a private email, phone number, or text; Facebook; Tik-Tok; Instagram; and other platforms crosses boundaries between the adult and the student. These private platforms are often used "innocently" to ask a question or make a comment. But the goal isn't innocent. It is to create a connection, get a response, and build a relationship.

Using a private platform is much like being alone with a student behind a closed, locked door. There is no monitoring method, and the interactions are hidden and secret. Students who spend their time saturated in the media don't experience a text from a teacher as anything unusual. In several cases I have studied, hundreds of text messages were exchanged throughout a school day. Back-and-forth texts escalate into more intimate and sexually explicit communications and often include exchanges of photos of body parts or other sexual displays. It is not uncommon for an abusive teacher to text a picture of his penis to a student and ask for a picture in return. When students reciprocate, some abusers use the images to blackmail the students into sexual cooperation. Female teachers are less likely to text pictures, but when they do, they are undressed or in sexual poses.

Trust is often built by supporting and encouraging students—an admirable teacher behavior but one that must happen within boundaries. Suzanne described herself as a high achieving student. She said, "I work hard. I have professional parents who expect a lot. I am always trying to get their admiration and approval. Most of the time, I fall short. They aren't the warm and fuzzy parents that some of my friends have." Ronald Askington held a Ph.D. in mathematics and taught advanced classes at Suzanne's school. She was in his tenth, eleventh, and twelfth-grade advanced math classes. Suzanne recalled:

> Dr. Askington would always tell me how intelligent I was and how far above other students. He encouraged me to compete in Mathletes. I hadn't considered myself a "math" person, but he said I was. He told me he thought of me as a daughter and was so proud of me. When I got a 760 perfect score on my PSAT, I was excited and stayed after class to show him my PSAT report. He was so happy for me. He hugged me and held on for a long time. Something changed then. He began to work with me more often before, after, and during school. He would touch, hug, and tell me how special I was. He was there for me, and I knew he cared about me.

In this case, Dr. Askington didn't start helping Suzanne for sexual contact. Initially, he supported a student who hadn't yet realized her talents. However, as the helping behaviors continued, Dr. Askington began to feel sexual attraction toward her and didn't provide the barriers to keep him from sexual actions toward her.

Trust-building happens a little differently in elementary school. Sometimes, it is built around identifying selected students as class helpers.

Harrington was a fourth-grade teacher who, according to students, each year chose a small group of students, usually three or four, as classroom helpers. These students were always girls. They were asked to stay in the classroom at recess or lunch to "help" Mr. Harrington with "teaching" tasks. Mr. Harrington also played "learning" games with them. One student, who was one of the helper group, described one of the games that they played:

> When I was in fourth grade, my teacher played games with the helpers when we would stay in during recess. One game was "the tasting" game, which was supposed to help us learn the five tastes. He

blindfolded us, and we had to taste something and decide if it was sweet, sour, salty, bitter, or savory. Sometimes we would lick something. Other times, chew or drink and swallow. It was weird, but he gave us candy if we got the correct answer. Once, my blindfold slipped down, and I saw Mr. Wright touching his "private," and white stuff was squirting into a glass. He handed the glass to Marylou, who drank it . . . I didn't say anything, but I didn't drink it . . . I never played that game again.

Another student describes how her offender built her trust by listening to her problems and offering her opportunities:

Mr. Rogart-Bizet was kind to me. He asked me to be his teacher's assistant and helped coach me with my forensic speech. At school, Mr. Rogart-Bizet spent a lot of time alone with me. He was a very attentive listener, and he allowed me to talk about my problems with my parents. He told me he had taken psychology courses in college because he wanted to be a psychiatrist instead of a teacher. In my mind, and with what was happening in my life, I thought, "Finally, here's someone I can talk to. Here's someone who listens and understands me."

Abusers violate the trust of students, not only by sexually abusing them but also by putting the student in a position where the student may conclude, as one, sadly, did, "There was nothing about me that was special. I see that now. He only paid attention to me to have sex with me. I feel so foolish. I thought I was someone. Now I realize I'm no one."

Trust and dependence are also built when adults become accomplices in illegal or banned activities, such as consuming drugs and alcohol. Jeglic et al. report that students sexually abused by "trusted other" adults are nearly fifteen times more likely to have been given drugs and alcohol.[9] This makes the student complicit in an illegal act and increases the barrier to reporting ("I won't tell if you don't tell").

Desensitization to Sexual Content and Physical Touch

The Jeglic et al. study showed the most differences between those who had been sexually abused and those who hadn't in their experiences with this grooming category (desensitization). Those who were sexually abused were fifteen times more likely to have experienced seemingly innocent or "accidental" touching and twenty times more likely to be told by the adult about the adult's sexual life.

Desensitization begins with a touch that can be considered normal. For instance, at a for-profit early-childhood education center, the children were gathered daily in a big hall to wait for their parents. All the teachers were expected to attend, and there were daily debriefs and chats between the teachers and parents.

One teacher, Mr. Yarrow (known as Mr. Y), was especially boisterous and physical in playing with his students. The parents watched as he tickled the little girls, swung the boys around by the ankles, and wrestled with the little boys and girls on the big floor. If skirts got pulled up or bottoms got grabbed, it was "all in fun," and it was all in public. The teacher was desensitizing the kids, the parents, and the other teachers. He was normalizing physical interaction that would compromise any child who might complain to a parent that "Mr. Y touched me" or "Mr. Y acts weird." Parents and teachers remembered these behaviors when Mr. Y was arrested, but before his arrest, when someone commented on the behavior, they explained it all with, "That's how he is."

Another example of desensitization was directed toward Hal, an up-and-coming high school wrestler and, eventually, the target of sexual misconduct by his coach. Even though he was in the eighth grade, he had a place on the JV team. His coach, Mr. Halverson, offered to work with him after practice to give him some extra experience. After practice, they would review basic skills such as stance, motion, and lift. Mr. Halverson would locate Hal's body in the proper stance and physically guide him through motions. His touch would often graze Hal's genitalia and buttocks, sometimes "longer than an accidental touch." Hal stated, "It felt creepy, but I didn't know if it was how coaches did things." After practice, Hal would take the required shower. During that time, Mr. Halverson moved in and out of the locker room, often stopping to say a few words to Hal as he was showering. One day, Mr. Halverson told Hal he had an appointment and, because he had stayed late to work with Hal, he would have to shower with Hal to be on time for his meeting. A shared shower after the other students had left soon became a regular practice. Hal was apprehensive about whether showering together was "normal" or something that shouldn't happen. Nonetheless, Hal wanted to stay on the JV team, and Halverson was the coach.

Sometimes, these forms of touch lead to sexual misconduct, and sometimes not. But there are always signs of boundary crossing that need to be prevented. Even if they don't lead to direct sexual misconduct, the behaviors disrupt comfortable and healthy teacher-student relations.

Jodi experienced desensitization that compromised her student-teacher relationship. Jodi especially liked Ms. Corey, her high school art teacher. They often talked during class and after school. Ms. Corey asked her if she had a boyfriend, and Jodi said she wasn't "into" boys. Ms. Corey laughed and said neither was she. Over time, Ms. Corey told Jodi about her relationship with women and invited Jodi to a lesbian bar. Jodi said she liked the atmosphere there. It felt very female-friendly. Over time, Ms. Corey began to touch Jodi, first "accidentally" and then more deliberately as in a hug hello and a hug good-bye, sometimes full-body and sometimes not. Ms. Corey told Jodi she was attracted to her and invited her to her home for dinner. Jodi was flattered but also nervous. She didn't know how to interpret Ms. Corey's invitation. Jodi said she "liked and was attracted" to her teacher but wasn't sure about a physical relationship. Because she felt uncomfortable and didn't know how to handle the situation, she told Ms. Corey she had a boyfriend (which she didn't) and dropped out of art so she wouldn't "hurt Ms. Corey's feelings."

Laura was similarly uncomfortable. She and her friends talked about how Mr. Spoonhaven always touched their hair while working on class assignments. He would stand behind girls with long hair and "fiddle" with it, wrapping it around his fingers. She stated, "He would tell me that I had soft, beautiful hair. He never did anything else, but still, that was creepy. I didn't like it. But I didn't know how to tell him to stop. It was just playing with my hair. I didn't know if teachers were allowed to do that. It was hard to concentrate on my schoolwork. I hated going to that class."

Texting sexual jokes and pictures is another way abusers try to desensitize sexual content by making these texts, pictures, and comments seem like "normal" teenage communication. This escalates to asking for pictures of students in stages of undress or sharing nude pictures with students. Technology makes it possible to desensitize from afar and then transition to in-person touch and sexual activity.

Maintenance

Once sexual contact is made, and most often at earlier stages, the abuser increases the manipulation through rewards and secrecy. The abuser works to convince the student that there isn't anything wrong with what is going on but that others might not understand. Therefore, both need to keep this behavior a secret. Jeglic et al. noted that students who were eventually sexually abused by an adult were 124 times more likely to be told not to tell anyone, even in the early stages of grooming.[10]

When the grooming begins, the abuser works to normalize the behavior and tries convincing the target and others that the behavior is ordinary teacher interaction. The abuser uses many of the above-described techniques in the maintenance stage to keep the "secret." Ways in which the school employee enforces the "don't tell" policy include not only affection and gifts. Often, the adult convinces the student that the behavior wouldn't have happened if the student weren't so "pretty," "mature," "willing," or "lovable." In other words, the adult is shifting the responsibility to the child. Not infrequently, the adult abuser will tell the student, "You know that if you tell, I can lose my job and go to jail." The abuser also threatens abandonment and rejection of the child if the child doesn't conform, thereby placing the child in the position of losing rewards, privileges, and "positive" attention and reinforcement.

WHAT IS TO BE DONE ABOUT GROOMING?

Grooming students for sexual exploitation is a heinous thing for a teacher to do. Recognizing the difference between good teaching and early-stage sexual manipulation can be problematic for faculty bystanders and some school building administrators. Who would not want teachers to pay attention to their students? To attend to the "whole child," not just academic performance but emotional well-being and social interactions? To spend time, even "extra" time, with them? The insidious aspect of grooming is that the sexually harassing teacher can put into play the same activities that other teachers use to excellent effect. The difference is in the purposes, the motives, and the follow-on actions, which are not readily apparent.

There are differences between the knowledge of and interaction with students expected of an effective teacher and the grooming behaviors of a predator. Good teaching can be distinguished from sexual harassment and manipulation. Making that distinction is a staple of graduate preparation for professional educators. Preservice and in-service programs for school administrators and schoolteachers regularly educate about how to recognize sexual harassment—and how to differentiate it from effective teacher-student interaction.

But what can those—both parents and other concerned school employee bystanders—do? They can observe, ask questions, and pursue their conclusions—a topic to which I turn in chapter 8. Questions that point to reporting include:

- Does the teacher have favorites among the students, and if so, are they only girls or only boys?
- Is the teacher singling out specific students for privileges, rewards, or treats—are they only girls? Only boys?
- Are new individuals or new small groups recruited each year?
- Are there meetings before school with individual students or perhaps with tiny groups of students? During recess? During lunch? During prep periods? After school?
- Does the teacher have access to private, uninterruptible spaces, and do they use them with students?
- Is the teacher "handsy?" "Touchy-feely?" "Warm and affectionate in physical encounters?"
- How does the teacher interact physically with students? High-fives or hugs? How frequent are the hugs? How long are the hugs? Who is initiating the hugs? Are they side hugs or full-body?
- How is the teacher communicating with favorites? Do they have the teacher's cell phone number? Does the teacher have theirs?
- How common or uncommon are the teacher's practices? If they are very unusual, very singular, why is that? Is it justified?
- How involved is the teacher in the lives of their favorites? Schools employ counselors and psychologists to help students with family crises, identity issues, and personal problems. Is the teacher inserting him or herself into those areas?
- Is the teacher known to give students rides? To take students on private outings? Sports events? Movies? Meals?
- What does the teacher say?
- What do the kids say? And how do you know what they are saying?
- What does the teacher's department chair say?
- What does the teacher's supervising assistant principal say?

- What does the principal say?
- And what does the district's designated Title IX compliance officer say if you're not satisfied?

Processing the answers to those questions requires judgment. No abuser is likely to be seen by the same person engaging in all of these behaviors. That's why reports of boundary crossing all need to end up in the same office and file. One person sees one thing. Someone else observes a different boundary violation. The reports are likely to be in shades of right and wrong. There are likely to be green-light, yellow-light, and red-light behaviors. Nonetheless, simply reporting to a central person and asking questions can have a deterrent effect. Asking the questions and pursuing the answers can advance the safety of children.

In my experience, students are most likely to know about an abusive teacher. But young children and even teenagers seldom describe what sexual abusers do in explicit and graphic language. Instead, they employ euphemisms like "creepy" and "weird." Those words still point to harassment and abuse. The US Court of Appeals for the Fourth Circuit approvingly quoted the observation of the National Women's Law Center that children "cannot be expected to articulate the sexual abuse and harassment they suffer in the same words as adults."[11]

The critical takeaway for school personnel, parents, and students is that sexual abuse of students by school employees happens because we let it happen. We see things but don't say anything about them. We allow red flag behavior to continue without a word of alert, caution, or disapproval. We fail to develop codes of conduct between adults and students, and even if we do, we forget to teach students, teachers, and employees what to do when they see such behaviors. Even if we do training, we only train adults about appropriate behavior. Students also need to learn the difference between appropriate and inappropriate behavior by school employees and what to do when they see it. While much (but not all) of the physical sexual contact occurs in isolated spaces, the red flags of boundary crossing happen in front of us. We need to see it, recognize it, and report it.

PART III

Standard of Care for Preventing School Employee Sexual Misconduct

CHAPTER 7

A Model for Prevention

T he one remark I hear the most regarding prevention is, "Well, it should be common sense for a teacher not to have sex with students." I agree. I completely agree. I couldn't agree more!

But clearly, common sense isn't working because it's still happening—all the time. Remember, the most conservative calculation of school employee sexual misconduct warns that at any one time, 5.2 million kindergarten to twelfth-grade students are dealing with this threat to their well-being.[1] Each year, abused students graduate or drop out of high school, joining the pool of survivors of sexual misconduct by school employees.

Pick a state from the table below. At any one time, the number of students still in school that a school employee has sexually mistreated is more than the total population of the state you chose.

Wyoming	Vermont	Alaska	North Dakota
South Dakota	Delaware	Montana	Rhode Island
New Hampshire	Maine	Hawaii	Idaho
West Virginia	Nebraska	New Mexico	Nevada
Kansas	Utah	Mississippi	Arkansas
Iowa	Connecticut	Oklahoma	Oregon
Kentucky			

If you live in one of those states, imagine that nationally, more children are victims of sexual abuse by a school employee than there are people who live in your state.

So, if relying on "common sense" is the extent of school districts' prevention, they are, by default and neglect, putting students at risk. An interview in a national magazine in 1984 reminds us that the profession has been aware of school employee sexual misconduct for decades. An experienced principal gave a chilling insider's view of what she had observed in her career in the 1960s, 1970s, and 1980s: "Child sexual abuse is the best-kept secret in American education. I have never lived in an area where some school employee—often a teacher or administrator—was not found to be sexually abusing students." She also pointed out that in the first five months of mandated background checks of school employees in four states, "over 6,000 job applicants were found to have criminal histories of child sexual abuse." "This isn't surprising," says a National Center for Missing and Exploited Children advisor. "If you want to ride horses, you go to a stable. If you want to molest children, you go to schools, camps and daycare centers."[2]

When I began studying school employee sexual misconduct in the late 1980s, I thought I could find someplace where the policy, regulatory, and administrative processes to protect children had been collected and codified. Those "standards of care" are common in different enterprises, such as health and wellness institutions.

As a profession, we in education are still assembling and refining our standard of care for all school practices, including preventing employee sexual misconduct. I searched for standards of care that would protect students from sexual misconduct by trusted others, including school employees. The phrase *in loco parentis* came from English common law, which accepted the notion that the authority of schoolteachers was as comprehensive as that of a parent. The requirement that the *school* had an obligation to protect students was institutionalized in *Gott v. Berea College* in 1913. This was followed by calls for those who teach students to be "better parents." Over time, some of the broad authority diminished, but not the notion that schools had an obligation to provide a safe environment for students who were required by law to attend school. As the safety and well-being of students moved more into the forefront, federal policies and laws have upheld the in loco parentis doctrine acts like the Gun-Free Schools Act of 1994, mandated reporting, Title IX, and other safety and human rights protections.

Over the years, I found guidelines that touched on student safety from religious organizations, accrediting organizations, the Centers for Disease Control and Prevention, sports associations, and schools. The guidelines were similar across categories of policies: screening, hiring, training, reporting, and investigating. Guidelines in these youth-serving organizations are not new. Boyle notes that as early as the 1920s, youth-serving organizations identified concerns about "motivated offenders" who might apply for staff and volunteer positions.[3] "In the 1970s, Big Brothers (now Big Brothers Big Sisters of America) began formally addressing CSA."[4]

The National Education Association's (NEA) "Code of Ethics for Educators" says that its three million members

- shall make reasonable effort to protect the student from conditions harmful to learning, health, and safety;
- shall not intentionally expose the student to embarrassment or disparagement;
- shall not on the basis of race, color, creed, sex, national origin, marital status, political or religious beliefs, family, social or cultural background, or sexual orientation, unfairly (a) exclude any student from participation in any program; (b) deny benefits to any student; (c) grant any advantage to any student;
- shall not use professional relationships with students for private advantage.[5]

The National Association of State Directors of Teacher Education and Certification (NASDTEC) first provided a "Model Code of Ethics for Educators" (MCEE) in 2015 and updated it in 2023.[6] The second edition of their Code includes expectations such as

- refraining from professional or personal activity that may lead to reducing one's effectiveness within the school community;
- refraining from using one's position for personal gain and avoiding the appearance of impropriety;
- staying current with ethics guidelines and decisions from professional organizations and other relevant sources;
- protecting students from any practice that harms or has the reasonable potential to harm;
- considering how appearance and dress can affect one's interactions and relationships with students;
- considering the implications of accepting gifts from or giving gifts to students;
- engaging in physical contact with students only when there is a clearly defined purpose that benefits students and continually keeps their health, safety, and well-being in mind;
- avoiding multiple relationships with students that might impair objectivity and increase the risk of harm to their well-being or decrease educator effectiveness;

- acknowledging there are no circumstances that allow for educators to engage in romantic or sexual relationships with students;
- considering the ramifications of entering into an adult relationship with a former student, including but not limited to any potential harm to the former student, public perception and the possible impact on the educator's career. The professional educator ensures the adult relationship was not started while the former student was in school;
- using social media transparently and primarily for teaching and learning per school and district policy. The professional educator considers the ramifications of using social media and direct communication via technology with one's interactions with students, colleagues and the general public;
- exercising vigilance in maintaining separate and professional virtual profiles and keeping personal and professional lives distinct.

Other professional organizations for school administrators, counselors, and other professional employees have similar codes, as do state education departments. Some include the overall well-being of the student as fundamental to decision-making, although they do not define or provide examples of their "fundamentals." (See, for instance, the American Association of School Administrators and the National Association of Secondary School Principals).

Up to the 1960s, it was common for individual schools and districts to issue codes of conduct for teachers. Daniel Klemm noted that codes of conduct became more common after World War I. Describing the ethical teacher, Klemm wrote, "[the person] must be so filled with devotion for those committed to his care, so interested in their highest good, and so impressed with the importance and sacredness of the charge entrusted to him that his attitude toward those who have delegated the task to him and to those with whom he works, will be one of sympathy and love, rather than of criticism and defense."[7] Klemm's 1938 synthesis of national standards, the first for teachers, had the following observations. "The teacher should recognize that the child's welfare is the principal obligation of his profession. Personal gain, pleasure, community responsibility, even the mastery of subject matter, are subordinate interests of the true teacher, while service to the child is his first responsibility."[8] An additional standard was, "The teacher should report corrupt or dishonorable practices known to exist in the profession to the proper authorities."[9]

Early regulations and codes of conduct at the local level often prohibited smoking and drinking for all teachers and required women who were married to leave teaching. Many included dress codes, particularly for women, and proscribed living and behavior requirements. Beginning in the 1960s, as these requirements began to conflict with changing societal values, they fell by the wayside.

PREVENTION

I began studying school employee sexual misconduct in the 1980s. My thinking benefited from the work of Robert Shoop, a researcher and professor of school leadership and school law, who, in the early 1990s, began guiding parents, teachers, and administrators in preventing and interrupting sexual harassment.[10] In 2002, he published a standard of care for school officials for student safety and provided more detail in his 2004 book, *Sexual Exploitation in Schools.*[11]

In 1991, the identification of child sexual abuse and maltreatment was documented as a public health problem. Over the years, the risks to lifetime health of child sexual abuse have been identified, and prevention research and implementation have increased. More recently, The Centers for Disease Control and Prevention in the US Department of Health and Human Services acknowledged that the sexual mistreatment of students by school employees is a problem of national proportions. I am a co–principal investigator of one of the CDC's initial study grants focused on sexual misconduct in youth-serving organizations. With colleagues at the School of Medicine at Virginia Commonwealth University, we began to study the prevention remedies based on the findings from the sexual misconduct civil cases that are the foundation of this book. From these cases, I identified four cornerstones for prevention:

1. Adopt prevention policies and monitor compliance.
2. Employ safe hiring procedures.
3. Provide training on red flags and reporting.
4. Investigate red flags.

In addition, if sexual misconduct has occurred, after-action is necessary:

1. Provide support services to the student(s) harmed.
2. Provide information to the school community and the public.
3. Conduct an after-action investigation to identify what went wrong and how to prevent future abuse.
4. Engage the entire school community in understanding expectations and consequences.

Examining what happened when a school employee sexually abused a student, I identified safety and prevention categories that were not in place. These findings recognize the lack of safety practices—including psychological safety—and strengthen the argument that school employees, students, and parents need training on red flags and bystander reporting of these red flags.

Table 7.1 illustrates that once the sexual misconduct is identified and reported to an administrator, most, but not all, school officials report it to the police. Remember, these are cases where a school employee has been found guilty of sexual misconduct of a student. In 70 percent of the cases, red flags had been observed by adults and students. The red flags were reported to adult employees, but nothing was done. Increased supervision occurred as a result of only 2 percent of the reports of a red flag. In nearly 75 percent of the cases, others had seen red flags. Only after someone finally reported and an investigation was conducted did the magnitude of the lack of reporting become apparent. In none of the cases did the administration provide training about the red flags that weren't reported and the procedures for supervision and reporting that should have occurred. When the abuse was uncovered, 10 percent of schools did not report it to officials. Sometimes, nothing happened to the abuser. Other times, the abuser was moved to another school or provided a glowing recommendation to help them find a job in another school district. Even when administrators were alerted to an employee crossing boundaries and possibly endangering students, only 2 percent of administrators increased supervision of the boundary crosser.

I also documented consequences for abusers since the risk of consequences is directly related to prevention and deterrence (table 7.2). Because my sample only includes cases where abuse of a student was found, it's not surprising that nearly 80 percent of the abusers who pled guilty were convicted and incarcerated. What is surprising, at least to me, is that of those who were found to have abused, 21 percent were not prosecuted.

When the police or the district took action, the abuse was stopped in the majority of cases. Of those not fired or terminated, 16 percent received no consequences and often moved to another school district.

Importantly, prevention matters to those who are abused. The abuse by the employee isn't the last betrayal a victim/target experiences. Staff and students often retaliate against a reporting student: a third of students are forced to seek schooling in a safer, more supportive environment. Families are forced to move to find safety for their children and themselves. In only 4 percent of cases, the schools provided counseling, class changes, or other

TABLE 7.1   Sexual misconduct by an employee of a student: Safety and prevention practices in place at the time of abuse

Safety factors	Percentage of cases employing safety factors
Policies	
Had some policies for the prevention of school employee sexual misconduct	10
If had policies, followed policies	0
Hiring	
Comprehensive application form	19
Comprehensive interview	15
References checked	19
Criminal background check completed	39
Training	
Provided employees with training about adult-to-student sexual misconduct	12
Provided training on red flags and boundary crossing	0
Provide training about mandated reporting	19
Supervision of employees	
Had received previous reports of red flags related to employee misconduct directed toward students. No investigation. No increased supervision.	70
Provided increased supervision of staff with previous reports of red flags	2
Reporting/investigating	
There were witnesses to the misconduct	74
Report made to law enforcement or Child Welfare	90
Investigated/followed up on reports/witnesses	4
Communication or reports of red flags across levels of school administration	0

TABLE 7.2   Sexual misconduct by an employee of a student: Consequences for the abuser

Consequence	Percentage
Pled guilty, convicted and incarcerated	79
Fired/terminated/	55
Resigned, not fired or terminated	29
No consequences or moved to another school in the district	16
Suicide	2.5

Note: There is an overlap of these categories. For instance, someone might have resigned, been fired/terminated, or moved to another school.

TABLE 7.3   Sexual misconduct by an employee of a student: Student experience after reporting

Student experience	Percentage
Student suffered from depression and anxiety	37
Student left school	33
Retaliation from staff to student after reporting	32
Student committed suicide	20
Student offered counseling, changes in classes	4

Note: There is an overlap of categories.

healing interventions. Recovery is hard for all the students; for a fifth of the students, recovery is impossible (table 7.3).

As I used these data to develop a model of prevention, I learned about Praesidium, a corporation that specializes in training to prevent child sexual abuse in youth-serving, religious, and educational organizations. Praesidium collected data from their customer organization's experiences and developed the Praesidium safety equation, which included eight components to promote a safe environment: (1) policies, (2) candidate screening and selection, (3) training, (4) monitoring and supervision, (5) internal feedback systems, (6) consumer participation, (7) responding, and (8) administrative practices. Praesidium's research and experience and my analysis, although based on different data, have identified similar components of a prevention model. Praesidium has further reified its components as online vignettes and learning experiences. Praesidium's training is available to school boards and school employees.

I hope that the previous chapters of this book have convinced you of the prevalence of school employee sexual abuse and the harm done. Many people continue to deny, diminish, or deflect the reality of educator sexual misconduct. Despite decades of abuse, the behavior continues. School administrators often believe that misconduct won't happen in their schools. They are likely wrong.

A comment on the idea of prevention: it is a goal for some of us. But can the aspiration of prevention be made real? Is prevention a possible solution to this problem, or are we merely thinking about the undoable? Appendicitis used to kill people until penicillin came along; those deaths were regarded as sad but unavoidable. Polio and TB were tragedies but not accepted as problems until vaccines and definitive medical interventions became available. Then, those hitherto unavoidable tragedies were reconceptualized as problems of public health. Without a solution, we see a tragedy but not a "problem." Child sexual abuse is a public health problem, and we have solutions.

The same dynamic appears in public decision-making, especially in resource competition. There are many potential problems, but getting policymakers to act is tough without a definitive fix. It is hard to justify attention and resources unless something works.

Claiming that adherence to a model can prevent or reduce employee sexual misconduct triggers queries about causality. I often get asked about individual components of the model. For instance, "Can policies alone prevent misconduct?" "Can training alone prevent misconduct?" My response is that prevention is not a one-event or one-strategy action. It requires a combination of actions: working together to provide the "rules," teaching about the rules, monitoring rule-following, and reporting when rules aren't followed. None of those levers have been strong in the cases I have studied. Attending to only one won't ensure safety for students.

- No law, no regulation, no threat of punishment has ever been 100 percent effective as a deterrent, including, for example, the death penalty. But no reasonable person argues that laws, regulations, and punishment are unnecessary. They are, in fact, both limited and helpful.
- A sad fraction of education jurisdictions have (1) only a handful of weak policies inadequately administered, (2) no relevant training, or

(3) no relevant supervision of staff or students or no history and practice of reporting. Those places have a higher incidence of substantiated allegations of employee sexual misconduct.

- The co-occurrence of weak policies and high rates of misconduct is just that—a correlation and not causation. In much social science and medical/public health work, we must look at relationships. I can't, for instance, set up an experimental study of school employee sexual abuse where some students are randomly assigned to a school with no policies, no training, no reporting, and no supervision of adults and others are randomly assigned to schools with some combination of prevention from one approach to all approaches. That would be unethical and put students at risk. However, we can examine the levels of all parts of the model of prevention and determine whether there is a correlation between the strength of prevention and the number of boundary crossings or cases of sexual abuse.
- No single policy is sufficient. Protecting children requires various components: screening job candidates, training, reporting, investigating, supervising, and curing the allegations and remedying the damage—all together.
- The evidence that supports the efficacy of prevention is likely to grow. In the meantime, millions of vulnerable children deserve to be protected with a repertoire of the best-documented components currently available.

I began this book by declaring that sexual misconduct can be prevented and that it isn't rocket science. As Amanda Lee Robertson, Danielle Arlanda Harris, and Susanne Karstedt write in their review of and suggestions for preventing sexual abuse in schools, "It's a preventable type of harm."[12] This section examines more closely what can be done and by whom to stop this harm to students in our nation's schools.

The sexual misconduct of some educators is like many complex threats—social and organizational dynamics bear it along; conflicting interests surround it; multiple players with different levels of self-interest interact, and there is much uncertainty. I have fielded phone calls from skeptical reporters, prurient media figures, ambivalent legislators, apprehensive school administrators, angry teacher organization officials, and tearful and frustrated parents. And, of course, student targets trying to heal.

In the following chapters, I draw on my experience with the crisis of educator sexual misconduct and its aftermath for administrators, teachers, students, the school community and the community at large.

FINKELHOR'S FOUR-FACTOR MODEL OF PREVENTION

More than four decades ago, David Finkelhor, Director of the Crimes Against Children Research Center at the University of New Hampshire, provided a way to think about the environment in which abuse occurs. Finkelhor's research on the four *preconditions* that facilitate the sexual abuse of children describes the conditions and encourages our thinking about responses.[13] Finkelhor makes a distinction between an inclusive or exclusive definition of pedophilia and inclusively defines pedophilia as any adult sexual contact with a child, regardless of the motive. That definition is appropriate for those who sexually abuse students in schools. Schools can deal with the internal and external factors that work together to drive or allow someone to abuse a child:

1. The adult must be *motivated* to sexually abuse a child. This motivation might be the sexual arousal of a fixated abuser or the incident that prompts an opportunistic abuser.
2. The adult must *overcome both internal and external inhibitions* against abusing.
3. The adult must have an *opportunity* to engage in sexual activity.
4. The adult must *overcome the child's resistance.*

Schools can create an environment that minimizes at least three, if not all, of these factors.

Motivation to Sexually Abuse

For fixated abusers, this is an internal desire that motivates action. However, many of these abusers don't want to abuse. Elizabeth Letourneau, director of the Moore Center for the Prevention of Child Sexual Abuse, and Michael Set, at the Royal Ottawa Health Care Group, have developed an online course "designed to provide the skills and tools necessary for adolescents and young adults with an attraction to children to live safe, healthy, and nonoffending lives.[14] In addition to training and support, schools can help to make it difficult for minor-attracted individuals to act on their attractions.

The majority of the cases that I have studied are not those of a minor-attracted individual abusing a child. Most of the abusers are sexually attracted to a range of ages and individuals but find it "easier" and "more convenient" to target students who are in a power relationship with them. Adults have the power. Students don't. These people don't identify as minor-attracted individuals. Thus, internal and external inhibitors, opportunity, and power of the student are more likely levers to prevent abuse.

Internal Inhibitors

Predators don't want to be caught. Fear of arrest and prison can derail the motivation to abuse. Shame, guilt, and fear of community opinion help control abusive actions. So, too, would training and support like that offered by the Moore Center.

The misconduct of those employees who sexually harass and sexually abuse students reflects badly on their colleagues and the institution. Preventing misconduct must begin with the uncomfortable business of calling out that misconduct. Acknowledging the need for prevention is acknowledging the fact of employee abuse. Predators rationalize their actions by using thinking errors such as, "She wanted me to do those things to her" or "I'm helping her to grow up." A climate that establishes that those explanations are faulty and unacceptable acts to strengthen internal inhibitors. Speaking out and being specific about permitted and forbidden adult-to-student interactions increase internal inhibitors. The more the predator is concerned with getting caught, the less likely the predator will be to abuse.

External Inhibitors

Good policies and procedures, annual and proper training, clarity about boundaries, parent awareness, and staff vigilance all work to minimize abuse. Knowing that other personnel will report inappropriate or questionable behavior or violation of policies can also inhibit an adult from inappropriate behavior with children.

Opportunity to Engage

Supervision of students and adults, monitoring empty rooms, requiring that teacher tutoring and office hours happen in a public space such as the library or cafeteria, where there is supervision, and prohibition of transportation of students are examples of ways to limit the opportunities for engaging in misconduct toward students.

Overcoming the Resistance

Educating students about what is and is not acceptable and safe interaction and conduct by a school employee helps both the targeted student and other students who see what is happening resist. Often, the targeted student does not realize or understand what is "wrong" with a teacher who tells her she is beautiful, special, and more mature than other students. Other students, as well, assume that the close physical and sexual behavior of a school employee toward a student is acceptable because, as they explain, "No one stopped it. Everyone saw it. We thought they were just dating, and it must be OK, or the principal would have stopped it."

CHANGING SCHOOL CULTURE

The interaction between sexualized popular culture and sexual abuse is as sad as the literature is enormous. A few aspects are particular to the culture of schools. The failure to act or even acknowledge child sexual abuse by school employees is reinforced by people who don't see what all the fuss is about. For instance, it's not unusual to hear that adolescents having sex can't be stopped, so why bother? Schools that look the other way about student-to-student harassment are more likely to treat adult-to-student harassment the same way. Creating a culture where harassment and a sexualized environment are the norm numbs everyone to the daily damage.

Or there is the leering if *sotto voce* observation that sex with a teacher must have been extra-thrilling. Or that sex with students, at least high school students, should not be criminalized "if the student was willing." If a drug dealer recruits a minor to sell drugs, do we excuse the dealer because the child agreed? Consent is irrelevant because minors are not able to give consent to an unlawful, illegal action.

The attitudes about verbal abuse are even more cavalier. When students report verbal sexualized language, their complaints are often ignored.

There are lots of ways to dismiss a student's concern:

- She's lying, he's lying.
- She got a bad grade and is trying for revenge.
- It was just teasing.
- It's a joke.
- He didn't mean it.
- You are wrong.
- He acts like that with everyone.
- No big deal.
- Ignore it.
- Why the fuss?
- Welcome to the eighth grade (or to middle school or high school).
- Grow up. You need to learn to handle these things.

Comments are about how the target, particularly a female, is dressed:

- You must have wanted the attention.
- What do you expect? Wearing that outfit!

Schools promote and protect the perpetrator—and discourage the abused child:

- The people in our school are so dedicated (caring, professional, progressive, sensitive, etc.) that they would never do such a thing.
- It's a compliment: I'd be happy if someone thought I was pretty (sexy, had great breasts, nice legs, etc.).
- We certainly would deal with it, but our hands are tied unless you file a written charge.
- I've got a school to run. Come back when you have something more than rumors.
- No one (else) has ever complained.
- I'll talk to him.
- This will ruin a good teacher's career.[15]

Pushback from Administrators

When they had to deal with allegations of staff-to-student sexual abuse, most superintendents reported being pulled in different directions. They were unsure about their duty. Was it to protect the alleged (student) victim or the alleged (adult employee) abuser? Both have rights (and one has an organization and the vote). Superintendents felt some empathy with the accused abuser, but only if the victim was female. In that case, they said, "What he did was wrong, but I can understand how it happened. He shouldn't have done it, but those girls wear such short skirts." Another explained that he could understand how teachers, especially young male teachers, could have sex with a student. That superintendent continued, "When I started teaching, I went to a bar and saw a girl. I gave her a line, and then I said, 'Don't I know you from somewhere?'" She said, 'Yes, I'm in your study hall.'"

Another superintendent portrayed male teachers as helpless, driven by id and ego. He told them to stay away from female students and said:

High school girls fall in love with teachers and flirt with them. It's appealing to the ego to have a pretty sixteen-year-old girl have a crush on you. Going home and feeling good about it is okay, but don't encourage those crushes. Smile and be flattered, but don't encourage it or do anything to facilitate it. Guys have let themselves fall into these mini relationships only one step short of sex. Driving girls home from games. . . . Who knows what can happen? If you encourage semi-innocent kinds of relationships, you can be in trouble.

Superintendents also reported being unable to believe the charges when first presented, especially if the accused was an outstanding teacher or a winning coach and the target, the accuser, was a marginal student. As one superintendent shared, "I couldn't believe it. The child was fifteen going on thirty. It turned out the teacher was having sex with both the student and her mother." In many cases, the superintendents or the principals were personal friends of the abuser and worked and socialized together for years. The prospect of investigating a friend is a painful dilemma.

One superintendent was typical of educators who worry more about adults than children. The superintendent echoed what many others said, "We need education and re-education of professional staff on how to protect *themselves* from accusations" (my emphasis). The policies of that urban district included the following (paraphrased) statement: "To protect against false child abuse accusations directed to school employees . . . training must include how to discipline students and maintain ethical relations with them." In these too common examples, there is no mention of protecting students from abuse, just protecting teachers from accusations. Another superintendent, in the wake of the sexual touching of elementary students by a fifth-grade teacher, described his plans for staff training: "In the future, we will meet particularly with male teachers to discuss people's perceptions when you touch youngsters. This can be misinterpreted. They must be sensitive to student vibes, reactions and how comfortable they [the students] are in a given situation. Female teachers can somehow warmly touch youngsters, and it is not as easily misinterpreted."

This superintendent, like many teachers and administrators, assumed that sexual harassment and abuse allegations come because female students misinterpret the actions of teachers rather than because those teachers initiated sexual contact. In this view, the problem is with the student's perception, not the adult's intent. When talking with staff, blaming the victim is easier than suspecting the perpetrator.

The Press of Other School Business

I was involved in a case where the HR director of an urban district called the HR director of another district—the conversation was on a first-name basis—to warn his colleague that he was about to hire a computer science teacher who had just been fired for sexual misconduct by the first director's district. The HR director in the receiving district responded, "We need computer science teachers." Within a year, one of the newly hired teacher's students committed suicide in despair over the computer teacher's sexual abuse. The hiring district settled the lawsuit for eight figures.

The same sort of school-over-student justification is common in abuses related to sports teams. Cases of male coaches touching male students hid the sexual abuse under the guise of coaching necessity to touch the athletes. In response to a question about physical "cup checks" by the coach, the athletic director responded, "Hockey? It's a brutal sport, and he was getting his kids ready." A wrestling coach demonstrated wrestling moves in private with his junior varsity athletes. When the head coach received a complaint about the way the junior varsity coach touched the athletes during practice, the head coach responded, "Get real: wrestling is physical and intimate. It goes with the sport; they're [coaches] all volunteers anyway."

Resistance from Teachers and Staff

If the response of some superintendents was ambivalent, staff responses to accusations that a colleague has behaved badly are less nuanced. The wagons get circled—fast. In my studies and practical experience, when a teacher is accused, most other teachers rally to the defense, often in ways that damage the victim, intimidate other students, chill reporting, and jeopardize the investigation. Many teachers conclude that the student reporter is lying and use that belief to justify their retaliation. Teacher anger overwhelms the Title IX prohibition against retaliation directed at legally protected reporters. Some teachers conclude that the investigation is a ruse to eliminate a teacher. Many of the teachers are angry that a charge is even investigated. Instead, investigations are coded as "antiteacher": they are rarely received as needed protection for both students and staff.

Even in cases where a teacher confessed to sexually abusing students, some of their colleagues maintained that it couldn't have happened. Colleagues were more likely to ascribe malicious behavior to the student accuser than criminal behavior to the adult. A common response was, "She [the student accuser] is trying to ruin the career of a good teacher."

The following describes how teachers in one district supported their accused colleague right up until the time he confessed:

> Two girls in elementary school told a guidance counselor that their male fourth-grade teacher was kissing them and touching their breasts and buttocks. The guidance counselor called the superintendent, who questioned the girls. During the interview, the girls said, "If you don't believe me, ask . . . [and they provided names of student victims who had moved onto

junior high school]." Interviews with the junior high girls confirmed that the same things had been done to them in the fourth grade, and they gave names of high school girls who had been kissed and touched. The high school girls described the same events and from the same perpetrator. By the end of the day, eight girls from fourth to twelfth grade had provided similar accounts of repeated kissing and touching by the fourth-grade teacher over the eight years. When the investigation was completed, the superintendent charged the teacher with sexually abusing students and began a hearing to terminate his employment. Other male teachers then sought out the student witnesses/accusers and tried to get them to change their testimony, saying they would be responsible for ruining the career of a perfectly fine teacher. One of these teachers said to the younger students, "I am your older sister's teacher, and I am shocked that you would do this. You are doing a bad thing." Current teachers of the student witnesses tried to attend the hearing when the students provided their evidence. The superintendent had to have them removed. (They could have been prosecuted for witness tampering—but weren't.)

In another school district where a teacher was arrested for sexual misconduct of a student, his colleague teachers collected money for his defense by putting jars on their classroom desks and asking students to contribute. The student who had been abused had to attend those classes and see other students and the teacher working to defend the employee who had abused her.

Similarly, in more than one school, teachers and staff wore armbands to show support for a fellow teacher who had been arrested for sexual abuse of more than one student. Students also wore armbands in support of the teacher. No one stopped this display, and no one did anything to support the students who had been abused by the teacher, who was later convicted.

Teacher Organizations

Teacher organizations exist to protect and promote their members. That is as it should be, and they have made welcome strides in fifty years of organizing for better pay and working conditions. There is still, however, work to be done, and part of that work is taking responsibility for policing the membership's ranks. There are local organizations that, faced with the evidence of some members' bad and criminal behavior, have concluded that to protect the other members; they must police their ranks. Scandals and prosecutions about teachers having sex with students damage the child-centered reputation of the profession and can anger taxpayers who vote on school budgets and impact teacher salaries. The teacher organizations that are taking responsibility for policing their members are also taking steps to complete the professionalization of teaching. Their leadership is praiseworthy, but it is not yet universal.

In listening to legislators and political staff at the national and state levels, I have concluded that they believe they will lose the teacher vote if they support legislation to protect students from the possibility of school employee abuse. And teacher organizations encourage that conclusion.

In 2011, the Virginia Board of Education sought to develop guidelines for the "prevention of sexual misconduct and abuse in Virginia public schools." This state Board of Education promulgates guidelines about at least eight different threats to children. The Department of Education had drafted research-based guidelines about how schools can prevent employee sexual abuse of students. The draft guidelines were posted for comment. As I read the comments—nearly all from educators and nearly all similar—it was clear that teacher respondents were working from a single set of talking points. Teachers seemed adamantly opposed to restricting social media use to school-approved websites and texting accounts. They wanted to preserve private personal platforms for teacher-student communication that could not be monitored. They also rejected the draft policies about reporting incidents because teachers might be falsely accused. Nearly all of the teachers who commented vetoed any boundaries, safeguards, or policy-directed limitations about how they might interact emotionally, academically, or physically with students. The reactions from the teachers were consistent and organized. That does not mean there weren't teachers who disagreed. But those teachers didn't post comments.

In an open hearing, the new guidelines, even though Department of Education professionals had developed them, received little support. The comments on the proposed guidelines put educators' protection before children's safety. Eventually, the Commonwealth's Board of Education watered down the proposed policies and published them. None of Virginia's "school divisions" were required to follow them.

Other legislators defend their failure to act because not enough is known about sexual misconduct by school employees to develop legislation—a "no solution problem." As this book documents, the conclusion is not accurate now, nor was it in 2011. But it again raises the question, How much do you need to know about the abuse that students suffer before you act? Twenty percent of high school students will experience a concussion while playing sports this year.[16] Schools have adopted almost universal and sustained interventions to minimize the damage of concussions. Are we waiting to go from 17 percent of students experiencing employee sexual harassment to 20 percent of students targeted before we conclude that their protection is warranted?

As some would have it, the teachers are vulnerable, not the students. In this narrative, teachers are helpless victims of students who want to retaliate for a low grade by making a false claim. Similarly, teachers are cast as victims who lack the judgment, strength of will, or professional ethics to resist "provocatively" dressed students who "tempt" the helpless teacher to break the law. In these storylines, students have all the power, the teachers are the victims and therefore can't be accountable for their actions. This narrative is never used when the student is male and the teacher is female. I appreciate the difficulties and stresses that teachers and administrators face. However, the defense that adult male professional educators are at the mercy of female students when it comes to sexual misconduct isn't supported by facts.

There is the mantra that teachers are caring people and that it is impossible to be caring if they can't hug a student, take them to lunch, or shut the door to the classroom so they can respect the student's privacy and listen to the student's problems. This viewpoint also includes the threat to parents that if codes of conduct interfere with how teachers interact with students, professional educators will stop caring, or there will be no more caring professionals in schools.

A more curious, and for me, disturbing, perspective is that preventing sexual misconduct interferes with the normal pedagogical eroticism that is present in most classrooms and that is a "natural outcome of the often intimate and intense pedagogical setting in which passion for subject matter blurs with passion for students."[17] While Tara Star Johnson, the author of *From Teacher to Lover*, admits there is a line between pedagogical eroticism and pedagogical abuse, she fails to explain how that "line" can be managed. She argues that teachers should not be constrained by rules preventing private interactions, time alone, out-of-school socializing, and intimate conversations with students. It is the asexual classroom, not the teacher, she blames for educator misconduct.[18]

Fear of False Accusations

Another common response is to shift attention from the harm done to students to the (potential) harm that may be done to adults. In my interviews and talks with whole faculty groups, many school people, especially male staff members, changed the conversation from children's safety to adults' safety. Female teachers were much more likely than male teachers to credit student allegations and maintain a focus on the damage done to student well-being and safety.

Male teachers prioritize the possibility that they may be falsely accused over the discovery of the truth of the allegations, and it is relevant to note that the purpose of an initial inquiry, typically by the principal, is to make a preliminary estimate of (1) "reason to believe." If that isn't established, the allegations do not usually proceed. If they do, a more comprehensive investigation looks for proof or its absence. The same "up or down" determination is the result of (2) law enforcement, (3) child protective services, or (4) a Title IX investigation. Nonetheless, virtually everyone who has introduced the topic of educator sexual misconduct and its reporting to a faculty meeting has the same experience. Despite the protections of the four possible investigations, people want to discuss the specter of false accusations more than the reality of valid accusations.

In the early 1990s, I worked on an advisory committee to the New York Public Schools led by Ed Stancik, the City's Special Commissioner of Investigation. I remember the beginnings of a contentious interaction between a spokesperson for the United Federation of Teachers (UFT) and me. He would regularly tell me that my research was wrong and that the reports being considered were false allegations. I always responded that I'd like to have the data to correct my research. Despite many requests for the data, I never received any documentation that the student allegations had been proven false. The UFT and other teacher professional unions' positive role is to ensure that those accused receive their due-process rights.

While false accusations are a legitimate concern, the chance of being falsely accused of sexual harassment is minuscule compared to the chance of a student being sexually abused by a teacher. The *American Journal of Psychotherapy* published an empirical study by Mikkelsen, Gutheil, and Emens that examined the prospect of false accusations:

> It is a common misconception that children lie about being sexually abused. Researchers have found that false reports are statistically uncommon, and estimates range from less than 1 percent to 10 percent of cases, depending partly on whether reports based on simple misunderstandings are included. *It is far more common for children to minimize or deny the extent of abuse they have experienced than to overstate what has occurred.* [Emphasis supplied.] Children will often test the waters by disclosing lesser offenses first

to see how the adult reacts. There are also many reasons why children recant after a disclosure (don't want to break up the family, don't like to see parents upset, feel out of control of events, etc.), and clinicians with expertise in working with child victims consider this to be a common part of the disclosure process rather than an indication that abuse did not occur.[19]

While there are cases of teachers who have been falsely accused of sexual abuse of students and who have suffered personal and professional consequences, these cases are rare. Not rare are the cases of teachers who sexually abuse students without ever being detected.

Teachers have protections that students do not—their unions, contracts, and licensing and certification. Regulations and guidance that provide safeguards for children are often opposed with exaggerated and unlikely situations. For instance, a school rule that disallows students riding in staff cars is often met with, "Oh so, if there is a blizzard and I pass a student without a winter coat, I'm just supposed to drive on?" Or "Well, it seems cruel that if a child falls and is bleeding and crying, I'm not allowed to touch him." These responses don't help children and aren't in the spirit of a safe school world for kids.

Physical contact and affection are healthy and educationally sound parts of teacher-student relationships. And there are safe ways to express approval and support. Of course, there are boundaries, but boundaries are not blanket prohibitions. Similarly, telling male staff members to never work with a single female student on a project doesn't help the learner, demeans the teacher, and overlooks the safety features that can be implemented. Rather than pretending to protect children by reducing adult contact to absurd and dysfunctional levels—levels that would and should be rejected—these jurisdictions would serve their staff and students better by investing in professional learning about the causes and prevention of sexual harassment and abuse.

Student Reactions

Some students whom an abuser violates are then revalidated by the adults and the system when they ask for help. Schools have discouraged students from reporting ("It has to be in writing." "You'll have to sign it." "This will follow you through your career here." "You must have done something!"). The adult's skeptical and even hostile reception of a report leaves the student feeling guilty for having "caused" their abuse. Unless the student reporter's confidentiality is rigorously respected, the reporter can be vulnerable to continued harassment by peers and adults.

When a popular educator is accused of abuse, some students rally around that person (often at the instigation of the accused adult) and call the target a slut or a troublemaker. Even when they recognized the truth of the accusation, students told me that the victim "deserved it" and that she had "brought it on herself."

Consider the case in which a teacher sexually abused an eighth-grade student for two years. Students knew what was happening but didn't report it at the school. Several students did talk with their parents, who told their children to "stay out of it." Nor did the parents tell anyone at the school or the female student's parents. When school officials learned about the abuse, they ignored the reports for a year. Finally, the girl's parents discovered what was being done to their daughter and went to the school to report the teacher. The administration responded by putting the teacher on paid leave, a contractual requirement, while an investigation occurred. Most students shunned the girl; others called her names. The student target was ostracized and blamed for "ruining the career of a good teacher." The school's several administrators looked the other way. The arrest and conviction of the teacher followed the investigation. The student and her parents moved to another school district.

When a peer supports a student victim, it tends to be personal and quiet. The more common response is to blame the peer, especially if she is female. One girl told me, "If girls are flirting or flaunting, then both guys and girls call her names, like 'ho.'" Another believed that anyone who "wears short-shorts is a slut." That girl and her friends wore short shorts, but she said, "We're not sluts. There are a lot of girls in our grade who are."

Community Reactions

Like teachers, communities and parents tend to rally around the accused teacher. Several superintendents reported being seen as the "bad guy" in the community for bringing charges against a popular staff member. Angry parents show up at board meetings to demand an end to the staffer's "persecution." Others professed concern for the schools' or the community's "reputation." For some, the concern about reputation is concern about property values.

For instance, one superintendent reported that scheduling a hearing to terminate a teacher for sexually abusing multiple students stirred up community unrest. In response, she and her attorney convened a public meeting where they were confronted by "200 furious parents who felt that the teacher was being falsely accused." Bound by confidentiality requirements, the school attorney could not provide details and could only say that the district was pursuing an investigation. The parents became increasingly angry, accusing the superintendent, who had only been in the district a few months at the start of this case, of being out to get the teacher. Finally, the superintendent faced the crowd, saying, "You are attacking me because I heard allegations of sexual abuse of a student by a teacher, and I am doing something about it. What kind of leader do you want? Do you want me to do nothing? I can't do that."

Another superintendent of an upscale school district, when she learned of allegations of sexual abuse of students by a drama teacher, immediately brought in outside consultants to help the district identify "what went wrong." Her first response had not been to doubt the student or the allegations but to examine the district's professional practices to find improvements to ensure that a student wouldn't be harmed again. After over a year of working with facilitators, the school staff redrafted their policies to protect students; provided training on prevention to staff, students, and parents; and helped the school community identify red flags and boundary-crossing behaviors. She, too, was met with community resistance and, along with two assistant superintendents, moved to other school districts.

Independent schools, both day and boarding, have experienced numerous reports of historical and current sexual misconduct by school employees. For independent schools, reputation is everything. Their parent clientele can easily transfer their children to alternate private schools. The National Association of Independent Schools (NAIS) has advised its members, "Schools must not confuse institutional integrity with institutional reputation. The truest measure of institutional strength is the integrity with which a school lives out its mission and values. In preventing and responding to educator sexual misconduct, a school may find its integrity tested."[20] Partly in response to numerous cases of school employee sexual misconduct, The Association of Boarding Schools (TABS) has worked to develop policies and procedures that provide students with a supportive and warm environment while ensuring that they are safe from boundary crossing and predators. A resource that many independent day and boarding schools have that public schools do not is the financial and institutional means to make changes quickly. The response of some schools has been not only to implement creative and regular boundary training but also to provide individual financial support for healing.

THE COMPREHENSIVE ECOLOGICAL PREVENTION MODEL: A WAY FORWARD

When educator sexual abuse happens, there is usually more controversy than functional resolution. Inappropriate or even illegal behavior of educators isn't unheard of. As with any enterprise with three million-plus employees, some teachers strike children or call them stupid. The organizational and administrative climate of many schools tolerates considerable adult-to-student disrespect, denigration, ridicule, humiliation, and even physical abuse. Why is it, then, that sexual misconduct is so often off the table when discussing, monitoring, or even—heaven forbid—regulating professional behavior? Especially when so many children, both male and female, students in gifted classrooms and those with special needs, are targets of sexual misconduct, from kindergarten to twelfth grade, in upscale suburban school districts and isolated rural ones.

Sexual abuse and exploitation of students by the adults who are responsible for teaching and protecting them is a crime. Sexual conduct directed toward students violates professional ethics and acceptable professional behavior and should be prohibited, reported, investigated, and punished in and by schools. The collective failure to prevent those abuses by educators, teachers' unions, politicians, and state and federal law enforcement and education agencies constitutes corruption. If the ultimate test of a moral society is the kind of world that it leaves to its children" then we are failing the test.[21]

So, let's not fail the test. We have ample support and evidence for measures of a comprehensive ecological prevention model.

The model of prevention that I have developed, beginning with my 2004 report to Congress and continuing to the present, relies heavily on reports and policies from youth-serving organizations and research on prevention, as discussed earlier in this chapter. I have more recently been informed by research funded by the Centers for Disease Control and Prevention and the Bloomberg American Health Initiative, as well as the work of Praesidium. Those resources are described below.

Assini-Meytin et al. (2021) indexed abuse-related prevention and policy areas in documents from seventy-four youth-serving organizations. They identified the following components in those documents directed at preventing child sexual abuse in the organization:

- statement of overall commitment to child safety: include a positive environment fostering children's positive development and preventing child sexual abuse
- codes of conduct that cover physical and verbal contact; inappropriate relations between staff and children; inappropriate behavior when children are present or on the organization's property; overnight activities with children; changing area, bathroom, and shower procedures; offsite activities; electronic communication; one-to-one interaction; out-of-program contact with children; communication with parents; code of conduct for parents/other adult participants; and a code of conduct for child members
- training and education: child sex abuse facts and prevention, codes of conduct and policies, responding and reporting. logistics and monitoring
- program assessment, implementation, and monitoring: quality assurance, monitoring program, and facilities; organization's supervision of staff/volunteers; staff's supervision of children; safe physical environment; line of sight supervision
- screening and hiring: background checks and criminal history, written application, personal interview, reference check
- reporting and responding to child sexual abuse: reporting documented by individuals and by the organization, responding by the organization, responding to policy violations[22]

The training company Praesidium identifies a "framework of seven organizational operations" related to a safe environment. Prevention requires all operations to be engaged in prevention, not just one or two. The synergy among them provides an environment that discourages sexual misconduct. My model is similar to Praesidium's model. I adopted Robert Shoop's *Standard of Care* manifesto from 2002, bringing together the research of others to include those who work in youth-serving organizations and those who work in schools. There is nothing new in these prevention approaches or the

FIGURE 7.1   Comprehensive ecological prevention model

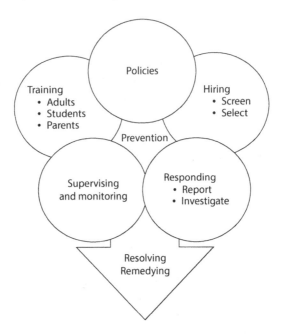

research. The following chapters describe the components of a standard of care, a framework I have used since 2004. These actions, in concert, provide strong protection for students and schools. Figure 7.1 displays the model components and how they interact to provide a comprehensive approach to prevention.

Policies for Preventing Educator Sexual Harassment and Abuse

Policies are the rules that members of an organization are to follow. They help people understand their rights, obligations, and restrictions. Policies are a necessary beginning for the prevention framework. A code of conduct for staff and students is a central policy. These policies include all aspects and functions of schooling where safety and prevention are needed.

Training and Education

School employees, students, and parents need training to understand the rules. What is allowed and what isn't? Under what conditions? And why? Policies without training are useless papers.

Screening, Hiring, Releasing

Hiring the right person for the job is a mainstay of any organization. Not only do employees need to understand the core knowledge and skills of their work assignment in school, but they also need to understand how to treat others, particularly students. Hiring properly ensures that those who would harm children are not employed. An appropriate release from employment ensures that a dangerous adult no longer is a threat to children in the school they are leaving but also that children in other settings are safe.

Monitoring and Managing Personnel

Supervision ensures that those hired don't cause harm. Supervision can be informal, as in noticing the behaviors of adults with students. It can also mean paying special attention to someone who seems too close to crossing boundaries. Supervision also means checking classrooms with closed doors, locker rooms, bathrooms, and other isolated places where harm might occur.

Reporting and Responding

Sexual misconduct usually begins with crossing boundaries, and that may violate policies but not necessarily criminal law. Policies, training, and close supervision lead to understanding and support for reporting actions that might indicate inappropriate behavior with students. Employees and parents must be taught how and when to report and to have reports taken seriously. They must also learn what a report from a child "sounds" like. Children use a different language to alert adults of inappropriate behavior, and adults need to learn their language.

Once there is a report or a concern, an investigation must occur. This might be done by a school employee or by law enforcement. If the school employee begins the investigation, it is only to determine if this is a law enforcement matter. It is better to investigate and turn the investigation over to trained people.

Resolving

Resolving and remedying are central to a school's response. If there is an incident of abuse, there are actions that must be taken to resolve and remedy it, not only for the victim of the abuse but also for the entire school community.

The next chapters explain how this model's components help keep students safe.

CHAPTER 8

Policies and Training

P olicies and training are foundational to the prevention of school employee sexual misconduct. They go hand in hand. There must be rules. And everyone needs to know what they are. In my work, that is the primary purpose of policies and training. This chapter identifies policies that need to be in place and then turns to the training necessary to understand and follow the policies.

POLICIES

A school can enter the prevention model at any point. I begin with policies—the rules of the organization. Some are based on state or federal laws, others on safety practices, and others on research on effective education practices. Policies come from many places, but they combine to tell us what behaviors and responses are expected by those who work in schools and those who attend schools.

While policies are the framework in which people in schools work and study, they are often not shared with employees, students, or parents. Step one in prevention is the adoption and implementation of comprehensive policies. Step two is teaching employees, students, and parents what the policies mean for them—in other words, training the entire school community on the policies that guide their actions.

I often hear that policies don't matter. "If any employee wants to abuse a student, policies won't stop that person." This response always annoys me. Some people run stop signs. Does that mean we should abolish all stop signs in the country? Of course not. Stop signs are one prevention mechanism, along with many others. The same is true of prevention policies.

A prevention model is more than policies, but it can't exist without the framework of expectations found in policies. Policies aren't only for the abuser; they are also for the bystander who sees something and knows to say something; for the student who understands what employee behaviors directed at them are prohibited; for the parent whose child regularly returns home from volleyball practice in the coach's car.

WHY HAVE POLICIES?

The research is clear. Organizations work better when there are rules. In schools without comprehensive policies for preventing sexual misconduct, appropriate hiring and supervisory practices, and comprehensive training, students are more likely to be sexually abused. As I noted in chapter 7, where a school employee abused a student, only 10 percent of schools or districts had policies, and none were comprehensive; 100 percent of those with policies didn't implement them sufficiently or guarantee compliance.

In their research on the efficacy of school policies, Grant, Haverland, and Kalbfleisch surveyed students about school policies and their own experiences of school employee sexual boundary crossing. They found that schools that did not

- distribute policies and materials to students on employee misconduct had twice as many incidents of student-reported sexual abuse by an employee than those that did distribute policies;
- adopt employee-to-student sexual harassment policies had nearly three times more incidents of student-reported sexual abuse by an employee than those schools that had adopted policies.[1]

Grant et al. documented that even though 22 percent of students identified some level of fear of being sexually abused by a coach and 21 percent by a teacher, 94 percent of students had no knowledge of their Title IX officer, and 70 percent had no knowledge of how to file a grievance. Of students who were friends with a school employee on social media, only 18 percent knew there was a rule against this.[2]

More than 94 percent of students in this study had no idea how to file a report or to whom the report would go. Not surprisingly, of the students who were targets of sexual misconduct, fewer than 2 percent reported to a Title IX officer, and only 4.7 percent reported to a school employee. Of the school employees who received the report of sexual misconduct against a student, only 21 percent reported the abuse to school authorities. In nearly 80 percent of the cases, the school employee to whom the student reported did nothing to act on the report. This study confirms that policies can't be helpful without communication. That is not evidence that policies are useless. It is evidence that the organization's policies must be communicated and understood by its students and employees.[3]

Just because policies are required under federal and many state laws, doesn't mean all schools have adopted these needed policies.[4] Thus, while federal law cannot protect students unless schools develop policies and train on them, until that is accomplished, students won't know the rules and won't know what their protections are.

It's not only students. School employees often don't know what is expected of them, particularly in reporting other school employees' boundary-crossing or red flag behaviors. In case after case of school employee sexual misconduct of a student, adult employee bystanders who saw red flags and boundary-crossing behavior didn't intervene. When questioned, they responded that they "didn't want to get involved" or "weren't 100 percent sure that the student was in danger" or said, "It's not my job." These employees were either unaware of their responsibility or deliberately chose to allow students to continue to be in danger.

BASIS FOR POLICIES ON SCHOOL EMPLOYEE SEXUAL MISCONDUCT

There are four historical expectations that influence policies required of schools for the prevention of sexual misconduct by school employees. *Age of consent laws* began in the United States in the 1800s and were enacted at the federal and state levels. As of 2023, all states have a minimum age of consent for sexual intercourse; in thirty-two states and the District of Columbia, the age of consent is sixteen; in eight states, it is seventeen; and in eleven states, it is eighteen.[5] In some states, consent considers both the age of the offender and the age of the victim. In schools, consent is a nonissue if there is a policy prohibiting sexual behaviors by school employees directed toward students, including, for example, those who may be eighteen-year-old high school students. This is one reason why a strong statement is necessary.

Relying only on the age of consent laws still puts youths at risk. Youths who are targeted are often led by their abusers to believe that they are in a special "loving" relationship, that the sexual contact is consensual, and that the adult will leave their spouse or partner for the student. Teenagers rarely understand that there is no such thing as consensual sex between a teacher and a student. Nevertheless, when this misconduct is uncovered, it isn't unusual for the target to believe that it is a consensual relationship because the target cares about the abuser. That is one of the reasons why laws that criminalize sexual misconduct with a student are necessary. Without them, the employee can quietly resign and move to another district. These individuals are not held accountable, and sadly, the students learn later that what they believed was a romantic relationship was just one in the abuser's string of inappropriate serial sexual encounters.

The next movement that affected the expectations of teacher behavior came through *codes of conduct*, which were formalized across schools after a 1913 court decision that defined the authority and responsibility of school personnel to be equivalent to that of parents while the students were in the school's care. In loco parentis stated that schools had an obligation to protect students from harm, acting in place of the parent.

Professional standards of care and codes of conduct are the third development. In loco parentis expectations were taken up by professional associations, and beginning in 1927, professional organizations developed standards and codes of conduct. In 1935, recognizing that the welfare of the child is the principal obligation "of the professional," the National Education Association (NEA), The American Association of School Administrators (AASA), and the National Association of Secondary School Principals (NASSP) were some of the organizations that adopted codes of ethics and behavior to protect children from harm and to report and stop harm if it occurred.[6]

The most recent requirements about school employee and student sexual interactions came with the passage of Title IX in 1972 and two Supreme Court rulings. In 1986, sexual harassment was defined legally as a form of sex discrimination. In 1992, K–12 students could file a Title IX action for damages if subjected to sexual harassment by school employees. Following these rulings, many youth-serving organizations began, in earnest, to provide guidance on boundaries and policies for preventing sexual misconduct of youth organization participants.[7] Other youth-serving organizations started in the 1970s, 1980s, and 1990s to develop codes of conduct and policies to prevent adult-to-child sexual misconduct.[8] The reports about the abuse of children by Catholic priests and other clergy members, Boy Scout leaders, employees in the Boys and Girls Clubs, and other organizations were occurring at the same time that schools were working to formalize prohibitions of boundary crossing and sexualized adult behavior.

In addition to Title IX, states have passed policies prohibiting school employees from sexual boundary crossing. Abboud et al., in their 2020 research on state-level educator sexual misconduct statutes, identified twenty-nine states that have adopted specific state laws prohibiting school employees from sexual acts with students. As the authors point out, the language of the statutes differs, as do the penalties: "The majority of the states fall on this spectrum: Some specific language about a certain classification of crime, possibility of imprisonment and/or fine, and registration as a sex offender. However, there was a wide array of differences between states, varying from in-house punishment to felonies, fines from nothing to up to US $300,000, and imprisonment from months to decades."[9]

The National Association of Independent Schools (NAIS) and The Association of Boarding Schools (TABS) developed a set of recommended policies and practices for independent schools that provide guidance specific to independent and boarding schools. In addition to recommendations for policies and practices, the guidance suggests that the school's insurance policies be evaluated for coverage. They also provide companion resources and a webinar.[10]

RESISTANCE TO POLICIES PROHIBITING SCHOOL EMPLOYEE SEXUAL MISCONDUCT

There has been some resistance to policies outlining appropriate boundaries and prohibiting specific interactions between educators and students. In 2018, for instance, the Portland Teachers Union objected to a proposed professional conduct policy after an investigation of sexual misconduct in the schools. The pushback was in response to concern that prohibiting grooming behaviors would make friendly, helpful behavior with students appear sinister. After community, school, and school board discussions, the policy was passed in 2019 and updated in 2021. The Portland professional conduct policy explains what is expected and why. It also includes the various reasons for exceptions in emergencies or other circumstances.[11]

Others claim such policies aren't necessary. "Everybody knows not to have sex with students," they say. Unfortunately, not everyone knows that. And, even if everybody did, that wouldn't stop some educators from crossing the line. A policy is a mechanism not only to make explicit expectations for employees and students but also to have the institutional power to take action.

WHAT SHOULD BE INCLUDED IN POLICIES FOR PREVENTION?

Schools and districts need clear policies that define and prohibit sexual misconduct, make it clear that the organization is committed to eliminating misconduct, require employees to report boundary crossing when they see it, encourage targets to come forward, and prohibit retaliation. These policies should be written in clear and straightforward language. Policies must also describe the personal, professional, and legal consequences of sexual misconduct.

Policies that prevent school employee misconduct are also policies about hiring practices, training requirements, supervision, investigation, and reporting. Policies should be in policy manuals, be posted where students and staff can regularly read them, and be distributed and used for training for staff, students, and parents annually.

There are many ways to construct and organize these policies. Some school districts include them in their Title IX policy sections, others as a separate policy on fraternization, and others in codes of conduct. Some have a separate "Sexual Misconduct Prevention" section and also include appropriate policies under Title IX, hiring, evaluation, retention, and other policy areas.

Many state school board associations provide members with model policies. These might be a good start, but they probably still need some work to respond to the specific school/district conditions. These policies often don't provide prohibitions and explanations in several areas: off-campus trip protocols, procedures to address non-school activities (babysitting for teachers, tutoring, coaching), gift giving, photographing and videoing students, prohibition of all but school-sanctioned and supported social media platforms, record retention of online communication, central record retention for complaints, and communication of boundary crossing across levels. Policies that don't give examples of boundary crossing and prohibited actions aren't helpful. Readers need examples and reasons why this is a policy to have a complete understanding of what is expected of them.

The following policy components come from several sources. The US Department of Education's Readiness and Emergency Management for Schools (REMS) has an excellent section on policies and training.[12] REMS is a guide for administrators and educators on addressing adult sexual misconduct in the school setting. This is a technical assistance center that serves "two critical functions aimed at helping education agencies, with their community partners, manage safety, security, and emergency management programs . . . [and] also serve as the primary source of information dissemination for schools, school districts, and IHEs [institutions for higher education] for emergencies via the REMS TA Center Website."[13] Based on my experience and research, I identify this site as the most thorough and informative resource for guidance for school administrators, policymakers, and staff. This resource points out that policies ensure that school personnel and volunteers receive consistent messages, understand the conduct that constitutes school employee sexual misconduct, and understand their duty to "prevent, report, and respond."[14] The policy components recommended in this chapter come from this and other sources.

WHAT'S MOST OFTEN MISSING IN POLICIES

A 2022 study by Russell et al. examined all Nevada school district policies and Nevada Law, which since 1997 (updated in 2017) has a law (NRS201.550) that prohibits all sexual contact between employees and students, regardless of age.[15] The authors note that Nevada "has been highly publicized" for school employee sexual misconduct, and they examined policies and employee handbooks to determine the extent to which Nevada schools have appropriate and complete policies for prevention.[16] Because early-career teachers are more likely to cross boundaries and engage in sexual relationships with students, Russell et al. stress the importance of policy training for new hires and continuing annual training.[17] Their research found the following omissions in several districts: lack of consequences to include criminal charges as well as loss of license, policies specific to home visits, transportation of students in personal vehicles, and social media use when communicating with students.

Protecting the Graduate

Russell et al. do not mention the importance of including policies related to graduates. A common practice I've documented is the grooming of a senior student in the final year of high school. The groomers in my study have been males, but the targets are both females and males. The grooming is intense throughout the academic year, with many boundaries crossed, but it stops short of identifiable sexual activity. That occurs soon after the student graduates. I believe that schools have an obligation to protect their graduates from exploitation and misconduct by teachers, especially by teachers who, after students have graduated, continue to exploit the access, roles, and authority granted to them by their schools.

The responsibility of schools survives the graduation of their students. Graduates can benefit from their former teachers, and those teachers can grant or withhold those benefits:

- Graduates continue to depend on the good offices of their former teachers for career and sometimes personal advice and counsel.

- Graduates can benefit from former teachers who connect them to career opportunities and provide recommendations and references.
- Former teachers can act as gatekeepers, granting or withholding access to the school where they continue working, which can, with the cooperation of faculty, benefit selected former students.
- The influence of teachers lasts beyond the classroom: former teachers have established themselves as people of influence.

Those characteristics continue the power differential that makes students—now graduates—dependent on and vulnerable to former teachers.

Schools—as they should—grant their faculty members the authority and privileges that give them influence over students. The complement to that grant is a responsibility to continue to monitor and sometimes govern the relationship between their faculty members and the school's graduates. Failing to do that puts current students and future graduates at risk from emboldened faculty member misconduct. It damages the teaching/learning interaction and negatively impacts the school's reputation.

The grooming and sexual harassment of students often does not stop but, rather, increases once they have graduated. The logic is "they're no longer students"—although the abuser remains a school employee. And "they're no longer minors," although the possibility of exploitation continues. Where schools have an absence or an inefficiency in hiring, managing, training, reporting, investigating, and supervising, those failures facilitate educator sexual misconduct. Had the school not allowed misconduct during the students' enrollment, the abuser would not have been able to exploit them as young adults. The lack of protection of students during their school years continues their vulnerability as graduates.

Policies for Coaches and Athletes

Sexual misconduct by coaches of student-athletes, both male and female, is not uncommon and not surprising. Coaches spend time alone with athletes; they develop strong relationships, and coaching often involves touching and strong emotions. Every school or district needs a policy on coach relationships with student-athletes in addition to the policy for all staff. Student-athletes are vulnerable to those adults who coach them, as discussed in chapter 5.

There are several model policies in the literature for coaches, both in K–12 and higher education.[18]

Codes of Conduct

Codes of conduct govern employee and student behaviors and clarify expectations. These are sometimes referred to as codes of ethics. In searching state codes of conduct, I found them in all states. Some were for educators in general; others were for teachers. In addition, some states had state laws prohibiting educator sex with students. All states had general sexual harassment policies. Not all provided a definition or examples. A little over half provided information about consequences, and one also included the possibility of teaching certification being suspended or revoked. Areas that the authors noted were most often missing included social media–friending students, consequences of sexual misconduct, teacher power and authority as a critical component of sexual harassment and misconduct, guidance on home visits, transportation of a student in a personal vehicle, and specific policies for interacting with students on social media.[19]

Policies Prohibiting "Passing the Trash"

A common practice in dealing with employees who cross boundaries with students is to ask the employee to find other employment with the promise of a positive reference. "Passing the trash" is so prevalent that Congress reauthorized the Every Student Succeeds Act (ESSA) to address this practice. In this reauthorization, Congress required that every institution that receives federal funding must have a policy that prohibits the school/district/organization from providing a recommendation for an employee, contractor, or agent when they know or have probable cause to believe that the person has engaged in sexual contact with a student or minor in violation of the law. While the employer could transmit administrative or personnel files, if necessary, the employer cannot do more than that to help the employee obtain new employment. A reference can be supplied if the employee was reported to law enforcement and acquitted or exonerated.

Policy Components for Preventing School Employee Sexual Misconduct

Table 8.1 includes policy elements that address school employee sexual misconduct.

Policies are necessary but not sufficient. I have seen jurisdictions with terrific policies. They are comprehensive, current with laws and regulations, briefly stated, and aimed at school employees. I've seen these strong policies because, in most but not all cases, the districts have been sued for educator sexual misconduct—and lost. But policies, like other components of

TABLE 8.1   Checklist of policies for preventing sexual misconduct

Policy component	Check if present
Educational, safety, and legal background for prohibition of sexual misconduct	
A foundational statement that references a code of conduct, civil and safe organization commitment, and respect for all	
Description of federal laws that prohibit educator sexual harassment/sexual misconduct of students are described; clarification that the term *sexual harassment in law* is called sexual misconduct when it applies to students	
Description of state laws that prohibit educator sexual harassment/sexual misconduct of students	
Statement distinguishing workplace adult-to-adult sexual harassment from educator sexual misconduct of students	
Zero-tolerance statement from the district prohibiting educator sexual misconduct of students; clarification that illegal and inappropriate conduct is not permitted and can lead to termination of employment	
Inclusion of a statement on grievance procedures for prompt and equitable resolution of complaints of sexual discrimination	
Statement on sexual relations with graduates to include a prohibition for up to two years after the student graduates	
Sexual misconduct: definitions and examples	
Definition of sexual harassment/misconduct of students by educators as stated in Title IX to include the applicability of Title IX prohibitions and procedures	
Definition of educator sexual misconduct to include physical, verbal, visual, and technological sexual misconduct	
Examples of educator physical, verbal, visual, and technological sexual misconduct	
Description of appropriate and inappropriate use of digital or social media	
Guidance on boundaries; description of acceptable and unacceptable behaviors	
Statement that there can be no consensual sexual relations—"welcome" or not—between an employee and a student	
Statement concerning the near- and long-term impacts of educator sexual misconduct on the student victims/survivors and their families	
Statement concerning the near- and long-term impacts of educator sexual misconduct on the school community of staff, students, and families	

TABLE 8.1   Continued

Policy component	Check if present
Statement of the legal and personnel consequences, sanctions, and penalties for educators who violate these policies and bystanders who do not report, including that educator sexual misconduct is a possible criminal offense for those who offend and those who don't report educator sexual misconduct	
Statement that sexual misconduct by educators with students is prohibited both on and off school grounds	
Transportation	
Prohibition of transporting a nonrelative student in a personal automobile or being a passenger in a student's automobile	
Boundaries for coaches and chaperones for sports and events when traveling that include transportation, activities, hotel rooms, and events that are not otherwise monitored	
After-school activities/interactions with students	
Statement on locker room supervision procedures	
Description of appropriate behaviors when meeting with students before and after school, for example, avoiding the following: conducting private conversations that are unrelated to school activities or the well-being of the student and that take place in locations inaccessible to others; inviting a student or students to your home; visiting the homes of students without knowledge of parents; inviting students for social contact off school grounds; physical contact with a student that could reasonably be interpreted as sexual harassment; showing pornography to a student; invading a student's privacy; singling out a particular student or a type of student for personal attention and friendship beyond the bounds of an appropriate educator-student relationship; conversation of a sexual nature with students not related to employee's professional responsibility; flirtatious, romantic, or sexual relationship with a student	
Description of when food and other extras can be provided to students; gift policies.	
Description of boundaries on hiring students for babysitting and other personal unsupervised work in the employee's home	
Bathroom policies for elementary and special needs students	
Supervision of bathrooms, which are used by which grades, and bathroom accompaniment; toileting and personal care guidelines for special needs students	

(continued)

TABLE 8.1   Continued

Policy component	Check if present
Communication	
Posting of boundary, classroom use, and social media/communication policies throughout the building	
Statement that communication between personnel and students must occur on school-approved platforms: email, texting, and other social media platforms	
Procedures and technology for monitoring district-supported phones and computers for suspected violations	
Hiring and managing personnel	
Hiring procedures, e.g., screening, interviewing, and selecting candidates, including attention to student safety and prohibited sexual conduct, described in operational detail	
Follow-up references from previous employers, including questions on why the candidate left and interactions with students	
Background checks including both criminal databases and previous employers	
Applications including questions about why the applicant left a previous position and interactions with students in previous jobs	
Interviews including questions/scenarios about student interactions	
Management of personnel, e.g., placing, reassigning, promoting, terminating, and retiring personnel, including attention to student safety and prohibited sexual misconduct, described in operational detail	
Required disclosure of formal reprimands or dismissals for violating policies on sexual misconduct to other schools seeking reference	
Prevention training and education	
Training for all staff that includes content specific to educator sexual misconduct, including its recognition, prevention, and deterrence; training that includes boundary crossing and red flags; training on reporter responsibilities for educator sexual misconduct	
Annual required training for all staff	
Additional staff training specific to roles and responsibilities, e.g., building administrators, central office administrators, Title IX coordinators, and support staff (bus drivers, aides, custodians, clerical personnel)	

TABLE 8.1   Continued

Policy component	Check if present
Annual training for students provided in an age-appropriate, clear, and understandable language, including boundaries with adults and examples	
Recommended and available training for parents about the recognition and prevention of educator sexual abuse	
Reporting	
Description of channels for reporting suspected educator sexual misconduct: to whom, how, and instructions for parents, staff, and students, including building-level, district-level, and extracurricular activity; Clarification that if a student reports to another employee, that employee must continue the report to the appropriate level	
Description of the requirements and obligations of mandated reporters with specific attention to educator sexual misconduct with students	
Description of the threshold for mandated reporting, e.g., "reasonable belief," "suspicion," etc.; clarification of the standard for a report: observation of red flags, boundary crossing, or other warnings of possible educator sexual misconduct	
Clear guidance on reporting to law enforcement	
Listing of identities of recipients of reports by name, role, and location	
The point of gravity for when the alleged offense requires Title IX reporting	
Description of the reporting requirements and procedures beyond the organization, e.g., central office, law enforcement, CPS, state departments of education	
Description of the reporting procedures available to students, including anonymous reporting (Verbal reporting is as binding as a written report or complaint. Students are provided with names and contact information for reporting. However, a student may report to any employee, and that employee must submit the report to the appropriate authority.)	
Description of the reporting procedures available to parents/caregivers	
Requirement of a report by the organization on the investigation of each allegation and the action taken; requirement of a written conclusion for every report, kept in a central place and distributed to those involved, including the building-level and central office supervisors	
Requirement that all reports be kept in a central location	

(continued)

TABLE 8.1   Continued

Policy component	*Check if present*
List of possible consequences of failing to report an allegation	
Statement about anonymity or confidentiality for victim and reporter	
Statement prohibiting retaliation for the victim and reporter	
Statement prohibiting malicious and deliberate false charges	
Mechanisms for reporting to the state education certification and licensure officials	
Communication of boundary crossing and other reports across administrative levels	
Investigating	
Description of the steps and timelines for the impartial investigation process and authority, including information on parental notification and updates	
List of the identities of those who can investigate allegations, when, and to what extent it is clarified responsibilities or exemptions for a duty to investigate described for the organization (faculty, building principal, central office personnel, Title IX coordinator), law enforcement, and child protective services	
Identification of the point at which a school-based inquiry, separate from and in addition to a law enforcement investigation, is to be initiated and continued	
Identification of the point at which a school-based Title IX inquiry, separate from and in addition to a law enforcement inquiry, is to be initiated	
List of requirements of an investigation, e.g., timely, impartial, thorough, and professional, specified in operational detail	
Specification of how and with whom the results of investigations are to be shared	
Specification of the possible consequences for failing to act promptly on the allegations are specified	
Supervision	
Specification of supervision of student safety, including attention to how, how often, by whom, and with what evidence; specification of how staff are monitored and evaluated in that supervision	
Specification of supervision of educators in their discharge of matters of student safety from predation by other educators; inclusion in job performance evaluations of how staff performance is monitored, assessed, and evaluated in that attention to colleagues' behavior	

TABLE 8.1   Continued

Policy component	Check if present
Prohibition of locked classrooms, obscured vision into the classroom, classroom furniture arranged to block the view of interactions, and uninterruptible spaces	
Regular monitoring of locked classrooms, storage rooms, and offices, both during school and before and after school	
Specification that school tutoring is to occur in public and supervised locations	
Resolutions/Remedies	
Description of acceptable uses of informal and formal resolution procedures	
Policy and administrative regulations that specify operational procedures for resolving allegations	
Statement requiring the provision of due process to both parties	
Procedures and obligations by role for preventing and stopping harassment and abuse and preventing its recurrence	
Procedures for preventing and stopping retaliation by staff against protected reporters or participants in the allegation and investigation	
Statement that the school must respond promptly and effectively to remedy a hostile environment	
Statement that the failure to take prompt action can create a hostile environment	
Description of the interim measures that will be taken to protect the alleged student victim(s), e.g., schedule modifications, adult escorts, etc.	
Statement outlining Title IX and legal remedies that are available to complainants	
List of support services available to victims, their families, and the school community, e.g., therapy and counseling services and support groups	
Plan for postincident policy review, evaluation, and improvement	

Sources: These guidelines have been gathered from various sources, including professional associations, the US Department of Education, the US Department of Justice, the Centers for Disease Control and Prevention, REMs, Praesidium, United Educators, religious organizations, and individual school districts.

a standard of care, do not ensure deterrence for employees or protection for children.

Policies have some particular properties. Chief among those is the difference between "paper policies" and administered, implemented policies. Asking employees fact-level questions at the end of training is helpful, but it measures recall, not action. School people may be able to recite a board policy on, for example, mandated reporting and still not "see something" and "say something." Policies must be implemented, and the supervision of knowledgeable and observant administrators and the concerns of knowledgeable and observant colleagues best gauge how well they guide employee behavior.

Most districts subscribe to a service that provides policy language, formatting, updates, and revisions. Those policy subscriptions often come from state-level school board associations. Receiving districts typically put recommended policy revisions on the board docket, adopt the policy, and require a district administrator or a clerk to update the district's policy book, add the language to the website, and alert employees to the changes and their location.

A reality of these policies is that they are often not specific enough. Strong policies are often described as "professional boundaries," and employees are warned against crossing those boundaries. A lawyer in the state capital can craft language that accurately reflects the amendment to a law. That legally accurate language may not illuminate what a second-year eighth-grade teacher should or should not do with three eighth-grade girls sitting in the stands at a volleyball tournament. Boilerplate policies often fail to identify the specific boundary behaviors in explicit language:

- Do not engage in dating, romantic relationships, or sexual activity with a student.
- Do not take any action that is or that can be interpreted as a sexual advance, including written, verbal, or physical actions, with students.
- Do not discuss sexual topics, including jokes, with students.
- Do not show or send sexually inappropriate pictures, images, or materials to a student.
- Do not be overly affectionate.
- Do not give personalized gifts to selected students.
- Do not share personal aspects of your private life with students, and do not encourage them to share personal aspects of their lives.
- Do not use phone calls or digital means to communicate with students except for school- and education-related purposes.

- Do not give students rides in your vehicle except in a health or safety emergency.
- Do not entertain students in your home or go to their homes except at the invitation and in the presence of the student's parents.

School districts are legally vulnerable if their employees should have but did not observe, recognize, discern, and report suspicious, possible sexual misconduct on the part of employees. The legal question is called *notice*— was the district on notice that something suspicious was happening?

The U.S. Department of Education's 234 CFR Part 106 discussion "Non-discrimination on the Basis of Sex in Education Programs or Activities Receiving Federal Financial Assistance" final rule provides regulations for implementing Title IX. The discussion of notice is similar to previous versions of implementing language for Title IX:

> Consistent with the 2020 amendments, the recipient need not have incontrovertible proof that conduct violates Title IX for it to have an obligation to respond; if the conduct reasonably may be sex discrimination, the recipient must respond in accordance with § 106.44. See 85 FR 30192 ("the recipient need not have received notice of facts that definitively indicate whether a reasonable person would determine that the complainant's equal access has been effectively denied in order for the recipient to be required to respond promptly"); see, e.g., *Doe v. Fairfax Cnty. Sch. Bd.*, 1 F.4th at 263–64 (citing *Davis*, 526 U.S. at 646–52) (holding that "a school's receipt of a report that can objectively be taken to allege sexual harassment is sufficient to establish actual notice or knowledge under Title IX—regardless of whether school officials subjectively understood the report to allege sexual harassment or whether they believed the alleged harassment actually occurred").[20]

A strong district policy might alert its employees as follows:

- A district has actual notice if employees "knew," or in the exercise of reasonable care, "should have known" that sexual harassment was occurring.
- This happens through a cumulation of activities. For example, (1) Did a school allow a sexually hostile environment to exist? (2) Did it not take immediate and appropriate action to correct that sexually hostile environment? (3) Were there employees who "should have known" about those actions and that environment but turned a "blind eye" or were "willfully ignorant"? (4) Was the offending employee's behavior

chronic (sustained over time), widespread (conducted in multiple sites), and notorious (unambiguously regarded as misconduct and discussed as such among students and faculty)? And (4) did the school or district know about the harassment but failed to conduct a "reasonable diligent inquiry?"

Those are necessary and helpful steps, but they are not sufficient, and they are not failproof defenses against lawsuits for educator sexual misconduct. The school board president still has to lean forward and say, "Dr. Mittel, thanks for calling our attention to those policy updates. Can you talk us through how you will measure the effect of the policy changes? Just an outline will be appreciated tonight, but let's calendar a report twelve months from now for you to talk us through how we're protecting our students."

Asking students, "Has a school employee sexually harassed you?" is not likely to yield valid indicators of the incidence of misconduct. The understandable barriers have been discussed in a previous chapter and include fear of retaliation, manipulation by the abuser, ignorance about what constitutes abuse, and shame. Moreover, for a student to respond truthfully to a district-sponsored inquiry requires a level of trust that may not be warranted or exist.

A resource for gauging the incidence of sexual misconduct in individual schools is available from the US Department of Health and Human Services. The Youth Risk Behavior Surveillance Survey (YRBSS) was initiated by the CDC in 1990 and has been fielded and refined annually since. The survey asks students empirically validated questions about aspects of their lives, including sexual misconduct. The results are returned confidentially from the CDC to the district, indicating how students' experiences in the participating district compare to similar districts. The YRBSS is provided at no cost to education entities to validate and reliably track their student's safety.[21]

Heads of schools or districts are advised to do the following to help students, staff, and parents understand district policies and procedures:

- Display posters, signed by the principal or superintendent, explaining unacceptable behavior in the school or district.
- On the poster, include the names of staff members who are available to hear complaints. This list should represent a range of adults in each school by position, sex, and age.
- Prominently show the name and phone number of the school or district's central reporting person, including the Title IX compliance

officer and the local or regional office of the US Department of Education's Office for Civil Rights.

- Involve teachers' organizations, parents, and boards in implementing these policies and in communicating them.
- Include policy information on district calendars. Include this in district publications on other matters.

Consistent Enforcement of Policies/Detection

Most students believe that districts won't do anything about sexual harassment, whether by staff or peers. Students often see cover-ups even when they don't exist, and most have little faith that their complaints, especially about school staff, will be taken seriously by school personnel. Because of this lack of faith in school district personnel, as well as personal issues around sexual harassment, many students won't report incidents directly. Therefore, district personnel must be aware of signs of inappropriate behavior by staff or changes in the behavior of students with staff. School personnel are responsible for "hearing" and "seeing" inappropriate or harmful behavior from staff to students, even if there is no direct complaint.

TRAINING

Training is a necessary partner to policies. Employees, students, and parents need to understand what the policies mean to them. Training on identifying and preventing sexual harassment, including school employee-to-student sexual misconduct, is required for all schools that receive federal funding—in other words, all public and some independent schools.

Who Needs Training?

Training needs to be done with all staff and students; it should occur more than once and should be annual and mandatory. Annual training sessions allow new staff members to learn about school procedures and expectations and remind veteran staff of the policies. Training sessions should help employees and students understand the sexual harassment policy and complaint procedures, should define sexual abuse and harassment, and should present examples of behavior that is not allowed.

Staff members need to learn how to help students talk about the issues of sexual misconduct and how adult employee language and behavior, no matter how well-meaning, can stop students from recounting their experiences. All staff, including teachers, administrators, support personnel, custodians, cafeteria workers, clerical workers, bus drivers, coaches, and any other adult who works with or comes into contact with students in the school setting, need regular training. Essential in staff training is a focus on the district's description of an appropriate staff and student relationship, an introduction to specific behaviors and language that might constitute sexual misconduct, a clear set of directives about how to respond when an allegation of sexual harassment is made or when staff see a sexually harassing behavior, and strategies for increasing the comfort level of students who do want to report an incident. District policies and procedures should be written for these workshops in clear, step-by-step language and discussed thoroughly.

Students also need help learning to identify boundary crossing by adults. They need a discussion vehicle to understand the "facts" and explore their emotional and sometimes ambivalent responses. Students should be clear about what is and what is not acceptable in their school and who they can and should talk with if something inappropriate has happened to them. Students also need to be able to communicate with others when they feel uncomfortable. The latter skill is challenging for most adolescents and will require much support within the school, especially when talking with an adult.

These messages can be communicated in several ways. A one-time large-group program is usually ineffective unless it is a play or presentation followed by a small-group discussion. This discussion should be ongoing since students need to think about these ideas and how sexual harassment may be part of their lives. Teaching about sexual misconduct can occur in almost any school environment, from the homeroom to the auditorium. A school might coordinate projects to accompany formal training as classroom assignments such as math problems that calculate the numbers of students who are targeted in their state, reading fiction/biography and discussion of themes, art projects on prevention, and other ways to continue learning to recognize and report boundary crossing. There are many web-based resources that can be found by searching "protect kids online" or "Internet Safety for Teens." The Crimes Against Children Research Center at the University of New Hampshire has links to preventing technology/internet victimization.[22]

Training explicitly targeted at school administrators and school board members has been less available. Jeffrey Thoenes surveyed Michigan principals regarding educator sexual misconduct and found that principals did not believe they were sufficiently trained to handle a case of misconduct by a staff member toward a student. The principals reported that neither their school district nor university training included this topic.[23]

School board training is also not widely done. However, school boards need to understand their oversight responsibility for the superintendent's implementation of prevention policies as well as the complexities that often occur in dealing with school employee sexual misconduct toward a student. Central office and school administrators, along with board members, are the focus of the volatile, contentious, and prospectively costly business of resolving allegations of educator sexual misconduct. They deserve to be prepared.

While the school cannot force parents to take training, they can offer the training through a link on the school webpage and during times when parents might be at the school, such as parent-teacher conferences and sporting and performance events. Research indicates that parents know little about school employee sexual misconduct and tend to overestimate the knowledge of their children, particularly elementary-aged children.[24]

Sadly, universities and colleges that prepare teachers and administrators have not enhanced their curriculums to include prevention training for school employee sexual misconduct. Its absence in the curriculums of preservice programs in higher education institutions is puzzling and borders on malpractice.

Available Training for Schools

Many training programs developed by organizations and vendors are available to schools and districts. Some require fees; others are free. Some are delivered in person, some can be inserted into the school curriculum, and most are offered online. Although not exhaustive, appendix 1 lists available training programs for students, staff, and parents. Several of these programs have been evaluated for effectiveness for fact-level content recall, although not for positive changes in prevention behaviors. This is partly because gaining institutional review board (IRB) approval or school participation in evaluating such programs is difficult.

The outcome research available on these programs indicates that training helps. Training, "in-services," and professional development are all essential components of a prevention framework.[25] Training needs to reach several audiences: students at every grade level, parents, and all staff, not just teachers, school administrators, and school board members.

Praesidium is one company that provides assessment guides for schools and an accreditation process that starts with a needs assessment. They also provide best-practice standards to help organizations develop robust prevention strategies. The three areas in which organizations that follow these standards report the highest compliance are policies that communicate zero tolerance for abuse, policies and practices that minimize barriers to reporting complaints, and systematic monitoring of high-risk activities. According to Praesidium, the three categories in which institutions are least prepared are (1) establishing and managing risk management practices with third-party providers, e.g., volunteers and on-campus vendors, (2) everyone's role in responding to allegations or incidents of abuse, and (3) how an organization defines everyone's role in student-to-student or adult-to-adult sexual activity.

Of all the training I have reviewed, the Praesidium package is the most comprehensive for staff, administrators, and school boards, providing the most potent prevention platform and the most extensive data, which it makes available in an annual report.[26] The Praesidium suite has two drawbacks: it does not train students on school employee sexual misconduct, and it is the most expensive.

However, it is not as expensive as even one negligence lawsuit. Praesidium annually analyzes the extent of claims payouts. In a study of 1,100 cases through 2021, 70 percent involved adult-to-youth abuse, and in many of those cases, there was a lack of comprehensive training on red-flag behaviors and reporting. In the two decades between 2000 and 2022, the *average* large-loss payout from schools and insurance companies for harm increased more than sixfold, from $8,193,207 in 2000–2005 to $49,941,987 in 2017–2022.[27] The 2024 Report documented that K–12 and faith-based organizations combined to make up 62 percent of all industries with large losses with average payouts of $64 million for negligent hiring, $38 million for negligent supervision, and $27 million for negligent training.[28]

A less expensive program comes from Enough Abuse, which has developed comprehensive school employee trainings and prevention strategies to address adult-perpetrated sexual abuse. Evaluation data of this program indicate an increased ability of school staff to identify boundary-violating behaviors that could lead to misconduct and confidence in and willingness to report these behaviors. Trainings for schools on how to understand and respond to Problematic Sexual Behaviors of children and adolescents (PSB) are also available to address the latest data documenting that over 70 percent of children harmed by sexual abuse are harmed by another peer or youth.

Enough Abuse also provides an interactive map showing where educator sexual misconduct has been criminalized at the state level, which states require child sexual abuse prevention training in schools, and which states have passed laws to strengthen screening of prospective school hires and to prohibit the practice referred to as "passing the trash." Its website links to a range of important school and prevention resources.[29] The website provides materials for parents and guides to conversations with their children.

More Training Options Are Needed

As noted above, training for students on school employee sexual misconduct is less available than training for adult employees. The same is true for parents. Universities and colleges, where teachers and administrators are educated and trained, must ensure that their graduates know about prevention and the limits of their behaviors.

Training Components for Preventing School Employee Sexual Misconduct

Annual training of all employees and students should be required. For staff, this training would focus on the dimensions of sexual misconduct, how to identify it, and how to report it. In addition to defining sexual misconduct examples and reporting responsibilities, administrators' training should include hiring and supervising issues. Student training should define sexual misconduct, provide examples, make clear that such behavior is prohibited, and teach students how to report it. Training for parents should be available and publicized, providing access to convenient online and in-person sessions. Training for volunteers should be required, including parent-teacher organizations, chaperones for student events, and volunteers at other school activities typically supervised by parents. All training should be offered annually and at the beginning of a new hire's employment or volunteer responsibility, with all materials edited to support the roles and responsibilities of each audience.

Training materials for all groups should be in everyday language and be age/role appropriate. For schools receiving federal funds, materials should outline the rights found in state law and Title IX related to sexual misconduct. Training on identifying, avoiding, and preventing sexualized behavior and harassment using technology and social media should be provided to all groups.

Training should be clear about the level of concern, suspicion, or belief that compels reporting and clear that the obligation to report does not depend on proving facts but on reasonable belief or suspicion. Training should also cover the barriers that prevent children and adults from reporting abuse.

TABLE 8.2 Checklist: training content for preventing school employee sexual misconduct

Training component	Check if present
Training: organization policies	
Train on the specific sexual misconduct policies of the organization and what they require. Use examples and plain language. Point out the relationship to Title IX, codes of conduct, and criminal laws. Describe policies and procedures involving transportation and the physical organization environment.	
Consider distributing a handout during training that describes policies and asking staff members to sign it.	
Employee training: description and examples	
Include a working definition of educator sexual misconduct; include examples and scenarios.	
Outline the harm to the student, the employee, and the organization if abuse occurs.	
Identify the warning signs of educator sexual misconduct, providing examples, when possible, from reported cases—examples of adult and student behavior that might indicate boundary crossing. Underscore the fact that some educator sexual misconduct behaviors (e.g., those meeting the legal definition of child sexual abuse) are criminal acts and that, therefore, educator sexual misconduct behaviors may lead to punishment under the law.	
Discuss trolling, grooming, and exploiting. Provide examples.	
Provide vignettes and situations where inappropriate and appropriate behaviors and boundary crossing might occur.	
Identify perpetrator behavior patterns, providing examples from local and national media accounts or case studies relevant to the organization setting and how and to whom they would be reported.	
Include information about which students are likely to be vulnerable targets for educator sexual harassment and what staff can do to protect these at-risk students.	
Reporting	
Explain the role and legal responsibilities of mandatory reporters and the organization's internal reporting procedures. Clarify the additional reporting responsibilities for all employees who witness boundary crossing by employees.	

TABLE 8.2 Continued

Training component	Check if present
Provide clear information about how and to whom educator sexual misconduct and sexual harassment reports should be made. Explain the organization's external reporting procedures, e.g., to CPS and law enforcement, and each person's reporting responsibility. Underscore that the original reporter must follow through to confirm that the recipient of the report has forwarded the report up in the organization and, as appropriate, out to law enforcement or CPS.	
Point out the consequences for failing to report educator sexual misconduct and sexual harassment, as well as protections for those who report in good faith when incidents of suspected educator sexual misconduct sexual harassment turn out to be unsubstantiated.	
Describe how organization policy prohibits making intentionally false educator sexual misconduct and sexual harassment complaints and the repercussions for doing so.	
Provide opportunities to practice reporting.	
Identify opportunities for students to report misconduct in cars, behavior on buses, and other transportation red flags.	
Take time to address questionable behaviors and reporting that are not criminal (i.e., the "gray areas" or the "red light," "yellow light," "green light" behaviors).	
Cover acceptable and prohibited in-person and electronic interactions of school employees between and among students.	
Provide clear information about how and to whom educator sexual misconduct and sexual harassment reports should be made.	
Discuss the steps employees are expected to take to reduce the risk of educator sexual misconduct and sexual harassment in the physical environment. For example, regularly monitor secluded, noninterruptible spaces like student restrooms.	
Describe how students usually report. Practice listening and responding to students' language that may be oblique but still has meaning for possible misconduct.	
Training process	
If training is from a vendor (online or in-person), ensure that an additional session covers areas the vendor doesn't include (organization policies, etc.). Use this session to practice intervening in boundary-crossing behavior to provide practice for employees and students.	

(continued)

TABLE 8.2 Continued

Training component	Check if present
Distribute and analyze a posttraining assessment mechanism, such as a survey, to gauge the impact of the training and determine the need for adjustments in content, approach, or format.	
Require and record training participation.	
Student training should be age-appropriate and provide a guide to boundaries, refusal, and expectations about educator-to-student interactions.	
Additional content for student training	
Describe the organization's educator sexual misconduct sexual harassment policies and procedures, including the steps for reporting incidents, how complaints will be heard and investigated, and how parents will be notified of investigations and outcomes	
Describe common patterns of behavior among educator perpetrators.	
Provide practice and language for avoiding, confronting, and reporting; provide a range of realistic scenarios that call on students to determine the appropriate actions, such as refusing inappropriate behavior, reporting suspicious incidents, or ensuring that a peer does not keep a secret about the educator sexual misconduct sexual harassment.	
Provide meaningful examples that will help students understand the gravity of educator sexual misconduct and sexual harassment.	
Provide respectful discussion about students who may be especially vulnerable to educator sexual misconduct and sexual harassment perpetrators and what their peers can do to support them.	
Provide real-world examples of past incidents if they have occurred (without names).	
Provide details about safeguards to protect students from retaliation when reporting incidents.	
Discuss the harms of false allegations and the punishment for making intentionally false reports or allegations.	
Additional content for parents	
Explain the organization's policies in plain language.	
Include a working definition of educator sexual misconduct; include examples, scenarios, and prevalence rates. Provide examples of boundary-crossing behaviors.	

TABLE 8.2   Continued

Training component	Check if present
Outline the harm to the student and the family if sexual misconduct occurs.	
Discuss trolling, grooming, and exploiting. Provide examples.	
Provide specific examples of the organization's efforts to monitor interactions between and among students.	
Encourage parents to ask questions after the training.	
Provide practice for parents to talk about educator sexual misconduct with their children.	
Explain reporting procedures to school and law enforcement.	

Sources: These guidelines have been gathered from various sources, including professional associations, the US Department of Education, the US Department of Justice, the Centers for Disease Control and Prevention, REMs, Praesidium, United Educators, religious organizations, and individual school districts.

Table 8.2 provides guidance on the content to provide in training to prevent educator sexual misconduct.

While central to prevention, policies and training need to be preceded by employee screening and supplemented by supervision, investigations, and internal communications. These are described in chapter 9.

CHAPTER 9

Personnel Management

M anaging employees is tightly connected to the prevention of sexual misconduct. Schools have layers of administrators, and three functions—hiring, supervising, and firing—are particularly important. Principals, assistant principals, and department chairs manage staff at the school level. At the district office, there are often "area superintendents" in charge of groups of schools or assistant superintendents for elementary and secondary schools. Special education typically has its top administrator. Most district offices have an assistant superintendent for human resources and a personnel director. Some district offices include curriculum topic specialists or directors, for example, in English language arts or math, who contribute to supervising. All of those specialists can be involved with managing the staff of schools, and they report to a superintendent of schools, who reports to the board of education.

Religious schools and nonaffiliated independent schools have similar structures, although depending upon the size of the organization, they might not employ as many people for these functions. However, independent schools, including boarding schools, have the additional task of working within organizations that emphasize teacher/staff relationships with students. This culture challenges the organization to find ways to support students without endangering them.

This chapter focuses on how personnel management can contribute to the prevention of school employee sexual misconduct.

HIRING

A thorough vetting of the candidate for each part of the hiring process is necessary to provide a safe approach to hiring, beginning with a description of the position that includes the expectation of ethical and appropriately demarcated interactions with students. This theme should run through the application, interviews, reference checks, and position offer. Stressing a culture in which supervision of adults as well as students includes not being alone with students in closed or uninterruptible spaces, prohibition of exclusionary behavior with selected students, and clear boundary guidelines both in and out of school sends a message that inappropriate behavior with students is not acceptable in this job.

Praesidium provides a list of high-risk characteristics of applicants for jobs, including the following:

- social isolation, difficulty with adults
- tendency toward excessive physical affection, tickling, wrestling
- difficulty with authority figures or working as a team
- permissiveness with children; failure to set limits with children
- applicant overqualified; will take any position; willing to accept lower pay
- difficulty with stress
- too involved with children
- tendency to give gifts to children
- poor role model with children
- poor judgement with children; harsh forms of discipline

Application

The application form needs to be complete and specific, with questions about work history, including dates of employment, supervisor contact information, and reason for leaving the previous position (table 9.1). Red flags on an application form include gaps in employment, lack of explanation for changing positions, and lack of contact information for previous supervisors. It is not unusual for an applicant to include a reference who did not supervise the person or is not even employed by the organization. Check with the personnel department to confirm that you are trying to reach the appropriate person. On the application form, inquire about adult volunteer or paid positions in youth-serving organizations and contact information for a supervisor. The application form should include a question encouraging the applicant to discuss their philosophy and practices when working with youths and how they maintain boundaries while providing support and supervision.

Red flags on an application include the following:

- gaps in years of work or just absence of years and information
- conflicting or incorrect information (school names wrong etc.)
- no reasons or vague reasons for leaving a previous position

TABLE 9.1   Items on application form

Item	Check if Present
Use a common form for all applicants	
Questions on work history	
Request for a list of past employment with contact information of supervisor	
Statement that past employers will be contacted	
Request to identify previous work or volunteer experiences with youth-serving organizations	
Questions on identification(s) that will facilitate background checks	
Statement that incomplete or false information can result in termination of the candidacy	
Question about if applicant has ever been convicted of a crime and, if so, what crime(s)	
Question asking if there has ever been an allegation of sexual misconduct with children	
Question asking if there has ever been an allegation of physical misconduct with children	

Sources: These guidelines have been gathered from various sources, including professional associations, the US Department of Education, the US Department of Justice, the Centers for Disease Control and Prevention, REMs, Praesidium, United Educators, religious organizations, and individual school districts.

- former supervisors not listed
- overeducated/prepared for the position
- willing to move to a lesser-paying position
- descriptions of children as needy, helpless, vulnerable

Screening

Screening happens when you are deciding who to interview. Read the application carefully, noting who is listed for a recommendation (or who has sent a letter). Read the letters to determine whether this is a pro forma letter or is from someone who knows the person's work experience. Note if there are references who did not submit a letter but were asked to do so or if the references listed aren't relevant to the applicant's work background.

Call all the references and interview others if the references listed aren't sufficiently appropriate. The application form should have asked why the candidate left a position. The hiring time should have been used to gather contact information on previous supervisors, even if those people aren't included in the reference list. Go beyond superficial reference checks to ensure that you are talking to someone who supervised the person and has knowledge of their interactions with students. Ask references directly about boundaries with students. Ask the references about the organization's and candidate's social media practices with students. Ask if the former employee was asked to leave the position.

Watch for red flags when contacting previous employers/references:

- Reference was not a supervisor.
- Reference is reluctant to talk.
- Reference didn't know the applicant well or had a very short-term relationship with the applicant.
- Reference won't answer particular questions.
- Information provided is different than that in the application or interview.
- Reference is evasive in responding.
- Reference is unwilling to go beyond sharing the individual's start and end dates for employment and most recent salary: limited cooperation from a previous employer often signals the boundaries imposed by a disputed departure from the previous job.
- Reference describes the applicant as having high-risk characteristics.
- Reference reports specific concerns they have.

Conduct internet and social media (Facebook, TikTok, X, etc.) searches for information about the candidate. All fifty states and the District of Columbia require criminal background checks for new employees. Screening for both criminal charges and licensure in the profession is necessary at both the state and federal levels, but even then, these approaches are inadequate, resulting in fewer than 0.2 percent of abusers being identified.[1]

Local criminal checks might not pick up illegal behavior in other states; the same is true for licensure. Different laws and regulations provide a flawed system and have allowed teachers disciplined for serious misconduct or those allowed to resign instead of being disciplined to move to another state, get a teaching license, and start again.[2] NASDTEC, the National Association of State Directors of Teacher Education and Certification, maintains a database of teachers whose licenses have been revoked. Because no federal government agency keeps these records, each state must work with other states to share their records, which they do through NASDTEC. A 2016 *USA Today* report indicated that at least 9,000 disciplined teachers were not in the NASDTEC system. Since that time, NASDTEC and state education agencies have worked to improve coverage.[3]

In cases I have reviewed, employees and applicants have used false social security numbers, fake names, and the credentials of others. Don't assume that everything in the application is accurate. Check and double-check. Examples of other screening sources for background information are listed in table 9.2.

TABLE 9.2   Sources for background checks

Name-based checks	Data sources
Social security number trace	County court records
Individual county criminal records search	State record repositories
Single-state criminal records search	Sex offender records
Multistate criminal records search	Administrative office of the courts
National sex offender registry search	Department of Public Safety
International criminal records search	Department of Corrections/Criminal Justice
Credit checks	State police agencies
Motor vehicle records search	Department of Probation, Parole, and Pardon
Professional license or education verification	Various state registries (abuse, drug, and violent crimes)
Employment verification	Various national security databases (FBI Most Wanted, Interpol Most Wanted, terrorist watch lists, etc.)
Personal and professional reference checks	Proprietary databases
Federal criminal and civil searches	
County civil records searches	
Search of social media such as Facebook, TikTok, Instagram, and others	

Sources: These guidelines have been gathered from various sources, including professional associations, the US Department of Education, the US Department of Justice, the Centers for Disease Control and Prevention, REMs, Praesidium, United Educators, religious organizations, and individual school districts.

Personality tests have been suggested as a screening device. At this time, there is mixed evidence on whether such tests would identify a child abuser. In one study, the Minnesota Multiphasic Personality Inventory-2 was tested with clergy members in the Catholic Church. While it did show small differences in the aggressive/sadistic scale between those who had sexually abused and those who hadn't, the authors "found relatively few differences in personality and psychopathology between a sample of clergy who have sexually abused minors and non-abusing clergy members." The finding suggests that "psychological impairment appears unlikely to contribute meaningfully to a model of initial sexual offending."[4]

Verifying information on the application form and in resumes submitted is important (table 9.3). Presidium notes that in an October 2022 survey, 58 percent of respondents seeking employment in education reported that they had lied on their resume at least once.[5]

TABLE 9.3   Screening process

Item	Check if present
Screen substitutes and volunteers.	
Make sexual perpetration history an automatic disqualifier.	
Make violent behavior an automatic disqualifier.	
Save background checks until the end of the screening and selection process.	
Verify social security number.	
Match employment history on the application with references listed to make sure references from all areas are included.	
Contact all references by telephone. Take notes and make them part of the personnel file of the candidate who is hired.	
Contact previous supervisor and two other references at the previous position held by the applicant, even if they are not on the reference list.	
Ask references about why applicant left previous position.	
Ask references if the applicant was accused of misconduct.	
Ask references about any gaps in employment in the applicant's history.	

Sources: These guidelines have been gathered from various sources, including professional associations, the US Department of Education, the US Department of Justice, the Centers for Disease Control and Prevention, REMs, Praesidium, United Educators, religious organizations, and individual school districts.

Interview

Before the interview, provide the applicant with information about the job description and the board policy on professional conduct between staff and students. During the interview, candidates should be probed about their views on boundaries with children and informed of the school's commitment to protecting children from employee abuse and boundary crossing. Include situation-specific questions to learn how the candidate would handle, for instance, a student who might need a ride home, who wants to talk to the teacher in private, who needs extra help with classwork, or who has a "crush" on the teacher (table 9.4).

Red flags in the interview include the following:

- defensiveness, anger
- evasiveness

TABLE 9.4 Questions and items for the interview

Item	Check if present
Ask the applicant to clarify and expand answers to questions from the written application.	
Ask open-ended questions to encourage discussion.	
Share the organization's code of conduct with the applicant.	
Inform the applicant of the organization's policies on boundaries for adult-student interactions.	
Ask about the applicant's views on the relationship between employees/volunteers and children.	
Ask the applicant about incidents or allegations of sexual or other abuse of children.	
Ask when it is appropriate to touch a child and why.	
Ask why the applicant is leaving/or left previous positions.	
Provide scenarios that require the applicant to explain how to handle being alone with a child, helping a child, responding to the special needs of a child. These should be situations that are red flags. For instance: A student knocks on your classroom door when you are in a free period. The student asks you for help with an assignment. What do you do?	

Sources: These guidelines have been gathered from various sources, including professional associations, the US Department of Education, the US Department of Justice, the Centers for Disease Control and Prevention, REMs, Praesidium, United Educators, religious organizations, and individual school districts.

- descriptions of children as helpless, vulnerable
- descriptions of patterns of gaining access to children
- patterns or descriptions of problems with authority
- willingness to accept any position to be around children

SUPERVISING

The most common supervision deficits I found in cases where a school employee sexually abused a student were ones of omission, overconfidence, and carelessness. Before any warning of boundary crossing or questionable behavior of a school employee, administrators identified supervisory responsibilities as only monitoring job-related responsibilities. For instance, classroom observations of teachers were used as a formal evaluation only of teaching, not of teacher-student interactions unrelated to the curriculum. Hall sweeps were about student infractions, not adult boundary crossing. Checking empty classrooms was rarely done except to see if the building had been cleared at the end of the day.

Supervising to prevent school employee sexual misconduct involves following up on comments about boundaries, creepiness, spending too much time with selected students, and what is happening in classrooms and other parts of the building when classes aren't in session. It is about listening to students' and colleagues' comments and asking questions. It is about noticing how and when students enter and leave the school building and student-employee interactions after sports and other extracurricular activities. If students arrive extra-early for school, do they bypass common areas and spend alone time with particular teachers? Is there a similar pattern after school? Supervision is about awareness of boundary crossing and intervention when it occurs.

The following things should be done when supervising to make the organization safe:

- Control access to the facility.
- Monitor high-risk locations: those that are remote, obscured, and uninterruptible.
- Strengthen formal surveillance, both of people and technology.
- Restrict personal telephones at work.
- Conduct risk assessments of programs and places that aren't easily supervised: after school, before school, on playing fields, in parking lots.

- Limit one-on-one tutoring, guidance, and transportation. Create and identify areas where tutoring and guidance can be done in an open space where others can monitor or where the interaction is publicly visible.
- Identify employees whose job it is to manage and supervise high-risk spaces. Be specific about those people's duties, such as their co-curricular activities, like sports, drama, and music.
- Add posters with reporting reminders. Make sure both employees and students can see these posters. Use posters to help students and staff think about boundary crossing and red flags.
- Remove excuses by uniformly and comprehensively enforcing formal protocols about conduct and reporting.
- Review training to ensure that it includes practicing reporting and understanding boundary crossing and red flags.
- Manage every day. Walk the halls and observe adult-student interactions; attend before- and after-school practices and events; sit in the cafeteria and observe adult-student interactions; check classrooms at recess and between classes.

REPORTING

This section is primarily about adult reporting and less about student reporting. In this book, I focus on organizational culture and responsibility. The organization's job is to create a culture that protects children, not one that requires children to be responsible for their safety from school employees. A culture where adults are in charge nonetheless encourages students to report their sexual harassment and their concerns about others.

Types of Reports

Reports are both internal and external:

- Notice of possible misconduct toward a student is reported to a school employee.
- The school employee who receives the report and who is also a mandated reporter makes sure the report is made to whomever the school-identified person is for such reports, as well as the principal of the school, the Title IX compliance officer, the assistant superintendent for human relations, and the superintendent.

- the superintendent (or other person designated as the organization's reporter) send a report to law enforcement or child protective services.
- If the misconduct is substantiated and is in violation of school, district, and state policy, a report must be made to the state education agency licensing office.
- A Title IX report and resolution must be made to the superintendent and school board.

Initial Report

The first report is from the student target or a bystander about possible boundary crossing or misconduct. Students typically turn to a trusted or accessible school employee. An aggrieved and upset ten-year-old student is not likely to request an appointment with an assistant superintendent to receive, complete, and submit the board-required "2207-G Sexual Harassment Report" form. "Reporting" from a child includes elliptical remarks, second-party "my friend" accounts, rumors, sentence fragments, and tearful and incomplete thoughts. Sometimes, it is a direct charge—"Mr. Smith keeps touching my breasts."—or an indirect but pointed comment—"Someone should look at Mr. Smith. He acts weird around the girls." Young children and even teenagers seldom describe what sexual abusers do in explicit and graphic language. Instead, they commonly employ euphemisms like "creepy" and "weird." Those words still point to sexual harassment and abuse. The US Court of Appeals for the Fourth Circuit quoted approvingly the observation of the National Women's Law Center that children "cannot be expected to articulate the sexual abuse and harassment they suffer in the same words as adults."[6] School employees who receive those often-vague accounts are still legally obligated to forward that information.

Official Channels Report

Because the initial report is not likely to be made to the internal offices that deal with employee misconduct, the next step is to ensure that the initial report gets to the right person in the organization. If the employee who first receives a report of possible employee misconduct is not the person in the reporting hierarchy who make decisions about investigation and next steps, that person should be contacted. The organization usually designates the "officials" who need to receive the report, which prior recipients must relay to that person or persons.[7] Most often, the people who "need to know" are the building administrator, the Title IX coordinator, the human relations administrator, and the superintendent. Sometimes, a union official is part of the reporting path. Different organizations may identify additional officials who should be informed.

Law Enforcement

After a cursory investigation, local law enforcement should be contacted. School employees are required to report, and school officials who did not contact law enforcement about possible school employee sexual misconduct have faced misdemeanor or felony charges.[8] Because all school employees are mandated reporters, if the school representative does not take action or the school or district does not move the complaint forward, the original employee who heard the complaint must contact law enforcement.

State Licensing Agency

If sexual misconduct is determined, and if the employee is a certificated employee, the state education office in charge of licensing and certification must be alerted about actions they may take to remove the employee's certification or license.

Title IX Investigation and Report

Sexual misconduct by an employee toward a student is not only a possible criminal offense, it is also a violation of Title IX. Therefore, federal law declares that each reported incident requires a Title IX investigation and a report on what happened and the resolution. The Title IX report does not require a new investigation and can use findings from the law enforcement investigation. It does, however, need to determine what the findings mean for the district's policies and practices and the resolution and support for the target of the abuse. The report includes the charges, the findings, and the resolution for the alleged abuser, the target, and any others involved.

What triggers a report? First, what the reporting requirement isn't; it is *not* having to know for sure that a school employee and a student are having sexual intercourse because you have seen it firsthand. The threshold is "reason to suspect" or "reasonable belief" that there might be abuse:

- Red flags and boundary-crossing behaviors are indicators that grooming of a child for sex *might* be occurring. That is a reason to report.
- If there are rumors and gossip among students and staff that a teacher is having sex with a student, dating a student, touching a student

inappropriately, or driving a student to and from school, those are reasons to report.

Staff often believe that certainty and irrefutable proof are necessary, which becomes an obstacle to reporting and facilitating continued harassment. Proof is not required at the early stage of reporting. A report essentially says, "There might be something going on here. Take a look. Make sure the student is safe." Title IX protects those who report "reasonable belief" in good faith. It isn't the responsibility of the bystander employee to investigate the veracity of the red flag or the report. That job is done by someone trained to provide a thorough and fair look at what is happening.

One of my cases demonstrates the tragic consequence of requiring proof at an inappropriately early stage. Carl Jabbia, an associate superintendent in a mid-size district, received several teachers' reports that a colleague was crossing boundaries. Instead of investigating the multiple reports, he told the teachers, "All you have are rumors. Come back when you have proof. If it's a rumor, you'll have to have facts before you can report." In Jabbia's district, the board policy was "reasonable belief," and the state's threshold for mandated reporting was "suspicion." Jabbia's instruction was not only wrong, but it also advised bystanders to do what they were neither trained nor allowed to do—investigate a colleague. As a result of the assistant superintendent's misdirection, the teachers backed off, and the abuser continued to abuse at least ten additional students before a better-informed administrator joined the district and a report—of "reasonable belief"—was made, investigated, and sustained with consequences for the abusing teacher.

The United States Court of Appeals for the Fourth Circuit addressed the issue of what counts as actual notice when a report is received. The court held that:

A school receiving a report or complaint alleging sexual harassment is sufficient to satisfy the actual notice requirement. . . . Furthermore, "[t]he consequences of [a subjective actual-notice standard] are especially concerning as applied to children, who cannot be expected to articulate the sexual abuse and harassment they suffer in the same words as adults."[9]

To the extent that the School Board suggests *that actual notice means a school official's subjective knowledge or conclusion that the alleged sexual harassment occurred, such a standard would be even more nonsensical* [emphasis in original]. Under Title IX, a school's actual notice of the alleged sexual harassment triggers its duty to investigate. . . . It would be illogical to require a school to investigate a complaint alleging sexual harassment only if it has already determined that such harassment did occur. . . .

Nor would it make sense to require a student alleging sexual harassment to bear the burden of substantiating their claim with adequate evidence at the time of their initial report before the school undertakes an investigation.

In response to the complaint that "allowing a student's unsubstantiated complaint to establish actual notice would mean that schools would be "liable based on mere gossip or rumor," the Court responded, "*This argument is meritless.*"

In other words, if there is a report of suspected or possible sexual harassment/abuse/misconduct, that is actual notice and must be investigated.

Typical Report Patterns

Students whom school abusers victimize have been manipulated into secrecy and illegal acts. A direct report rarely comes from the student who has been targeted. But victims do tell their friends, and friends and other students often see what is being done to another student. Those bystanders are the most frequent source of reports. It is rare for either a female or male victim to come forward while they are being abused. Rather, it takes time for student victims to recognize the damage done to them. As a result, states across the country have waived or "tolled" their previous statutes of limitations for reporting educator sexual abuse. Hundreds of former victims have benefitted from this opportunity at justice.

Studies of student reporting indicate that students believe they have reported and that no one listened to them.[10] When students do report, it is most often indirect, through comments like, "That teacher is weird," "I don't want to be in that class," or "Something creepy is going on between my friend and [school employee name]." Other observations from a student that constitute a report might be that "there is a student who calls Mr. Smith by his first name," Ms. Brodson stands too close to the boys in the class," "Mr. Garrison takes pictures of us. You should look into him," "Coach Roster is doing some weird things," and "Ms. Costello acts like she is our age when she talks with the boys."

In one school district I studied, a male industrial arts teacher, Mr. Baldwin, sexually abused eight boys over the years. Students described him as "faggy" and "weird." Boys in his class talked about visiting his vacation house on a lake. Both students and adults described his closeness to male students as "odd" and "creepy." The principal described a series of red flags and his and the school's inadequate responses. In his deposition, the principal testified:

> [Within the first year of employment], other administrators and teachers began to develop feelings that Baldwin was potentially a pedophile, that something was wrong, as Baldwin was too friendly with the students, and there may have been something going on that they didn't know about. Within two years after his hire, he was observed to allow the students to get personal with him and he was "too open with students." Five of his colleagues and supervisors in the school talked about him as "odd" and questioned his behavior. In response to his "undue closeness with students," he was given a "professional improvement plan." [An incident in the school] resulted in a letter in his personnel file. The letter cited his favoritism, protecting particular students from board policies and hosting students at his private vacation home. While we gave him an "improvement plan" every few years, we didn't follow up on them.

Thus, even in this case, with observations, intuition, and actions leading colleagues and supervisors to suspect that the teacher was abusing students, there was no reporting, no investigation, no meaningful follow-up, and no close monitoring.

No matter how the information comes to an employee, it must be further reported and investigated. All too often, in the cases I studied, school administrators peremptorily rejected the report and stopped protecting students at the early stages.

Anonymous and School Tip Reporting

School policies often include a statement such as "Anonymous complaints involving inappropriate boundary invasions by a staff member with students will be investigated as if a student, parent, or staff member reported the violation." There are vendors for such web-based anonymous systems. In the cases I've studied, these reports provide more information for investigation and almost always identify actual school employee misconduct. One of the arguments against anonymous reporting is that it can lead to "witch-hunts." I have never encountered such an event.

The US Department of Justice provides a blueprint for school tip lines. Recognizing that students have information about potential threats and risky behavior, the tip line helps them get that information to the right person. Staff often volunteer to collect, verify, and route the tip to the most appropriate person at the school, a mental health professional, or law enforcement responder. The Department of Justice's case analysis study of 998 schools with tip lines found 1,410 tips that served nearly 500,000 students. Of the number of tips that students reported, half related to sexual abuse, sexting, harassment, and sexual assault.[11]

BARRIERS TO REPORTING

There are reasons why people don't report. Fortunately, those barriers can be removed or altered to encourage rather than discourage reporting.

School Culture

Expecting teachers to "report" on their colleagues is asking a lot. But what is the purpose of the "report"? I suggest a report can be considered an "alert." Think of the alarm service that many of us have in our homes. When it goes off, it alerts us that something may be wrong. Do you ignore or dismiss it like many school people do with student accounts? Do you jerk the electrical connections out of the wall? Do you conclude that the alarm company is trying to mislead you or that it has an ulterior motive? Do you think, "I have a perfectly sound house? Why is the alarm company trying to ruin the reputation of my house with my neighbors?" Do you wait for "proof" (i.e., flames and smoke and the sound of breaking glass)? More likely, you treat the report of the alarm company's sensor as an alert that warrants your attention.

Getting your attention to a possible danger is where the analogy ends. Checking the basement steps for smoke is what a homeowner should do. Checking Mr. H's after-school classroom—and the little cubicle with a windowless door that he uses as an office just off his classroom—is the responsibility of a supervisor or administrator. Nonetheless, passing along the initial information about possible abuse is how school employees should alert others to a report. Imagine a principal talking the faculty through a fall session review of their reporting obligations. Not many principals will say, "I want you to report on your colleagues." Many more principals would tell the faculty, "I want you to alert me if you see something that you think is amiss or suspicious. Alert me, please. My job is to figure out the likely reality."

Why Student Targets Might Not Report

There are many reasons that students don't often report their abuse: fear that they won't be believed, belief that it was their fault or they will get in trouble, fear of harm from the abuser to them and their families.

Students who are abused often tell their friends, and because these students have information that adults don't, the culture of the organization can encourage or discourage children from telling adults. *Students* don't report because

- abusers manipulate them;
- they don't interpret the interaction as abuse;
- they want to protect their abuser;
- they are intimidated and afraid;
- they feel shame and embarrassment;
- they blame themselves and feel guilty;
- they believe that in a student-versus-adult employee situation, they will lose;
- they don't want to "get in trouble";
- they believe adults will not act;
- they fear reprisal by the abuser, the school, or their peers;
- they fear the organization will not protect them;
- they don't know what to report;
- they don't know how to report;
- they don't know to whom to report;
- they've been asked by the victim to keep the information secret;
- they want to protect their student colleague/victim;
- they don't understand that, even if it is happening to another child, they must report.

Shame

Some targets of adult sexual abuse keep quiet because they fear the shame of being labeled a "whore" or "slut." The abuser convinces many that the sex is their fault. "If you weren't so darned sexy, this would never have happened."

Sexual reputation matters to girls, and the threat of being labeled a "ho" or a "slut" looms large. The threat of sexualization and social derogation is often a barrier to rape reporting. Within the slut-shaming behavior, there are differentiated statuses. One student, April, differentiated herself from Sara: "There's a rumor going around saying that Sara had sex with him and so did I and that [she's] a slut and all this stuff." April insisted the rumors about her were untrue because, unlike Sara, who let "it just happen," she "said no." Using these "rules," any girl who is persuaded into sexual activity is weak and to blame, as is a female who enters a situation where she can be raped.

No One Will Believe Me

There is evidence to support students' fear that they won't be believed. In nearly every case I studied, when students initially reported, they were not believed. Studies of who believes reports of child sexual abuse identify women as more likely than men to credit student reports and to respond with empathy. Men are more likely than women to believe (1) that the damage of sex abuse is not serious, (2) that the child is at fault, and (3) that the reporting child is not credible.[12] Those attitudes discourage inquiry and further reporting to, for example, law enforcement.

Female students are more likely to disclose to friends than male students, and often, the female friend of an abuse target is the one who makes a report about the harm being done to her friend. As illustrated earlier in this chapter, these reports are often discounted because they are second-hand. At best, the reporter is told to "tell your friend to come forward if she has a problem."

No One Will Think This Is Serious

When reporting, students are already nervous. They usually start with ambiguous, indirect descriptions. They back off when met with a rebuttal or what feels like a "doubting" question.

In a suburban school district case I reviewed, a teacher began sexual contact with a fourteen-year-old girl. By the time his victim was in the eleventh grade, he had bragged to another teacher about his misconduct. He also told a marriage counselor what he had been, and was still, doing to the student. The mandated reporter, the marriage counselor, reported the teacher's admissions to the school superintendent. Instead of picking up the phone and calling the police, the superintendent ignored the report. In his deposition, the superintendent described the convicted teacher as "local; I've known him since he was five years old." The superintendent decided that this was a consensual "relationship" and, therefore, he didn't need to report.

Something Bad Will Happen to Me if I Report

Targets of sexual abuse are often told that if they let anyone know what is happening, harm will come to them or their family. In one case, the teacher told the student that if she ever told anyone what they were doing, he would kill her. In several other cases, the abusers threatened the students' families: "I will kill your parents." "I know where your niece lives." "I was in the military, and you have no idea what I can do to you." "I will hurt your sister." These threats are not uncommon or empty. In at least three cases I studied, the educator abuser did try to harm members of the student's family. In one case, he killed the student he had been abusing.

In another case, the abusive teacher was worried about being caught. He persuaded his victim to protect him by writing texts and emails that he could use as evidence that the girl was stalking him rather than that he was abusing the girl. He dictated the language of scores of messages that the girl dutifully sent to him.

Other threats came in the form of "protecting" the abused student. "Don't tell anybody because they won't believe you and will call you names." "Don't tell anyone because they will all say you are a slut, and it is your fault." These threats are used to protect the abuser. But the abuser is right. When students do report, other students, parents, teachers, and the community take sides. If the abuser is popular—and even if not—the criticism from a proportion of these communities turns on the reporter. "You are a slut, you would sleep with anyone." "You are making this up." "You led a good man down the wrong path. It's all your fault." "If you didn't wear [short skirts, tight shirts, slutty clothes, make-up], this wouldn't have happened." "You are just a boy toy, and you wanted more." "You tricked him into having sex with you." "You should have known better." "What do you expect when you act the way you do?"

Some results of indirect reporting harmed students' grades and opportunities. For instance, a band director in a midwestern district sexually abused a girl who was trying to prepare for a music career. She told a friend, but no one else, what the director had done. Schools are dense communication networks, and the friend was not as guarded as the abused girl. One friend told another, and the band director heard the rumors. He demoted her from first chair; he created reasons to exclude the girl from prize competitions and never completed the scholarship recommendations she and her family had asked him to provide.

Similarly, a female basketball player was abused by the head coach at the school and after practice. She trusted an assistant coach with whom she was close. And she knew that the assistant coach had seen the head coach take her into his office and close the door. The assistant coach, a mandated reporter, was a drinking buddy with his boss, the head coach. He warned the head coach about what the girl had told him. Fearful that the girl would report to someone else, the coach increased his manipulation of the abused player, including threats to her and her ability to play her sport and the consequences for college scholarships. Knowing what had happened after she told the assistant coach, this athlete never told any other school employee. The coach continued his abuse. It is relevant that the school did not provide an anonymous, confidential reporting capability nor the locator information for "official" report recipients, such as the district's Title IX compliance officer. She had nowhere to turn for protection from the authority figure.

Students' believing they are in a love relationship is another reason they don't report. A teacher who was arrested for sexual misconduct with a student shared his views about why some students might not report:

> Most teachers do not have relationships with students because they are attracted to high school students; they have relationships with students because they view the students as peers—equals—rather than products of their occupation. . . . These teachers are not becoming attracted to students because they see them as children; teachers are becoming attracted to students because they see them as adults. . . . I believe that is every bit as dangerous. She was just another woman to me, and I ignored everything else because I viewed her as a peer, not a student, so age was never a factor.[13]

Unsurprisingly, the students believed they were in a "real" boyfriend-girlfriend relationship and were in love. Treating students as equals gaslights the student, who has feelings for the adult. Those feelings keep the student from even imagining that there is something to report. And when someone else reports concerns, the victim often denies them, at least initially. One teacher who reported concerns about a colleague to the principal relates her experience: "Our principal [at the time] was a real jock and a real 'man's man.' When he [the principal] talked to the teacher, he said something like, 'What the hell do you think you're doing?' . . . Told him to cut it out . . . that's as far as it went . . . no follow-up."

Adults Know and Don't Report

The message to students is that adults won't help. A student who was the target of a high school principal reported that many adults in the school knew what was going on between the principal and her. She noted that a police officer, also serving as the high school resource officer, stopped her for speeding in the principal's car. The officer was concerned and reported this to the assistant principal as well as to his own supervisor. The student talked with a school social worker, telling him that the principal gave her gifts and talked sexually to her. The student asked the social worker (a mandated reporter) if this was allowed. The social worker assured her this was "normal." "He's just trying to be a father to you." Teachers complained to the assistant principal that this student missed class because the principal called her to his office.[14] They complained, but they did not follow up. The girl concluded that there was nowhere to turn.

Students are made to feel they are blowing things out of proportion. When students tell an adult, they are often told that they are exaggerating, misinterpreting the employee's behavior, and just blowing things out of proportion. One student complained to her teacher that the PE teacher was touching her vagina. She was told, "He does it to everyone; it happens sometimes." Another student said she didn't like how her band teacher hugged and kissed her. She was told that it was just "typical male behavior. He just wants you to know you are doing a good job." The adults normalized touching and boundary crossing. The girl concluded that she, an adolescent, was immature and inexperienced and that these behaviors were what adults did. The school's authority figures must be right; she must be wrong.

For many victims, it takes decades to report. For many survivors of childhood sexual abuse, the willingness to disclose changes between childhood and adulthood. Growing up provides a more complete perspective on what was done to them, and once the awareness sets in, many people speak up. It is essential to understand how the disclosure process changes with age.[15] Many child sexual abuse survivors don't disclose until they are adults, if ever. Because disclosure was so long after the abuse, for years, there was nothing that could be done to hold the abuser or the school accountable because the statute of limitations on the crime had run out. For that reason, Child USAdvocacy has led a successful campaign for states to open up the statute of limitations for allegations of childhood sexual abuse to allow criminal and civil charges to be brought.[16]

Males abused by males have historically been reluctant to report their abuse. Often, they are unclear about their sexuality, and the abuse by the male teacher interrupts a healthy understanding of their sexual preferences. It is not unusual that a drastic act, such as a suicide attempt, moves the victim of child abuse into therapy and self-discovery: "I wanted to tell someone and make it stop, but I knew if I did, everyone would call me gay and a fag. I didn't know what I was then; the experience confused my sexual identity development. As a child, I wasn't attracted to males and certainly not to my abuser. As an adult, I identify as heterosexual. But it took a lot of time to work through this."

Amy Hestir (her real name) is a survivor of childhood sexual abuse and an advocate for the protection of children in Missouri. Ms. Hestir's grooming and abuse began when she was twelve. "I was a shy, awkward kid." She said she was flattered that an adult told her he loved her. He then convinced her that "having sex was what people in love do." She reflected that "I thought it was all about love. . . . The Cinderella movie played in my head." He further instructed her to keep everything secret because "it would hurt my family if anybody found out. . . . [I] didn't have the maturity level for this . . . even though I thought I did. At thirteen, kids cannot handle an adult relationship. They aren't equipped to make the best choices for themselves."

This survivor decided to speak out and work to change the law in Missouri. The legislature passed the Amy Hestir Student Protection Act, which required districts to "provide information about former employees to other school districts if the employees have been fired or resigned because of substantiated sexual misconduct allegations."[17] A similar process was written into federal law in the Every Student Succeeds Act of 2015.

Why Bystanders Don't Report

Across my cases, many bystanders who students told about sexual misconduct by another teacher explained that they didn't understand what the student was telling them. "I didn't realize that when she said he was weird and made her feel creepy, that she was telling me there was sexual abuse," a teacher explained after the abuser had been arrested. "We weren't trained to understand what a student might be telling us. We didn't know to ask questions like, "What do you mean he is weird?' or 'What does she do that makes you feel uncomfortable?'"

Bystanders also lack knowledge about what behaviors are red flags, described in more detail in an earlier chapter. Common red flags of actual sexual abuse of the student in the cases I studied include:

- touching and hugging a "target" student;
- meeting a student in closed rooms, with doors locked and windows covered;
- driving a student in personal vehicles;
- sitting with a student on an event bus;
- calling a "target" student by a nickname;
- giving gifts to an individual student;
- holding a student back from the passage of classes and providing them with late passes to their next assigned class;
- meeting with a student alone before and after school, during lunch, or during a prep period.

One teacher described how her principal dealt with her reports of boundary crossing of a male teacher who was too close to a female student. "His behavior toward her, how he stood beside her, was always with her . . . in his car, after school. I shared my concerns with the principal." The principal told her that she was "making a very serious accusation, and if it couldn't be proved," she—the reporter—would lose her job. (Title IX and many district policies prohibit retaliation against those who report misconduct allegations.) The principal said he would look into it and counseled her not to speak about it. The principal did not investigate.

But sometimes, it is the principal who is the abuser. In this case, a school principal, who I will call Mark Robbeler, was grooming a male student, I have named Martin:

> The principal spent a lot of time with Martin; at some point, teachers began talking. They remembered that incidents of inappropriate

behavior were reported to three different superintendents about Mr. Robbeler's boundary-crossing with male students. Each superintendent explained the incidents as Mr. Robbeler being a caring [teacher, promoted to assistant principal, and then principal]. Nothing was left in writing for the next superintendent, and no mention was ever made of the reports.

Teachers had noted to each other that Mr. Robbeler was especially fond of Martin but didn't see that as a problem. When police investigated, they found a display of photographs of Martin in Mr. Robbeler's office, which the police detective noted. "It was peculiar that he had what looked like a little shrine on display on his bookshelf. There was a collage of pictures of Martin and thank you letters from Martin. No such displays were focusing on other boys in Mr. Robbeler's office." The superintendent and teachers had often been in Mr. Robbeler's office, where this "shrine" was located and yet none of them noted the inappropriateness of the display, or if they did, none of them reported Mr. Robbeler to appropriate authorities.

Martin assumed the teachers thought Mr. Robbeler's behavior was acceptable. "The teachers saw it. Teachers recognized Mr. Robbeler always coming up to me and whispering in my ear, taking me to lunch, or taking me out of class." His teachers confirmed that they had seen these behaviors but never assumed that anything inappropriate was happening.

The superintendent told police that Mr. Robbeler was friendly with parents and students and, as a result, he was popular. She was aware that Martin was in the principal's office alone with him on several occasions. Once, when she had inquired, Mr. Robbeler told her that Martin's mother had asked him to meet with Martin because he was having difficulties related to his father's death. This made sense to the superintendent since she knew Mr. Robbeler was friendly with the mother and occasionally had dinner there. She thought perhaps "Mark and [Martin's mother] were dating."

Even if they weren't dating, the superintendent noted that this was a small school district, almost like a private school and that it was not "an uncommon practice for administrators to meet with students alone in their offices or to take a personal interest in a family dealing with tragedy." The superintendent explained, "I probably would not notice an administrator putting his or her arms around the same child repeatedly because we put our arms around so many kids all day. Very, very routine for us."

The more teachers and administrators reflected on Mr. Robbeler's interactions with Martin and other male students, the more they realized they should have acted. Several teachers blamed themselves for not intervening. "I should have said something. I don't know why I didn't. I guess I didn't think anything was going on. I didn't imagine someone with a reputation for doing good could be doing bad."

But overall, across cases, bystanders don't report primarily because they are protecting the reputation, job, and well-being of the colleague over the child's safety. It is easier to believe that a colleague is just a friendly, helpful teacher than to believe the colleague is a child molester.[18] It is easier to convince oneself that the harm of a false report does more harm to the adult than sexual abuse does to the child. It is easier to stand by and believe it is someone else's job to report, say, a guidance counselor or a school building administrator, or even a parent. Or to say, "I mentioned it. It's out of my hands now."

Reporting Takeaways

Organizational policies should follow state regulations and professional practices developed across schools and other child-serving organizations. Organizations that protect students emphasize reporting, not only reporting by adults but also reporting by students. Reporting is a bulwark against educator sexual misconduct. The prospect of reporting has a deterrent effect—not sufficient but important, nonetheless.

Organizations that protect children emphasize reporting by employees "who have reason to believe" that a child might be the target of sexual misconduct or that the behavior exhibited could lead to sexual misconduct. That threshold for teachers and other general employees is purposefully established to be short of the evidence that can be developed by school administrators, that is, a preliminary inquiry to estimate the probability of an allegation's occurrence. And it is far short of the evidence that can be developed by professional and independent investigators—especially law enforcement, children's protective services, and some state education agencies. Those groups have the resources to investigate the potential result of bringing charges and substantiating allegations:

- If a report suggests abuse, don't investigate; contact the appropriate state certification and licensing agency (for certified and licensed employees).
- Communicate reporting procedures in policies, posters, and public spaces in the school and district. These well-publicized procedures for receiving complaints and grievances should include the identification and contact information for a compliance officer, usually the Title IX coordinator, as one of the organization's designated report recipients. All people who receive reports should communicate them with the compliance officer, who takes the next step.
- Teachers, school support staff, students, and parents/caregivers should report suspicion, rumors, and gossip at the point of "reasonable belief."
- Policies should guide in identifying and reporting behaviors that might indicate sexual exploitation and make it clear that the entire organization is responsible for identification and reporting.
- Policies about reporting that are intended to prevent sexual misconduct on school sites need to be separate and distinct from (although related to) policies that require mandated reporting by personnel if abuse is suspected in domestic settings. Organizations need to outline the specific reporting steps required by the organization.
- Reporting guidelines need to consider why both adults and students might not report and require practices to counter these barriers.
- Training on reporting should include the signs of red flags and inappropriate behavior, the damage to students caused by not reporting, and the understanding that reports and investigations protect both the student and the adult accused.
- Contact the parent and keep the parent and (age-appropriate) child informed about the report.
- Communicate up and out in the organization: inform the principal, department chair or other supervisory personnel, district communication head, superintendent, board president, and school attorney.
- Document the report. Keep a copy in a central location.
- Whatever the outcome, prepare a Title IX report describing the complaint, the investigation, and the outcome. Keep this in a central location where all Title IX reports are stored.
- Use the event as a teachable moment for the students, parents, and school employees.

INVESTIGATING

There are three types of investigations: (1) a preliminary inquiry, (2) a full-fledged investigation, and (3) a postincident, local summary inquiry. Each is triggered at a different phase in resolving an allegation.

(1) Preliminary School-Based Inquiry

At the point of initial reporting, the school can conduct a preliminary inquiry to estimate "reasonable cause" to report, although that does not extend to definitively proving the validity of an allegation—that is the responsibility of professionals (see below). Additionally, the school should record its own preliminary and necessarily cursory inquiry for, among other things, the postincident refinement of its policies and procedures as indicated and for reports of the investigation, consequences, and resolutions. Nevertheless, if the initial inquiry raises concerns, law enforcement should be contacted, and the employee should be removed from the classroom (and all contact with children) and placed on administrative leave until the law enforcement investigation is completed.

If an adult is possibly sexually abusing a student, that is a criminal act and requires a criminal investigation. School personnel aren't trained in criminal sexual abuse. It is important to remember that what a school principal or Title IX officer might do in the way of an investigation is to comply with district policies and regulations for personnel purposes and Title IX accounting, not for determining criminal action.

Dr. William Pelfrey, Jr., professor of criminal justice and homeland security and emergency preparedness at Virginia Commonwealth University, noted, "Law enforcement personnel who conduct investigations, particularly sex crime investigations, receive specialized training and mentorship. The laws and ethical practices around questioning victims, especially minor victims, are complicated, and a case can quickly fall apart if a defense attorney starts asking questions about how evidence was secured, how the witness was questioned, and the experience/training of the investigating officer. If a school police officer conducts these investigations without proper training, the odds of a conviction plummet."[19]

In addition to a lack of skill, administrators and other school personnel might have a conflict of interest when investigating an employee. "There is a perceived lack of objectivity when one investigates coworkers. Indeed, a school official could be inappropriately lenient on a coworker or inappropriately vindictive. The important part is whether a jury will believe that an administrator or even a school resource officer who is technically a member of the police force but has relationships within the school can objectively investigate coworkers. There is an important reason police departments partition internal affairs officers from other officers—real or perceived compromised objectivity is anathema to a conviction."[20]

In the preliminary "investigation" to determine what happened and if law enforcement should be called, the school representative should do the following:

- Take notes on all interviews and telephone calls. Make sure the date and time are on the notes. Write a summary of each interview.
- Ask specific questions about behaviors—but just enough to determine whether something has happened. Err on the side of contacting law enforcement.

After law enforcement has completed their investigation and for the Title IX report and personnel decisions, use law enforcement records for the following:

- Develop a chronology of events of the investigation by law enforcement and the actions in the complaint that are being investigated. At what time? Where? What happened? What happened after? What did you do? What did the child do?
- Determine who else was present or might have walked by or seen what was happening.
- If there are people who might have witnessed the event, red flags, and boundary crossing and weren't interviewed, talk with them.
- Interview teachers and administrators to determine if there have been previous allegations about the adult.

(2) Comprehensive Investigation by Law Enforcement or Central Administration

Some large school districts can mount an investigation with the district's police department, and many have school resource officers stationed in the schools. As noted above, it may not be appropriate to investigate an employee for sexual misconduct of a student.

Most reports go from the school to local law enforcement, which is the appropriate protocol. School personnel investigating allegations of employee criminal conduct are likely to be perceived as having a conflict of interest. If the school or central administration undertakes a more detailed investigation, then that investigation should be impartial, objective, thorough, and professional. Ordinarily, these investigations should be conducted by law enforcement or legally authorized state or county child protective services. Law enforcement ordinarily directs schools to suspend school-based investigations so as not to interfere with law enforcement efforts.

(3) Postincident, Local Summary Inquiry

However, after the law enforcement investigation has resulted in either charges or dismissal, the school or district should complete its inquiry about school practice and its adequacy. Some dismissals conclude that the misconduct did not constitute criminal behavior. But that same behavior may well violate school or district policy. Law enforcement investigations may develop incident descriptions sufficient for legal purposes but fail to understand the school circumstances that facilitated or enabled the misconduct. A guilty verdict will not often illuminate what a school or district should do to strengthen its prevention and protection efforts. For these reasons, a school should complete an internal inquiry about the alleged and resolved misconduct.

The ability to investigate depends on the prior act of reporting. The ability of a school or district to further the protection of students by investigating allegations depends on what has been reported, and that depends on what has been recognized or discerned. If employees, students, and parents/caregivers are not trained to recognize the signs of abuse, they may see abuse or its precursors but not recognize their significance. Without recognizing or discerning, there is no reporting; without reporting, there is no investigating. And without those linked activities, there is no stopping harassment and abuse.

In general, investigations should be the province of professionals in that work. The exception is early on in the reporting process when, typically, a report has been made, and a school building administrator is involved. The school can do an initial inquiry to estimate "reasonable cause" to report. This limited activity is called an "inquiry" to distinguish it from the more comprehensive and detailed "investigation." The school administrator's job is to take the report and turn it over to law enforcement. While the person taking the report might ask some basic questions, overall, the process demands more than can be reasonably expected from a school building administrator. The sole purpose of the school-based inquiry is to confirm "reasonable cause," although that does not extend to definitively proving or disproving the validity of an allegation—that is the responsibility of professional investigators. Suppose the initial inquiry confirms the reported concerns. In that case, it should be immediately forwarded outside the district, and the district should remove the employee from all contact with children and place the person on administrative leave until the investigation is completed. The school or district should preserve a record of its own preliminary and necessarily cursory inquiry for, among other purposes, the postincident refinement of its policies and procedures as indicated and for documentation of the inquiry, consequences, and resolutions.

Investigations should be impartial, objective, thorough, and professional. There are 18,243 local education agencies in the United States, but only a small fraction are large enough to warrant a dedicated investigation staff. For investigations, most school districts should rely on law enforcement.

Except for the districts that support a staff of trained professional investigators, school personnel should not investigate a report of school employee sexual misconduct because they aren't trained in investigating this type of crime. Law enforcement and child welfare investigators receive specialized training in investigating allegations of child sexual abuse. Both school resource officers and Title IX compliance officers/coordinators are often called upon to investigate. Studies of both indicate that these incumbents are not trained to do investigations of child sexual abuse and that school districts should not rely on them. Compare, for example, the preparation and experience of an assistant superintendent for human resources—a role often designated as the Title IX compliance officer—with the preparation and experience of a specialist in the forensic interviewing of child victims of sexual abuse employed by a local children's advocacy center. The assistant superintendent has many responsibilities and limited time: the forensic interviewer is a dedicated specialist.

A 2023 scoping review that examined research on the role of forensic interviews in child sexual abuse cases identified thirty different procedures for taking testimony from the victims of child sexual abuse. The National Institute for Child Health and Human Behavior interview protocol was frequently mentioned.[21]

The Faux Investigation

What usually happens is what I call the faux investigation. It seldom uncovers abuse, it delays effective investigation, and it prolongs the abuse of a child. It is typical that a concern is finally reported to a principal. The report usually says, "Mr. X spends a lot of time with student A." or "Mr. Y isn't doing his recess duty. He says he must stay with a student on a special project." Or "Ms. Z sure is flirty with three senior boys." The principal usually talks with the teacher in question but doesn't directly express a concern or remind the teacher of boundary expectations. Sometimes the principal says, "Someone saw you alone with a student in your classroom with the door shut." Mr. X or Y explains, "Yes, she's been having a lot of trouble with her work and at home. I've been giving her some extra help to catch up." Or from Mr. Y, "A couple of students are working on a special project, and I don't want to take time away from others in class to help them." For Ms. Y, there is rarely any follow-up, with the excuse that "she's young and the younger teachers dress differently and are used to more informal interactions. It's normal for them." And that's the end of it. No cautions, extra supervision, or warning about the consequences if it happens again, and no note in the personnel file memorializing the concern.

When the principal takes a bolder step, it's the same result. The actions of a principal who had a report of time alone with a student by a male elementary teacher are not unusual. The principal asked the teacher if he was "inappropriately touching" any of his female students, and when the teacher said no, the principal concluded that the case was closed. Did she talk with students? Did she interview other teachers? Did she increase the observation and monitoring of the teacher? Did accepting the denial of a school employee, at face value, protect the child?

In these situations, none of the principals involved law enforcement resources. They discounted the reports and trusted the teachers, who continued to abuse their students year after year.

Reporter Bethany Barns (at the time working at the *Oregonian*'s Oregon Live website) described how the Portland School District investigated a report against a "charming educator and coach," Mitch Whitehurst, by seventeen-year-old Rose Soto. Her friends told her not to report because no one would listen and that "it will come back on you." Finally, after one sexual transgression too many, Rose reported Whitehurst to school officials. She produced a two-page, handwritten statement about all the sexually suggestive comments and behaviors. The district investigator checked Whitehurst's personnel file and talked with him. The next day, Whitehurst "was back at school." Ms. Soto's complaint was one of many reports over the years about Whitehurst. At one point, the school's attorney investigated internally. Reporter Barns could find no records that the attorney had ever spoken to the seventeen-year-old student who had made a formal, written report. As the years passed, other complaints were brought, but nothing was done. Fifteen years after Ms. Soto's complaint, the teacher left the school and surrendered his teaching license. A male colleague had reported that Whitehurst tried to abuse him. At the time of Whitehurst's departure, there were three student complaints in the record, and the reporter found two additional targets. The district had not taken action to protect the students, but they did protect another employee.[22]

Investigation Takeaways

Whether the complaint is direct or inferred, allegations must be reported immediately to the district or school's compliance officer and then to law enforcement. While most school district officials will call the district/school's attorney, the attorney should not investigate. Very few attorneys are trained to investigate, and if they are counsel to the district, an investigation presents a conflict of interest.

The following checklist may be useful in assessing the adequacy of any investigation:

1. Was the investigation timely?
2. Was the investigator unbiased and objective?
3. Was the investigator trained in documenting allegations of employee sexual abuse of students?
4. Was the investigator experienced in documenting allegations of employee sexual abuse of students?
5. Were interviews guided by a protocol that enhanced fairness and consistency?
6. Was the investigation recorded, transcribed, and otherwise noted and documented?
7. Were parents notified and invited to be present for student interviews?
8. Did a person of the same sex interview the student victim, and did the interview team include same-sex representation?
9. Was the interviewee promised confidentiality to the extent feasible?
10. Was the interviewee promised protection from retaliation?
11. For interviews with student victims, were they apprised of their rights under Title IX?
12. Was the investigation conducted in a way that complied with Title IX requirements?
13. Did the investigator select and interview other students who may have been victims of sexual misconduct by employees?

14. Did the investigator interview teachers and other staff members who knew the alleged perpetrator and knew about his/her interaction with students?
15. Did the investigation include attention to the alleged harasser's previous conduct?
16. If the investigation was school-centered, did it involve district resources, including the district's Title IX compliance officer?
17. Were the files that support the investigation retained in a central location?
18. If law enforcement investigated criminal or otherwise illegal conduct, did the organization conduct a parallel or phased inquiry about district policy and regulation violations?
19. Were the involved parties—the victim(s), their family(ies), and the respondent—kept apprised of the progress of the investigation?
20. Were the involved parties—the victim(s), their family(ies), and the respondent—notified of the investigation's outcomes or results?

REMOVING SEXUAL HARASSERS FROM EMPLOYMENT

An employee who has crossed sexual boundaries with a student does not belong in a school. While removing an offending employee from service is not always easy, the effort should be made. If that is not possible, the employee should be closely supervised and moved into a position that provides the most safety to students. I am not talking here about an employee accused of a fabricated story, but rather an employee who has continued boundary crossings and does not stop.

Passing the Trash

When an employee is accused of sexual misconduct toward a student, districts are supposed to contact law enforcement. Law enforcement then investigates and makes a determination. If a crime has been committed, the school employee will be charged with a criminal offense. If not, the charges will be dropped. That does not mean that the employee has done nothing wrong. In fact, in most cases, the employee has crossed sexual boundaries with students, and the district attorney, for many reasons, does not want to prosecute.

The police/district attorney's decision not to prosecute does not end the school's responsibility. The school district has a job to do as well. Under Title IX, the district must determine the consequences of any action. If the action violates school district policies or state law, the school must take action and keep records. Law enforcement might determine that something doesn't reach the level of a criminal offense, but the behavior might still violate school policies. Texting a student regularly about sexual topics might not persuade the district attorney to bring charges, but it violates school policy and Title IX requirements and is grounds for termination for cause.

In June 2023, the US Office of Education reported the results of the Department's study of state-adopted policies under the Elementary and Secondary Education Act, reminding states and school districts that a report completed in 2017 has implications for State laws and school district practices.[23] The US Department of Education examined state policies and practices and found that California is among many states that "does not prohibit the suppression of information about Employee misconduct." California is one state in which there are several school employees who sexually abuse in one district, quietly resign, and get a job in another district, where they sexually abuse students again.[24]

Like most states, California has a teacher credentialing office (California Commission on Teacher Credentialing, CTC) responsible for keeping track of teacher's employment status changes due to misconduct allegations. As in most states, the CTC investigates and makes a final determination, which is then, if sustained, recorded publicly as an adverse action. Sexual misconduct is one of those adverse actions.

However, for any name to appear on the registry, it must first be reported and investigated. The San Francisco Standard documented some areas where this system fails students. For instance, a teacher was hired in 2019 while he was under investigation by the CTC. Two years later, a record of the investigation's findings was published. That teacher abused students in two districts before he lost his teaching credentials.[25]

Some states counter this problem by prohibiting education officials in a school or school district from entering into any agreement that "suppresses information." Missouri's Amy Hestir Student Protection Act addresses non-disclosure agreements where abuse of a student has occurred. Districts are required to have a policy prohibiting educator sexual misconduct, with all reports investigated by an outside agency; they must include in policies what information will be provided about former employees, with school officials granted civil immunity for providing information on the employee; school districts may be civilly liable for failing to disclose information about a former employee who was dismissed or resigned after a charge of sexual misconduct; and districts must have a policy regarding the use of electronic media between staff and students.[26]

Other states are beginning to adopt similar legislation as well as more up-to-date data for those who have been found to have abused a child. But state laws and school policies often fail to include those who don't hold the status of professional, such as bus drivers, custodians, and others who work in schools and who might also abuse a child.

A not-atypical example of passing the trash was reported in North Carolina. A high school coach recommended someone for a middle school teaching position. That person had been fired "a year earlier for seating young girls on his lap and rubbing their backs, and sexually harassing two female colleagues."[27] Two months after he was hired, there were complaints from students and colleagues who called him creepy. He was indicted for attempting to get a thirteen-year-old student into his office to look at nude photographs. No one checked on his background or why he left six previous positions and stopped teaching for six years in between positions. A later investigation found that he had forged his teaching license.[28]

Led by Senator Pat Toomey, Pennsylvania was the first state to adopt passing the trash legislation and has been followed by other states.[29] This legislation was adapted and included in federal education law, Section 8546 of the Elementary and Secondary Education Act (ESEA), which addresses "aiding and abetting of sexual abuse of students in K–12 schools."[30] This legislation was later incorporated into the Every Student Succeeds Act (ESSA) and "requires all states receiving certain federal funding from the Department of Education to enact policies, laws, or regulations to explicitly prohibit the practice of allowing teachers with a history of abusing students to transfer schools without facing any consequences. Despite this statutory requirement, three-quarters of all states have not yet enacted legislation while continuing to receive federal funding."[31]

As of 2022, Senators Toomey and Manchin were pushing the US Department of Education to enforce the education law.

In 2002, MassKids, the oldest, state-based child advocacy organization in the country, received a five-year grant from the CDC with the challenge to "build adult and community responsibility to prevent child sexual abuse."[32] Executive Director Jetta Bernier worked on all angles to meet the prevention challenge. She partnered with several organizations in Massachusetts to launch the Enough Abuse Campaign as a community mobilization/citizen education and action initiative. Bernier then pushed prevention efforts from the community level to the national level, disseminating Enough Abuse training, policy, and prevention resources to other states (e.g., New Jersey, Maryland, New York, Nevada, ten Greater Bay California counties, South

Dakota, and more). MassKids rebranded in 2024 as Enough Abuse to reflect the organization's broader reach with sites now in Nigeria, Sierra Leone, Ghana, and India.

Its national "A Call to Action" report issued in 2021 was the first effort to document and track a range of child sexual abuse prevention legislative efforts in all fifty states. Ongoing updates on state and federal legislative efforts can be found in a set of interactive maps on the Enough Abuse website.[33] These maps let readers know: if their state has laws criminalizing educator sexual misconduct (thirty-eight states and Washington, DC, do; my state, Virginia, does not), laws that require screening of school employees to prevent educator sexual misconduct (sixteen states and Washington DC), and legislation mandating state task forces to address child sexual abuse (seventeen states and Washington, DC).[34]

PART IV

Going Forward

CHAPTER 10

Institutional Courage and Societal Change

S chools act in loco parentis. John Dewey argued that we should want for all children what the best parents want for theirs. Professionally trained and state-certified teachers and administrators should not function simply in loco parentis but *in loco optimae parentis*, not in place of the parent but in place of the best parent.[1]

Previous chapters have addressed what schools in the US are doing to prevent school employee sexual misconduct, and it is clear that US schools still have work to do. However, there are additional prevention levers that can be enlisted.

HEALING AND REPAIRING

The prevention framework-suggested actions are largely directed toward people within the organization with the goal of prevention. This chapter suggests additional prevention levers outside of schools and describes the necessary work to heal those harmed.

Heal All Who Are Harmed

Across the cases that I have reviewed, one response requirement stands out as the most neglected: healing and restoration. Healing begins with attending to the well-being of the harmed children but doesn't stop there. Others need our attention: the family of the child who has been harmed is spotlighted, blamed, and shamed; the school community is traumatized and divided; the families of the abuser are shunned and confused.

It isn't uncommon to believe that if a person is prosecuted and found guilty, the victim is the victor. While it might be reaffirming, it doesn't substitute for the healing and support necessary to help the child become whole. For any crime, even child sexual abuse, the state is considered the injured party. The victim is just a witness. The community is harmed when one violates the law. However, the interests of the state and the interests of the survivor do not always coincide. It is the responsibility of the school community to attend to the interests of the harmed child. Victims are likely to feel isolated and disrespected unless there is a concerted and sustained effort to reinforce and embrace the child who is healing. The betrayal of the bystanders who didn't speak up or protect often feels like a worse betrayal than that of the perpetrator. The survivor is isolated when bystanders don't support the survivor. Bystanders need to recognize this and be part of the healing process.

Accountability to students targeted by employee sexual misconduct is a promise under Title IX, but healing and change must go even further. Remember, it is not just the abuser who has harmed the child. It is also those in the school who didn't believe the child or acknowledge the damage to the child who have contributed to the child's injury. Judith Herman reminds us that victims of sexual abuse need acknowledgment of the harm, in addition to vindication by the community, an apology, fair restitution, and prevention of future harm. Add to that a path to asserting their dignity, power, and control; respect for their narrative; and limited exposure to trauma reminders.[2]

Students who have been harmed must receive supportive therapy and protection against retaliation. They need repeated attention and assurances of support and safety. Their long-term mission is to feel safe and whole. Their families also need kindness, support, and answers. Parents and siblings often feel guilty and judged.

Although the primary person in need of support, the student victim is also part of a larger school community that has been betrayed. The abuser violated the trust of the profession and the community. The school community needs answers, honest responses, and a space in which to talk and heal. Refusing to address what has happened with the whole community results in suspicion, rumors, cynicism, and continued misconduct.

We don't often think of the family of the abuser. It is not unusual for the abuser to have children in the school system and spouses who haven't come to terms with betrayal from the person they married. Those children and the family also need care and support.

A Thorough Analysis of School Culture and Practices

When knowledge that a school employee has abused a child becomes public, it is common to hear, "How could this have happened?" It's a good question that needs an answer and a plan. Instead, the typical responses are silence, excuses, or defensiveness.

Once the investigations of the allegations have occurred and action has been taken against the offender, there is more to do. School leadership must begin an inquiry and provide a plan to correct what went wrong. Whether it is an internal or external process, this review should be conducted in a way that builds trust. The purpose is to identify what needs to change to prevent another student from abuse:

- Are the policies sufficient?
- Do people understand the policies?
- What training was provided, and was it effective in communicating appropriate boundaries and reporting responsibilities for crossing boundaries?
- Are there environmental and space conditions that helped to hide the abuse?
- Why didn't people report?
- Why did the supervision and monitoring of adult-child interactions fail?
- What do parents and students believe should be done?

Sexual abuse of a student by an employee is not just the case of a "bad apple." It is a sign of an unsafe culture. It is too simple to just blame the abuser. The responsibility for student safety belongs to everyone.

Data need to be collected. Surveys of parent, student, and employee knowledge, practices, and suggestions will help identify needed policies and training. Practice in reporting should happen. Culture change is necessary not only to atone for the harm but also to prevent future abuse. Cultural change needs to be anchored, directed, and monitored in a school or district-wide committee that collects data, evaluates progress, and keeps the focus on safety.

When a report of school employee sexual misconduct was made in the Shoreham-Wading River School District in New York, Superintendent Gerald Poole immediately began a review of policies and practices. Below is an accounting of the review and changes put into place. Superintendent Poole ensured that the district did all it could to prevent this harm from happening again.

Policy

Revise district fraternization policy.

Revise district electronic communication policy.

Adopt a sexual misconduct policy.

Hiring

Implement additional background checks for all hires.

References to be asked if the employee was ever accused of misconduct.

Before hiring, all final candidates will be run through the Raptor License check system.

The committee candidate rubric will be revised to include an evaluation of the candidate's ability to maintain appropriate student relationships.

Training

Annual staff training for sexual harassment will include an increased emphasis on inappropriate fraternization, sexual misconduct, and reporting. Training will shift to in-person presentations.

- Partner with PTA/O on parent workshops for student safety.
- Review the current K–8 curriculum for child safety. Revise as necessary.
- Review the current grades 6, 8, 10 (health) curriculum for sexual harassment/misconduct instruction.
- Implement annual assemblies/workshops for students in grades 7, 9, 11, and 12 for sexual harassment/misconduct instruction.

Monitoring/Prevention

- Install large flat-panel monitors in all building administrators' offices for a cyclical view of all building cameras.
- Ensure that all high school students' locations are always registered, including for any "non-instructional periods" formerly known as open periods.

Other actions were also taken. The point is that this superintendent and his board immediately turned to prevention rather than defensiveness to protect children by changing the school district's culture and practices.

Changing School Culture

In 2016, The National Association of Independent Schools (NAIS) and The Association of Boarding Schools (TABS) appointed an Independent School Task Force on Prevention of Educator Sexual Misconduct. The Task Force included twelve members who, along with professional staff from NAIS and TABS, developed a set of guidelines for prevention. I was privileged to be among those on the task force. The recommendations for independent and boarding schools are as comprehensive as any I've seen and are appropriate for public schools.

Central to prevention is culture change. Developing a safe and responsive organizational culture is not easy and requires commitment from leadership. The report notes, "A foundational element of a positive culture is the clear understanding that each community member has permission to report any concerning conduct without fear of retaliation. To create and maintain a culture of student safety, schools need to develop policies and attitudes that encourage and reinforce reporting of such conduct."[3]

The betrayal by the organization in not keeping students safe is often as potent or even more so than the actual abuse. Studies have documented the long-term effects of institutional betrayal on sexual abuse targets and the realization that the promise of safety was false. One response to institutional betrayal is institutional courage. Alec M. Smidt, Alexis A. Adams-Clark, and Jennifer J. Freyd studied institutional courage to alleviate the effects of institutional betrayal. Institutional courage is another way to describe a "supportive response and a climate characterized by transparency and proactiveness" that provides a healing and compassionate culture.[4] These behaviors of institutional courage attenuate many of the negative outcomes.

Simona Giorgi, Christi Lockwood, and Mary Ann Glynn describe organizational cultures as conceptualized in five ways: values, stories, frames, toolkits, and categories. Enter any elementary school, and you will likely hear, "Children come first."[5] And yet, these same organizations may have a culture that leads people to announce, "I don't interfere with what my colleagues do in the classroom, even if I disapprove." "I respect my colleagues." "I wouldn't feel comfortable pointing out to a colleague that she or he is crossing a boundary with a child." "I would never report a colleague unless I actually saw them in the sexual act with a student."

In reading the interviews of school personnel by police officers about why an adult employee didn't report the suspicious behavior of another adult, the frame most often used provides more care and protection to the adult than to the child. "I wasn't sure anything was going on. I mean, it looked suspicious, but it could also have been nothing. If I reported my suspicions and they were wrong, then a good teacher's career and life would be ruined." The frame, like the others, puts the comfort of the reporter and the well-being of the adult ahead of the effects of long-term abuse of the child.

Engage Students and Parents in Culture Change

The Boulder and Denver school districts and many others have found how potent engaging students in prevention can be.[6] Focused on both peer- and adult-to-student sexual misconduct, student groups are filing Title IX complaints to prod districts to do more. While it is the job of adults to keep students safe, it is also true that student peer support and action can stop abuse. Students often see what adults don't (even though the adults should). Engaging students in prevention through student organizations is powerful.

Stop Sexual Assault in Schools (SSAIS) is a national organization to educate students and families to respond to and prevent sexual assault. Started by parents of a student who had been sexually assaulted in school, the organization helps students organize SSAIS student chapters to make changes in their school. SSAIS provides a toolkit for students and parents to change the culture and make the school safer for students.[7]

Keep Track of Progress

Under federal law, all schools receiving federal funds must conduct an annual student climate survey. By adding questions about adult boundary crossing and misconduct to this annual survey, schools can keep track of prevention progress and areas that need attention.

Work with Teacher Unions

Teacher unions are often seen as a block to prevention. But just because the job of a teacher's union is to protect teachers' rights doesn't mean the union can't also work with their members to protect students. Protecting teacher due process is not at odds with training on boundaries and policies. Teachers' unions can lead teachers to honor appropriate boundaries with students.

Repair

When school officials don't comply with a standard of care for preventing school employee sexual misconduct, the school and district are responsible for repairing the damage done. Under Title IX, in *Gebser v. Lago Vista Independent School District*, "the Supreme Court . . . held that money damages were indeed an available remedy to individual litigants under Title IX."[8]

It should not require a civil lawsuit against the school district for school leaders to work with those targeted to help them heal and thrive.

Title IX provides standards and regulations for compliance, but there is very little risk of punishment with Title IX, except for a lot of paperwork and negative press. No school has ever lost federal funding based upon Title IX violations, and the Office for Civil Rights (OCR) generally works to develop an agreement for change. Because of this, parents of students who have been harmed are likelier to call an attorney than file a Title IX complaint.

Both are important, and they can work in tandem. Many attorneys focus on school liability and don't base the suits on Title IX, particularly after the 2022 Supreme Court ruling that emotional distress damages are not recoverable under Title IX (and Title I and the Rehabilitation Act).[9] While I believe that is a misguided ruling, it doesn't prevent financial recovery in civil suits against the school district and federal sanctions in a separate Title IX complaint.

BEYOND THE SCHOOL

School practices aren't the only lever that must change. Prevention help can come from external sources that provide the pressure to help schools change.

Adopt Laws and Enforce Them

In 2015, a provision was added to the Elementary and Secondary Act (ESEA) of 1965 requiring states to prohibit schools from assisting or "aiding and abetting" school staff in obtaining a new job if they are known or believed with probable cause to have engaged in sexual misconduct with a student or minor in violation of the law.[10]

Researchers at Policy Studies Association, Magnolia Consulting, and SRI International completed a study for the US Department of Justice on states' conformity to the new law. Seven years after the legislation was adopted, most states have not complied (table 10.1).

Only eighteen (36 percent) state education agencies monitor adherence to state laws and policies that prohibit aiding and abetting sexual misconduct in school districts.[11]

Use Existing Laws Such as Title IX

Title IX coordinators are street-level bureaucrats who can intervene with training and support.[12] They can do much more in most school districts to prevent employee sexual misconduct. Problems include the following:

TABLE 10.1   States' failure to implement federal law prohibiting aiding and abetting school employee sexual misconduct

Number and percentage of states that do not comply	Federal law requirement
Prospective employer requirements	
31 (62%)	Request information from previous employers
36 (72%)	Check the applicant's eligibility to teach
39 (78%)	Require a written statement from the applicant
Job applicant requirements	
36 (72%)	Authorize disclosure of previous employment information and records
36 (72%)	Provide written statement of any investigations or disciplinary actions
41 (82%)	Provide contact information for current/former employers
Current or former employer requirements	
32 (64%)	Disclose an allegation investigation
35 (70%)	Respond to information requests within a specified time
45 (90%)	Respond to any follow-up requests
Prohibitions in information suppression	
26 (52%)	In termination, resignation, or severance requirements
39 (78%)	In personal files (information expunged)
47 (94%)	In letters of recommendations
47 (94%)	In private settlements

- Most students and staff don't know who the Title IX coordinator is, nor that part of the job is the prevention of and response to sexual misconduct.
- Many Title IX coordinators aren't aware that they have been appointed to the position.
- The job is often tacked on to full-time and consuming administrative responsibilities. There is no time to do the Title IX job. Ambiguous job descriptions and duties are piled high onto other job responsibilities.

- Most Title IX officers in K–12 schools are untrained and inexperienced. They often continue to believe Title IX is "just about sports."
- Title IX coordinators are reactive, not proactive. They need to move from compliance to prevention.

A 2023 newspaper story demonstrates what can happen when a school district encourages Title IX investigations. Kate Cimini wrote that Florida's Lee County School District's Title IX coordinator and director of positive prevention, Chuck Bradley, led a move to make students aware of their rights and protections. As a result, the Lee County district sees eight Title IX complaints per 100,000 students compared to the Florida average of two complaints per 100,000 students. That might seem like Lee County is heading in the wrong direction. Just the opposite is true. More awareness and reporting lead to safer schools and changes in the culture and behavior of adults and students.[13]

Insurance Company Support

An increasing number of schools and school districts are being held responsible for the abuse of students by school employees, resulting in large monetary settlements. Insurance companies and pools can reduce settlement costs by supporting prevention and requiring schools to have thorough and regular training on boundaries and reporting as a condition of insurance coverage. Some companies, such as United Educators, work with school districts and provide online training in boundary identification, safe hiring for people who work with minors, and identification of the red flags and warning signs of sexual abuse by adults.

The Washington State Schools Risk Management Pool (WSRMP) was an early advocate for training and supported the development of training on preventing school employee sexual misconduct. Similar to other insurance pools and providers, WSRMP has experienced an increase in sex abuse claims costs, 952 percent, between 2010–2014 and 2014–2018. Like all of us, they have an investment in reducing abuse and, thus, reducing civil cases and hefty awards or settlements.

Civil Suits

The targets of school employee sexual misconduct are increasingly using civil lawsuits to hold school districts accountable for the abuse. This is a courageous response for both the child and the family, and juries have consistently been sympathetic toward the child in finding that the school or school district had not met their obligations to the safety of students. An additional opportunity for those bringing a civil suit is using a settlement agreement to change school practices. If these are part of the settlement agreement with a monitor to ensure they happen, the organization becomes safer.

Enlist the Press

The majority of information on school employee sexual misconduct has come from the local and national press. The free press does not face the same difficulties from school districts and universities in gaining permission to study school employee sexual misconduct as do academic researchers. Newspaper reports of sexual assaults of students by school employees help raise awareness of the issue and often bring forth increased reporting. Courageous reporters have done a great deal toward prevention.

Require Accountability for Abusers and Enablers

Rather than moving victims to forgiveness, we need to think about moving perpetrators to contrition and changed behavior. Prosecutors often won't prosecute unless they think they can win or because they don't want bad press, even when police departments recommend pursuing charges. If the abuser is an otherwise well-regarded coach or teacher, charges are often dropped. In a study of 500 child sexual abuse reports forwarded to prosecutors after a police investigation, fewer than 20 percent of cases were prosecuted.[14]

A mock juror study found similar conclusions by 541 mock jurors who analyzed a hypothetical case of teacher-student sexual misconduct. The gender and age of both teacher and student were systematically manipulated. When guilt and sentencing were determined:

- perpetration by males or older teachers resulted in greater sentences than for women and younger teachers;
- victimization of younger versus older children resulted in greater sentences;
- student age was most consistently related to findings of teacher guilt and greater sentences;
- same-gender abuse was not judged differently than male-to-female or female-to-male abuse;
- male students victimized by female teachers were "judged to have wanted the contact more than any other gender combination, especially by male mock jurors."[15]

Provide Reliable and Consistent State and Federal Data

In 2024, no reliable sources of comparable data over time would allow us to know if we were making progress in reducing school employee sexual misconduct. Most of the data available is regional or contained in empirical studies that ask similar but different questions. The most efficient and effective way to collect data is to use existing initiatives that regularly report on school enrollments and trends.

Civil Rights Data Collection (CRDC)

In 2017–2018, CRDC surveyed public schools and districts in all fifty states, the District of Columbia, the Commonwealth of Puerto Rico, and other US schools operated by the Department of Interior's Bureau of Indian Education and schools operated by the Department of Defense. There was a 2020–2021 follow-up. Questions asking for the number of school staff incidents of rape and sexual assault were included. Also included was whether the staff member was held responsible and whether the person was reassigned, retired, or resigned. However, the publicly available data do not include those variables because the questions were optional. In the next data collection (i.e., the 2021–2022 CRDC), those optional items will be required for the school districts to complete, and the data will be released to the public."[16] Those data should be available in 2024.

Other national surveys from the US Department of Education and the Department of Justice could include questions like the CDC's Youth Risk Survey. There are multiple public surveys of school practices and student experiences funded at the federal or state level that could include these questions and keep track of school employee sexual misconduct.

IT'S NOT ROCKET SCIENCE

We can reduce the sexual abuse of students by school employees. Institutional courage, individual responsibility, and shining a light on the abuse of children can prevail. It takes all of us: school employees, students, parents, community members, legislators, attorneys, judges, and the press. Each action makes a difference: your action can make a difference.

Methodology

My analysis used case study methodology to examine a selection of schools and districts that have had adjudicated experience with sexual abuse of students by school employees. I reviewed the methods used to study legal proceedings. One approach that is particularly strong for investigating processes is case study methodology. A Rand Corporation monograph report, *Class Action Dilemmas: Pursuing Public Goals for Private Gain,* exemplifies this approach and provided me with additional methodological insights.[1]

Case methodology allows for individual incident descriptions as well as a synthesis of variables across cases. Court and legal records are common sources of data in social science and historical research. Records for this study are both public and private and have been accessed through a number of approaches but were primarily provided by plaintiff and defense attorneys in civil litigation for which I have served as an expert. These documents lend themselves to case analysis and the documentation of variables across cases.

SAMPLE OF CASES

Sampling multiple cases allowed me to look at a variety of similar and contrasting cases. Demonstrating that a finding shows up in more than one place strengthens the validity, stability, and reliability of the conclusions I draw from the findings.

I applied six parameters for selection of cases for this book: (1) a student has been sexually abused by an employee of the school; (2) the employee has admitted the sexual abuse and been found guilty in criminal court; (3) the school is a pre-K–12 public or independent school; (4) sufficient documents are available to detail patterns of abuse, school district conditions, and response or nonresponse of those involved; (5) consent for use of documents has been given by the plaintiff attorneys; and (6) both the criminal and civil cases are closed. Although this sample is not random (a technique not available in these circumstances), it is a purposeful selection that has characteristics of both snowball and judgment sampling and is a selection strategy that includes cases that are both deep and broad. The cases listed are varied and are from thirty-five states; represent both state and federal complaints; include elementary and secondary student plaintiffs; are from urban, rural, and suburban school districts; contain both high- and low-income school districts; and include jurisdictions that serve predominantly white, predominantly Black or Latina/o, or mixed-race students. The victims in these cases are males and females, and the predators are males and females. The cases have been drawn from the fifty-year timespan of Title IX and its evolution, all litigated from 2004 to 2023. Thus, the sample replicates the socio-demographic properties of school districts and plaintiffs from the country as a whole.

DATA SOURCES

Litigation and trial data are commonly used in other disciplines, but rarely in education research. Nevertheless, the public has a qualified right of access to court proceedings and records rooted in the common law. Legal records and documents support the development of good policy by providing details and motivations of actors. Informational scarcity is a barrier to better policymaking and advocacy, particularly for understanding school employee sexual misconduct. My research has access to a full complement of school cases through the use of these litigation documents and provides an understanding of the similarity of patterns across schools and states.

Each site of past civil litigation included in this book is a source of extensive data. As indicated previously, the data being used are the original school documents and sworn depositions of persons involved in the case. The multiple data sets comprehensively present the perspectives of all who might be able to shed light on what policies and procedures were in place at the time of the abuse, how the abuse occurred, and how the school district responded.

The data sources are all of the documents used in both discovery and trial, such as depositions, police records, school district policies, school district training materials, reports from medical and liability experts, pictures and maps of the site, personnel files, school records, faculty handbooks, parent and student handbooks, and any other materials produced in discovery or at the trial.

Table A.1 displays the data I have collected and analyzed.

TABLE A.1   Data sources

Type of source	Description
Depositions, both in transcript and video	Victim, abuser, building principals, assistant principals, superintendent, guidance counselors, HR representative, supervisor of abuser, teacher and staff bystanders, classmates, parents of victim, medical/mental health experts, detectives who investigated
Handbooks	School, district, student, parent, staff
Personnel file	Abuser
Student records	Victim
Pictures, emails, texts	Abusers, victim, classmates, others
Memos, correspondence	Administrators, parents, teachers, abuser, victim
Policies and regulations	District and school plus relevant state and federal laws and regulations
Building layout, classroom set up	Site-specific
Training materials and schedules	School and district-provided training on educator sexual misconduct, sexual harassment, and mandated reporting; materials from state, regional, and local sources and from vendors

DATA COLLECTION AND CODING

Documents and depositions were analyzed using thematic data-analytic codes that relate to the objectives of this book and recorded in reports. The analysis focuses on patterns across schools and types of misconduct.

Training Programs

Addressing and Preventing Adult Sexual Misconduct in the School Setting	
Creator/ distributor	Readiness and Emergency Management for Schools (REMS)
Website	https://rems.ed.gov/trainings/CourseASM.aspx
Contact information	https://rems.ed.gov/trainings/CourseASM.aspx
Program is for:	
School staff: teachers/ general	Yes
School staff: administrators	Yes
School staff: coaches	Yes
Students: elementary	No
Students: middle school	No
Students: high school	No
Delivery	Online
Description	The content of this training is broken into four phases: (1) Understanding Adult Sexual Misconduct (ASM) in Schools, (2) Recognizing and Reporting ASM, (3) Integrating ASM into School Emergency Operation Plans, and (4) Try it! Choose What to Do. Throughout the training modules, you are asked questions about your school policies, and you review the content through multiple choice and true/false questions.

Enough! Preventing Child Sexual Abuse in My School	
Creator/ distributor	Enough Abuse
Website	https://enoughabuse.org/get-trained/ enough-course-for-schools/
Contact information	info@enoughabuse.org (617) 742–8555
Program is for:	
School staff: teachers/ general	Yes
School staff: administrators	Yes
School staff: coaches	Yes
Students: elementary	No
Students: middle school	No
Students: high school	No
Delivery	Online
Description	"Enough!" is a one-hour interactive course for schools that integrates latest knowledge in the field with an effective and engaging e-learning format. Research documents highlight increases in learner knowledge, ability to identify boundary-violating behaviors early, and willingness/confidence to report suspected cases. Learner satisfaction rate is over 98%. Pre- and post-tests and self-reported evaluations are included. A Resource Bank with downloadable booklets, handouts, videos and policy resources is included to promote follow-up discussions among school staff and administrators.
Sexual Misconduct Prevention and Response Training	
Creator/ distributor	TABS and RAINN
Website	https://www.tabs.org/sexual-misconduct-prevention -and-response-training/
Contact information	TABS@TABS.org (8280 258–5354
Program is for:	
School staff: teachers/ general	Yes
School staff: administrators	Yes
School staff: coaches	Yes
Students: elementary	No
Students: middle school	No
Students: high school	No

Delivery	Live virtual training
Description	TABS and RAINN have partnered up to create a training program addressing educator sexual misconduct in residential learning environments. The objectives addressed in this program include (1) understanding the foundations and complexities of sexual misconduct, (2) understanding trauma and its impact on survivors, (3) identifying and reinforcing healthy boundaries, and (4) understanding trauma-informed responses.

Protecting Children Course

Creator/ distributor	United Educators
Website	https://www.ue.org/risk-management/online-courses/collections/protecting-children-higher-ed/
Contact information	(301) 907–4908

Program is for:	
School staff: teachers/ general	Yes
School staff: administrators	Yes
School staff: coaches	Not specified
Students: elementary	No
Students: middle school	No
Students: high school	No

Delivery	Online
Description	United Educators offers four courses that are categorized by audience and content: (1) Boundary Training for Educators, (2) Identifying and Reporting Sexual Misconduct, (3) Hiring Staff Who Work with Minors, and (4) Shine a Light Video

Title IX: Preventing Sexual Misconduct for Faculty and Staff

Creator/ distributor	Traliant
Website	https://www.traliant.com/courses/title-ix-training/
Contact information	info@traliant.com (929) 202–7288

Program is for:	
School staff: teachers/ general	Yes
School staff: administrators	Yes
School staff: coaches	Not specified
Students: elementary	No
Students: middle school	No
Students: high school	Yes (grade not specified)
Delivery	Online
Description	Traliant offers four 30- to 40-minute courses all regarding Title IX, but specific to adult sexual misconduct: (1) Preventing Sexual Misconduct for Faculty and Staff, (2) Preventing Sexual Misconduct for Students, (3) Preventing Sexual Misconduct for Faculty and Staff with Reporting Obligations, (4) Online Title IX Training.

Voice Up! - Sexual Abuse and Molestation Prevention Training

Creator/ distributor	Community Matters
Website	https://community-matters.org/programs-services /voice-up-sexual-abuse-molestation-prevention/
Contact information	(707) 823-6159
Program is for:	
School staff: teachers/ general	Yes
School staff: administrators	Yes
School staff: coaches	Not specified
Students: elementary	No
Students: middle school	Yes
Students: high school	Yes
Delivery	Online or in-person
Description	This program offers training along with supplemental materials for students, school staff, parents/guardians, and administrators. Their program works to educate, empower, and guide students, parents, and school personnel to prevent sexual misconduct within school systems.

Sexual Harassment: Not in Our Schools!	
Creator/ distributor	Stop Sexual Assault in Schools (SSAIS)
Website	https://stopsexualassaultinschools.org/metook12 -resources/
Contact information	info@stopsexualassaultinschools.org
Program is for:	
School staff: teachers/ general	Yes
School staff: administrators	No
School staff: coaches	No
Students: elementary	No
Students: middle school	Yes
Students: high school	Yes
Delivery	Online
Description	SSAIS offers two video trainings: (1) about the history of Title IX and sex discrimination and (2) about sexual harassment.
Child Sexual Abuse Prevention Boundaries for Youth-Serving Organizations	
Creator/ distributor	TAALK
Website	https://www.taalk.org/training/45-training/240-child -sexual-abuse-prevention-boundaries-for-youth -serving-organizations-module-2-part-1
Contact information	(949) 495-5406
Program is for:	
School staff: teachers/ general	Yes
School staff: administrators	Yes
School staff: coaches	Yes
Students: elementary	No
Students: middle school	No
Students: high school	No
Delivery	Online
Description	This four-part course is designed to teach youth-serving organizations about boundaries as well as legal boundaries and on-site access boundaries.

Prevention and Correction	
Creator/ distributor	National Association of State Directors and Teacher Education and Certification (NASDTEC)
Website	https://www.nasdtec.net/page/CPCourse
Contact information	support@nasdtec.org
Program is for:	
School staff: teachers/ general	Yes
School staff: administrators	Yes
School staff: coaches	Yes
Students: elementary	No
Students: middle school	No
Students: high school	No
Delivery	Online
Description	NASDTEC offers a four-hour online course broken up into four modules: (1) The Model Code of Ethics for Educators, (2) Overview of Educator Ethics, (3) Educator Relationships and Boundaries, and (4) Cybertraps for Educators.
Everything Everyone Needs to Know to Prevent Child Sexual Abuse	
Creator/ distributor	Prevent Child Abuse Vermont (PCA)
Website	https://www.pcavt.org/upcoming-training-of-trainers?
Contact information	1-800-CHILDREN
Program is for:	
School staff: teachers/ general	Yes
School staff: administrators	Yes
School staff: coaches	Yes
Students: elementary	No
Students: middle school	No
Students: high school	No
Delivery	Online via Zoom
Description	PCA-Vermont offers a six-hour live training for parents, teachers, caregivers, and other personnel to teach topics regarding boundaries, reporting, and child abuse prevention.

Safe Touches	
Creator/ distributor	NYSPCC
Website	https://nyspcc.org/what-we-do/training-institute /professional-trainings-and-resources/safe-touches/
Contact information	(212) 233–5500 ext. 248 (Jessica Trudeau, director of training institute)
Program is for:	
School staff: teachers/ general	No
School staff: administrators	No
School staff: coaches	No
Students: elementary	Yes (K–3)
Students: middle school	No
Students: high school	No
Delivery	Live classroom training or virtual
Description	Safe Touches is a forty-five-minute workshop for children in grades kindergarten through third grade. The program is designed to teach children what safe body touches are and what to do if personal boundaries are not obeyed. In addition to the course, children are given an activity booklet called "My Body Belongs to Me."
Mandated Reporter Training	
Creator/ distributor	Making Right Choices
Website	https://makingrightchoices.com/online-courses/
Contact information	(844) 672-3377
Program is for:	
School staff: teachers/ general	Yes
School staff: administrators	Yes
School staff: coaches	Yes
Students: elementary	No
Students: middle school	No
Students: high school	No
Delivery	Online
Description	This training focuses on teaching how to recognize grooming patterns and the responsibilities of mandated reporters.

Stewards of Children	
Creator/ distributor	Darkness to Light
Website	https://d2l.csod.com/ui/lms-learning-details/app/course/4d2f0ac6-c056-4e0e-84f9-3dd5a589c1a9#t=1
Contact information	(843) 513-1614
Program is for:	
School staff: teachers/ general	Yes
School staff: administrators	Yes
School staff: coaches	Yes
Students: elementary	No
Students: middle school	No
Students: high school	No
Delivery	Online
Description	This prevention training teaches adults how to prevent, recognize and react responsibly to child sexual abuse. The program is designed for individuals concerned about the safety of children as well as organizations that serve youth.
Stay KidSafe!	
Creator/ distributor	BeKidSafe at the Center for Child Counseling
Website	https://www.centerforchildcounseling.org/programs/kidsafe/staykidsafe/
Program is for:	
School staff: teachers/ general	Yes
School staff: administrators	Yes
School staff: coaches	Yes
Students: elementary	Yes
Students: middle school	No
Students: high school	No
Delivery	In person, online, and zoom
Description	Be Kid Safe offers many different trainings revolving around abuse prevention, child safety, and adverse childhood experiences.

Body Safety Training	
Creator/ distributor	University of Colorado
Contact information	Dr. Sandy K. Wurtele, swurtele@uccs.edu
Program is for:	
School staff: teachers/ general	No
School staff: administrators	No
School staff: coaches	No
Students: elementary	Yes (three to seven years of age)
Students: middle school	No
Students: high school	No
Delivery	In person
Description	The Body Safety Training Program is designed to teach children that they are in charge of their body, the proper terminology for their body parts, and when being touched or touching someone is acceptable or not.
Child Abuse Prevention Program (CAPP)	
Creator/ distributor	Jeanette Collins, International Center for Assault Prevention (ICAP)
Contact information	childassaultprevention@gmail.com
Program is for:	
School staff: teachers/ general	No
School staff: administrators	No
School staff: coaches	No
Students: elementary	Yes
Students: middle	Yes
Students: high school	Yes
Delivery	In person
Description	The purpose of this program is to teach children and youths how to set boundaries and how to distinguish between appropriate and inappropriate behaviors, to teach response skills, and teach how to under-stand grooming tactics and understand if abuse occurred.

Child Safety Matters and Teen Safety Matters	
Creator/ distributor	Monique Burr Foundation
Website	info@mbfpreventioneducation.org
Program is for:	
School staff: teachers/ general	No
School staff: administrators	No
School staff: coaches	No
Students: elementary	Yes
Students: middle school	Yes
Students: high school	Yes
Delivery	In person
Description	This program includes lessons about child safety, shared responsibility for safety, safe adults, types of abuse, red flags, safety rules, bullying, cyberbullying, digital abuse and safety tips, and digital citizenship.
"It's Not Just Jenna"	
Creator/ distributor	Enough Abuse, MassKids/EnoughAbuse Campaign
Website	info@enoughabuse.org
Program is for:	
School staff: teachers/ general	No
School staff: administrators	No
School staff: coaches	No
Students: elementary	No
Students: middle school	Yes
Students: high School	Yes
Delivery	In person
Description	This video and discussion feature a compelling true story about a family whose lives were changed after sixteen-year-old Jenna Quinn shared that she had been sexually assaulted by a trusted family friend. In its discussion section, it includes behaviors in adults that could signal abuse, grooming tactics, behaviors in children signaling that they have been abused, and how to respond to signs.

Abuse Prevention Training	
Creator/ distributor Website	Praesidium https://www.praesidiuminc.com/services/academy/online/

Program is for:
  School staff: teachers/ general
  School staff: administrators
  School staff: coaches
  Students: elementary
  Students: middle school
  Students: high school
	
	Yes
	Yes
	Yes
	No
	No
	No

Delivery	Online or in-person
Description	This program uses skill-based content to educate staff on how to prevent abuse and create a culture of safety. They offer many different training programs including online training, custom training, and DIY group training.
Safer, Smarter Kids	
Creator/ distributor Website	Lauren's Kids, Florida safersmarterkids.org/teachers/curriculum/

Program is for:
  School staff: teachers/ general
  School staff: administrators
  School staff: coaches
  Students: elementary
  Students: middle school
  Students: high school
	
	No
	No
	No
	Yes
	Yes (called Safer, Smarter Teens)
	No

Delivery	In person
Description	This program is designed to teach children about safety rules, understanding strangers versus trusted adult risks, listening to intuition, body boundaries, safe versus unsafe situations, and tattling versus reporting.

Second Step Child Protection Unit	
Creator/ distributor	Committee for Children, Washington State
Website	www.secondstep.org/child-protection
Program is for:	
School staff: teachers/ general	Yes
School staff: administrators	Yes
School staff: coaches	No
Students: elementary	Yes
Students: middle school	No
Students: high school	No
Delivery	In person
Description	This program is designed to help teachers analyze their current policies and procedures for protecting students against adult sexual misconduct. There is also a classroom-based program designed to teach children about not keeping secrets, safety rules, and crossing boundaries.
Speak Up, Be Safe	
Creator/ distributor	Childhelp, Inc.
Website	www.childhelp.org/subs/childhelp-speak-up-be-safe
Contact information	1-480-922-8212
School Staff: Teachers/General	No
Program is for:	
School staff: administrators	No
School Staff: coaches	No
Students: elementary	Yes
Students: middle school	Yes
Students: high school	Yes
Delivery	In person
Description	This program teaches children and teens the skills to prevent or interrupt cycles of neglect, bullying, and physical, emotional, and sexual abuse.

Safe to Compete	
Creator/ distributor	The National Center for Missing and Exploited Children
Website	www.safetocompete.org
Contact information	(703) 224–2150
Program is for:	
School staff: teachers/ general	No
School staff: administrators	No
School staff: coaches	Yes
Students: elementary	Yes
Students: middle school	Yes
Students: high school	Yes
Delivery	Online
Description	This program for children, teens, and coaches is designed to help teach coaches and children how to avoid being kidnapped, trafficked, and exploited in youth sports.

Note: Not all programs have been included in this list. These are examples. Over time, links might change.

Notes

Chapter 1

1. *Sutedja v. University of Southern California et al.*, 2:18-cv-04258-SVW-GJS (C.D. Cal.) (Dkt. 167–1).
2. Victor J. Ross, "The Broken Taboo: What You Can Do When Teachers Get Too Cozy with Their Students," *Executive Educator* 3, no. 3 (1981): 23–25.
3. A description of my research methods can be found in appendix 1.
4. Institute of Education Sciences, "Public and Private School Comparison," IES Fast Facts, https://nces.ed.gov/fastfacts/display.asp?id=55#:~:text=Overall%2C%2053.9%20 million%20K%E2%80%9312,were%20enrolled%20in%20public%20schools.
5. Tuyen K. Dinh, Lauren Mikalouski, and Margaret S. Stockdale, "When 'Good People' Sexually Harass: The Role of Power and Moral Licensing on Sexual Harassment Perceptions and Intentions," *Psychology of Women Quarterly* 46, no. 3 (2022): 278–98.
6. Maya Riser-Kositsky, "Education Statistics: Facts About American Schools," updated January 9, 2024, *Education Week*, https://www.edweek.org/leadership/education-statistics-facts -about-american-schools/2019/01#:~:text=In%20America's%20public%20schools%20 there,2020%2D21%20numbers%20from%20NCES%20.
7. Jennifer J. Freyd, *Betrayal Trauma: The Logic of Forgetting Childhood Abuse* (Cambridge, MA: Harvard University Press, 1996).
8. Carly P. Smith and Jennifer J. Freyd, "Dangerous Safe Havens: Institutional Betrayal Exacerbates Sexual Trauma," *Journal of Traumatic Stress* 26, no. 1 (2013): 119–24.
9. Based on Smith and Freyd, "Dangerous Safe Havens," and first presented in Marina N. Rosenthal, Alec M. Smidt, and Jennifer J. Freyd, "Still Second Class: Sexual Harassment of Graduate Students," *Psychology of Women Quarterly* 40, no. 3 (2016): 364–77.
10. Carly P. Smith and Jennifer J. Freyd, "Insult, then Injury: Interpersonal and Institutional Betrayal Linked to Health and Dissociation," *Journal of Aggression, Maltreatment & Trauma* 26, no. 10 (2017): 1117–31.
11. Monika N. Lind, Alexis A. Adams-Clark, and Jennifer J. Freyd, "Isn't High School Bad Enough Already? Rates of Gender Harassment and Institutional Betrayal in High School and Their Association with Trauma-Related Symptoms," *PLOS One* 15, no. 8 (2020): e0237713.
12. Caitlin J. Pinciotti and Holly K. Orcutt, "Institutional Betrayal: Who Is the Most Vulnerable?" *Journal of Interpersonal Violence* 36, no. 11–12 (2021): 5036–54.
13. Smith and Freyd, "Dangerous Safe Havens," 119–24; Smith and Freyd, "Insult, then Injury," 1117–31.
14. Lindsey L. Monteith et al., "Assessing Institutional Betrayal Among Female Veterans Who Experienced Military Sexual Trauma: A Rasch Analysis of the Institutional Betrayal Questionnaire.2," *Journal of Interpersonal Violence* 36, no. 23–24 (2021): 10861–83.

15. Morgan E. Pettyjohn et al., "Secondary Institutional Betrayal: Implications for Observing Mistreatment of Sexual Assault Survivors Secondhand," *Journal of Interpersonal Violence* 38, no. 17–18 (2023): 10127–49.
16. Josef Spiegel, *Sexual Abuse of Males: The SAM Model of Theory and Practice* (New York: Brunner-Routledge, 2003), 318.

Chapter 2

1. Katrin Chauviré-Geib and Jörg M. Fegert, "Victims of Technology-Assisted Child Sexual Abuse: A Scoping Review," *Trauma, Violence, & Abuse* 25, no. 2 (2023): 1335–48.
2. There are 950,000. Alaska Trekker, "Alaska Caribou (Reindeer)," https://alaskatrekker.com /alaska-wildlife/alaska-caribou-rangifer-tarandus/#:~:text=The%20Alaska%20Caribou %20(Rangifer%20tarandus,32%20herds%20(or%20populations.
3. The lack of documentation of the number of students sexually abused in schools isn't the same as an absence of studies on sexual abuse of children by trusted others. We know a lot about how, where, why, and the harm to children occurs. It is recordkeeping of the extent of the abuse that is missing.
4. For instance, the Youth Risk Survey, National Crime Victimization Survey, School Crime Supplement, etc.
5. American Association of University Women (AAUW) and Harris Interactive, eds., *Hostile Hallways: Bullying, Teasing, and Sexual Harassment in School* (Washington, DC: American Association of University Women Educational Foundation, 2001); Charol Shakeshaft, "Educator Sexual Misconduct: A Synthesis of Existing Literature," US Department of Education, 2004, https://files.eric.ed.gov/fulltext/ED483143.pdf; Billie-Jo Grant, Jeffrey Haverland, and Jessica Kalbfleisch, "Title IX Policy Implementation and Sexual Harassment Prevalence in K–12 Schools," *Educational Policy* 38, no. 2 (2023): 1–38; Elizabeth L. Jeglic et al., "The Nature and Scope of Educator Misconduct in K–12," *Sexual Abuse* 35, no. 2 (2023): 188–213.
6. Shakeshaft, "Educator Sexual Misconduct."
7. AAUW and Harris Interactive, *Hostile Hallways*. This was the second survey by the AAUW on sex harassment in schools. The first was published in 1993. The data collected then used the same survey instrument as 2000 and were published with the same title, *Hostile Hallways*.
8. Frank Hernandez, Jonathan McPhetres, and Jamie Hughes, "Using Adolescent Perceptions of Misconduct to Help Educational Leaders Identify and Respond to Sexual Misconduct," *Educational Administration Quarterly* 557, no. 4 (2020): 507–35.
9. Grant, Haverland, and Kalbfleisch, "Title IX Policy," 19–20.
10. Examples of inappropriate touching include hugging, playing with hair, hands on back and shoulders. Examples of physical sexual contact are kissing, touching breasts, and anal, oral, and vaginal intercourse. Hernandez, McPhetres, and Hughes, "Using Adolescent Perceptions.
11. Four state universities in New York, New Jersey, Texas, and California.
12. Jeglic et al., "The Nature and Scope of Educator Misconduct in K–12."
13. Collected in 2002, published in 2004.
14. Most recent data available at the time of writing; National Center for Education Statistics, "Back-to-School Statistics," IES Fast Facts, https://nces.ed.gov/fastfacts /display.asp?id=372#:~:text=PK%E2%80%9312%20EDUCATION,-Enrollment&text =How%20many%20students%20attended%20school,including%20ungraded%20 students%20; 49.5 million pre-K–12 public school students; 4.7 million K–12 private

school students in 2019; National Center for Education Statistics, "Private School Enrollment," updated May 2022, https://nces.ed.gov/programs/coe/indicator/cgc/private -school-enrollment.

15. A. Gewirtz-Meydan and D. Finkelhor, "Sexual Abuse and Assault in a Large National Sample of Children and Adolescents," *Child Maltreatment* 25, no. 2 (2020): 203–14.

16. These responses include all adult contact, not just school employees.

17. These particular units are for all misconduct, including school employee sexual misconduct.

18. Special Commissioner of Investigation for the New York City School District, "History," NYCSCI. https://nycsci.org/history/.

19. Special Commissioner of Investigation for the New York City School District, "Reports," NYCSCI, https://nycsci.org/reports/.

20. New York State Education Department, "NYC Public Schools Enrollment (2021–22)," https://data.nysed.gov/enrollment.php?year=2022&instid=7889678368.

21. Students abused over several years are only counted once.

22. Anastasia Coleman, "Special Commissioner of Investigation for the New York City School District," 2022, https://nycsci.org/wp-content/uploads/2023/03/SCI-2022-ANNUAL -REPORT.pdf.

23. David Jackson et al., "Betrayed: Chicago Public Schools Fail to Protect Students from Sexual Abuse," *Chicago Tribune*, updated July 27, 2018, graphics.chicagotribune.com/chicago -public-schools-sexual-abuse/index.html.

24. Jackson, "Betrayed."

25. *Fiscal Year 2022 Annual Report*, Office of Inspector General (Chicago: 2022), https://cpsoig .org/uploads/3/5/5/6/35562484/cps_oig_fy_2022_annual_report.pdf.

26. I divided these numbers by 13 (K–12 grades).

27. Molly Henschel and Billie-Jo Grant, "Exposing School Employee Sexual Abuse and Misconduct: Shedding Light on a Sensitive Issue," *Journal of Child Sexual Abuse* 28, no. 1 (2019): 26–45.

28. Barna Group, an evangelical Christian polling group.

29. Brian D. Ray and M. Danish Shakeel, "Demographics Are Predictive of Child Abuse and Neglect, but Homeschool Versus Conventional School Is a Non-Issue: Evidence from a Nationally Representative Survey," *Journal of School Choice* 17, no. 2 (2023): 176–213.

30. Kelly Malone, "'Tip of the Iceberg': Report Finds 252 School Personnel Accused of Sexual Offences," *Toronto Star*, November 2, 2022, https://nationalpost.com/news/canada/tip-of -the-iceberg-report-finds-252-school-personnel-accused-of-sexual-offences.

Chapter 3

1. Maria H. Nagtegaal and Cyril Boonmann, "Child Sexual Abuse and Problems Reported by Survivors of CSA: A Meta-Review," *Journal of Child Sexual Abuse* 31, no 2 (2021): 146–76.

2. Victim statement is confidential.

3. "Fast Facts: Preventing Adverse Childhood Experiences," Centers for Disease Control and Prevention, updated June 29, 2023, https://www.cdc.gov/violenceprevention/aces/fastfact .html.

4. Vincent J. Felitti, "The Relationship of Adverse Childhood Experiences to Adult Health: Turning Gold into Lead," *Zeitschrift für Psychosomatische Medizin und Psychotherapie* 48, no. 4 (2002): 359–69 (in German).

5. "Data Visualizations: Adverse Childhood Experiences (ACEs)," Centers for Disease Control and Prevention, updated November 5, 2019, https://www.cdc.gov/vitalsigns/aces/data-visualization.html.

6. "We Can Prevent Childhood Adversity," Centers for Disease Control and Prevention, updated November 17, 2023, https://vetoviolence.cdc.gov/apps/aces-infographic.

7. Kerri Garbutt, Mike Rennoldson, and Mick Gregson, "Shame and Self-Compassion Connect Childhood Experience of Adversity with Harm Inflicted on the Self and Others," *Journal of Interpersonal Violence* 38, no. 11–12 (June 2023): 7193–214.

8. Michelle Schoenleber, Howard Berenbaum, and Robert Motl, "Shame-Related Functions of and Motivations for Self-Injurious Behavior," *Personality Disorders: Theory, Research, and Treatment* 5, no. 2 (April 2014): 204–11; Ana Xavier, José Pinto Gouveia, and Marina Cunha, "Non-Suicidal Self-Injury in Adolescence: The Role of Shame, Self-Criticism and Fear of Self-Compassion," *Child & Youth Care Forum* 45, no. 4 (August 2016): 571–86.

9. Maria Miceli and Cristiano Castelfranchi, "Reconsidering the Differences Between Shame and Guilt," *Europe's Journal of Psychology* 14, no. 3 (August 2018): 710–33.

10. Jeffrey A. Walsh and Jessie L. Krienert, "Innocence Lost: Educator Sexual Misconduct and the Epidemic of Sexually Victimized Students," in *Invisible Victims and the Pursuit of Justice*, ed. Raleigh Blasdell, Laura Krieger-Sample, and Michelle Kilburn (Hershey, PA: IGI Global, 2021), 249–73.

11. Carly P. Smith and Jennifer J. Freyd, "Dangerous Safe Havens: Institutional Betrayal Exacerbates Sexual Trauma," *Journal of Traumatic Stress* 26, no. 1 (2013): 119–24.

12. Smith and Freyd, 122.

13. Kurt Brundage, *After 3 PM* (New York: Morgan James, 2018), 96.

14. Brundage, 110.

15. "Stop Educator Child Exploitation—EDUCATOR SEXUAL MISCONDUCT AND ASSAULT—A Crisis in the Canadian School System," Canadian Centre for Child Protection Inc., 2022, 1–13, https://policycommons.net/artifacts/3781938/stop-educator-child-exploitation/4587700/; Brundage, 6.

16. Janet Currie and Erdal Tekin, "Understanding the Cycle: Childhood Maltreatment and Future Crime," *Journal of Human Resources* 47, no. 2 (2012): 509–49.

17. Elizabeth J. Letourneau et al., "The Economic Burden of Child Sexual Abuse in the United States," *Child Abuse & Neglect* 79 (2018): 413–22.

18. Letourneau et al., 413–22; "Value of 2015 US Dollars Today," Inflation Tool, https://www.inflationtool.com/us-dollar/2015-to-present-value; the calculation for 2023 dollars used the 2015 dollar value reported in the article multiplied by $1.28, using a May 2023 inflation calculator.

19. Letourneau et al., 413–22; Lance Lochner and Enrico Moretti, "The Effect of Education on Crime: Evidence from Prison Inmates, Arrests, and Self-Reports," *American Economic Review* 94, no. 1 (2004): 155–89.

20. Margaret C. Cutajar et al., "Suicide and Fatal Drug Overdose in Child Sexual Abuse Victims: A Historical Cohort Study," *Medical Journal of Australia* 192, no. 4 (2010): 184–87.

21. John Robst, "Childhood Sexual Abuse and the Gender Wage Gap," *Economics Letters* 99, no. 3 (2008): 549–51; Bernadette D. Proctor, Jessica L. Semega, and Melissa A. Kollar, "Income and Poverty in the United States: 2015," U.S. Department of Commerce, September 2016, https://www.census.gov/library/publications/2016/demo/p60-256.html.

22. Samantha Bouchard et al., "Child Sexual Abuse and Employment Earnings in Adulthood: A Prospective Canadian Cohort Study," *American Journal of Preventive Medicine* 65, no. 1 (2023): 83–91.

23. Bouchard et al., appendix table 4.
24. "Value of $247,250 from 2017 to 2023," CPI Inflation Calculator, https://www
    .in2013dollars.com/us/inflation/2017?amount=247250.
25. This is an organization of school districts that pools their insurance risks. These insurance
    pools are common across the United States.
26. In 2016–2017, the amount was $8.2 million.
27. Deborah Callahan and Dana Grandy, "Tool Kit for Mitigating & Managing SAM Claims,"
    Washington Schools Risk Management Pool, presentation.
28. "Large Loss Report 2023," United Educators, https://www.ue.org/496c42/globalassets
    /global/large-loss-report-2023.pdf.

Chapter 4

1. James Martin, "A Priest's View of Penn State," Bishop Accountability, November 13, 2011,
   https://www.bishop-accountability.org/news2011/11_12/2011_11_13_MartinSj_APriests
   .htm.
2. In my studies and cases, a "he" was always the person who fit this pattern.
3. Charol Shakeshaft, "Educator Sexual Misconduct: A Synthesis of Existing Literature," US
   Department of Education (DOE), 2004, https://files.eric.ed.gov/fulltext/ED483143.pdf.
4. Billie-Jo Grant et al., "A Case Study of K–12 School Employee Sexual Misconduct: Lessons Learned from Title IX Policy Implementation," Office of Justice Programs, September 15, 2017, https://nij.ojp.gov/library/publications/case-study-k-12-school-employee
   -sexual-misconduct-lessons-learned-title-ix. In total, from January 1, 2014–May 31, 2023,
   there were 4,601 reports from all 50 states; Molly M. Henschel and Billie-Jo Grant, "Exposing School Employee Sexual Abuse and Misconduct: Shedding Light on a Sensitive
   Issue," *Journal of Child Sexual Abuse* 28, no. 1 (2019): 26–45.
5. Simon Fletcher, "Touching Practice and Physical Education: Deconstruction of a Contemporary Moral Panic," *Sport, Education and Society* 18, no. 5 (2013): 694–709.
6. Erin Vogt, "12 Accused 'Perv' Teachers, Coaches Busted in NJ Just This Year," New Jersey
   101.5, December 23, 2022, https://nj1015.com/nj-teachers-coaches-arrested-past-year-sex
   -crimes/.
7. Christine Willmsen and Maureen O'Hagan, "State Failing to Weed out Unfit Coaches,"
   Seattle Times, December 16, 2003, https://special.seattletimes.com/o/news/local/coaches
   /news/daythree.html.
8. Christopher Keizur, "Fourth Victim Alleges Sex Abuse by Principal," *The Outlook*,
   August 18, 2020, https://www.theoutlookonline.com/news/fourth-victim-alleges-sex-abuse
   -by-principal/article_1fa1d2a4-1ed8-50f3-8aaa-734c77bb607e.html.
9. In my own research as well as research by others, I have not seen a case of sexual misconduct by a transgender person, nor research substantiating that transgender sexual misconduct is occurring. That does not mean that there might not be such a boundary crossing. I
   mention this because, despite any evidence, it has become a common theme among those
   who oppose transgender identification by both students and employees to charge that hiring transgender employees or allowing students to identify as transgender will cause
   increased sexual abuse of students.
10. These are cases brought to me as an expert witness.
11. Shakeshaft, "Educator Sexual Misconduct."
12. Henschel and Grant, "Exposing School Employee Sexual Abuse," 26–45.
13. US Department of Health and Human Services, Administration for Children and Families,
    Administration on Children, Youth and Families, Children's Bureau, "Child Maltreatment

2013," 2015, http://www.acf.hhs.gov/programs/cb/research-data-technology/statistics -research/child-maltreatment.

14. Franca Cortoni, Kelly M. Babchishin, and Clémence Rat, "The Proportion of Sexual Offenders Who Are Female Is Higher Than Thought: A Meta-Analysis," *Criminal Justice and Behavior* 44, no. 2 (2017): 145–62.

15. Cortoni, Babchishin, and Rat.

16. Shakeshaft, "Educator Sexual Misconduct"; The proportions of female abusers reported by victims for this study and the Shakeshaft 2004 study are not directly comparable because the definition of sexual misconduct used by Shakeshaft for school predation includes more boundary-crossing behaviors than does the definition in the Cortoni et al. study.

17. Billie-Jo Grant et al., "A Case Study"; Henschel and Grant, "Exposing School Employee Sexual Abuse," 26–45.

18. V. Young, "Women Abusers: A Feminist View," in *Female Sexual Abuse of Children: The Ultimate Taboo*, ed. Michele Elliot (Essex, UK: Longman, 1994), 100–12.

19. Based upon the 2004 Shakeshaft USDOE study. There are no recent national studies of student reports available. There are recollection studies of regional samples as discussed in chapter 3.

20. Charol Shakeshaft and Audrey Cohan, "In Loco Parentis: Sexual Abuse of Students in Schools. What Administrators Should Know," US Department of Education, 1994, https:// eric.ed.gov/?id=ED372511.

21. Shakeshaft and Cohan.

22. Larissa S. Christensen and Andrea J. Darling, "Sexual Abuse by Educators: A Comparison between Male and Female Teachers Who Sexually Abuse Students," *Journal of Sexual Aggression* 26, no. 1 (2020): 23–35.

23. Louise Rooney, "Gendered Perceptions of Child Sexual Abusers: The Paradox of the 'Vulnerable Other,'" *Journal of Contemporary Criminal Justice* 36, no. 4 (2020): 559–81.

24. Mollee Steely Smith, "'I'm Not a Child Molester, but a Victim Myself': Examining Rationalizations Among Male Sex Offenders Who Report Histories of Childhood Sexual Abuse," *International Journal of Offender Therapy and Comparative Criminology* 67, no. 12 (2022): 1.

25. Christensen and Darling, "Sexual Abuse of Educators," 23–35.

26. "Child Sexual Abuse Statistics," National Center for Victims of Crime, https://victimsofcrime .org/child-sexual-abuse-statistics/.

27. "Statistics About Sexual Violence," National Sexual Violence Resource Center, updated 2015, https://www.nsvrc.org/sites/default/files/publications_nsvrc_factsheet_media-packet _statistics-about-sexual-violence_0.pdf.

28. Jan Hindman and James M. Peters, "Research Disputes Assumptions About Child Molesters," National District Attorneys Association (July–August 1988); These results were also published in James M. Peters, Janet Dinsmore, and Patricia Toth, "Why Prosecute Child Abuse," *South Dakota Law Review* 34 (1989): 649 and under the same title in *The Prosecutor* 23, no. 2 (1990): 30, 33.

29. "Award-Winning Teacher Guilty of Sexually Abusing 11 Students," Fox News, September 2007, https://www.foxnews.com/story/award-winning-teacher-guilty-of-sexually-abusing -11-students.

30. Rose Kim and Liz Willen, "He's Haunted by Memories," *Newsday*, September 14, 1994, A8.

31. Baron and Carey-Place, "Final Report of Special Counsel to the Anne Arundel County Board of Education," Maryland, 1993, p. 3, cited in Shakeshaft, "Educator Sexual Misconduct."

32. Shakeshaft case study.
33. It is worth mentioning *Lolita*, the story that had such cultural impact that *Webster's* defines the word as "a precociously seductive girl" (https://www.merriam-webster.com/dictionary /Lolita), which of course, obscures the story of the real victim, Florence Sally Horner, who inspired the book.

Chapter 5

1. Charol Shakeshaft, "Educator Sexual Misconduct: A Synthesis of Existing Literature," US Department of Education, 2004, https://files.eric.ed.gov/fulltext/ED483143.pdf.
2. Elizabeth L. Jeglic, Georgia M. Winters, and Benjamin N. Johnson, "Identification of Red Flag Child Sexual Grooming Behaviors," *Child Abuse & Neglect* 136 (February 2023): 105998, https://www.sciencedirect.com/science/article/pii/S0145213422005324. Or maybe they aren't careful and target all types of people, but those who succumb to grooming are more likely to have specific characteristics.
3. Billie-Jo Grant et al., "A Case Study of K–12 School Employee Sexual Misconduct: Lessons Learned from Title IX Policy Implementation," Office of Justice Programs, September 15, 2017, https://nij.ojp.gov/library/publications/case-study-k-12-school-employee -sexual-misconduct-lessons-learned-title-ix. From January 1, 2014–May 31, 2023, in total, there are 4,601, from all 50 states.
4. Shakeshaft, "Educator Sexual Misconduct."
5. Caroline Hendrie, "Cost Is High When Schools Ignore Abuse," *Education Week*, December 9, 1998, https://www.edweek.org/leadership/cost-is-high-when-schools-ignore-abuse /1998/12; Kelly Corbett, Cynthia S. Gentry, and Willie Pearson, "Sexual Harassment in High School," *Youth & Society* 25, no. 1 (September 1993): 93–103 (reported, 77%); Bernard Gallagher, "The Extent and Nature of Known Cases of Institutional Child Sexual Abuse," *British Journal of Social Work* 30 (December 2000): 795–817 (reported, 54%); Charol Shakeshaft and Audrey Cohan, "Sexual Abuse of Students by School Personnel," *Phi Delta Kappan* 76 (January 1995): 513–20 (reported, 66%).
6. Davey M. Smith, Nicole E. Johns, and Anita Raj, "Do Sexual Minorities Face Greater Risk for Sexual Harassment, Ever and at School, in Adolescence? Findings from a 2019 Cross-Sectional Study of U.S. Adults," *Journal of Interpersonal Violence* 37, no. 3–4 (2022): 1963–87.
7. Richard Sobsey, *Violence and Abuse in the Lives of People with Disabilities: The End of Silent Acceptance?* (Baltimore, MD: Paul H Brookes, 1994); Dick Sobsey, Wade Randall, and Rauno K. Parrila, "Gender Differences in Abused Children With and Without Disabilities," *Child Abuse & Neglect* 21, no. 8 (1997): 707–20; P. M. Sullivan and J. F. Knutson, "Maltreatment and Disabilities: A Population-Based Epidemiological Study," *Child Abuse & Neglect* 24, no. 10 (October 2000): 1257–73.
8. Bernard Gallagher, "The Extent and Nature of Known Cases of Institutional Child Sexual Abuse," *British Journal of Social Work* 30, no. 6 (December 2000): 795–817.
9. Mary Lou Bensy, "Lending My Voice Outloud: The Sexual Abuse of Students with Disabilities in American School Settings" (PhD diss., Hofstra University, 2011).
10. S. Mansell, D. Sobsey, and P. Calder, P., "Sexual Abuse Treatment for Persons with Developmental Disabilities," *Professional Psychology: Research and Practice* 23, no. 5 (1992): 404–409.
11. I don't have any further information on Betsy.

Chapter 6

1. "Grooming: Know the Warning Signs," RAINN, July 10, 2020, https://www.rainn.org/news/grooming-know-warning-signs.
2. Usually for liability reasons in the case of an accident.
3. Additional examples in a previous publication: Charol Shakeshaft et al., "School Employee Sexual Misconduct: Red Flag Grooming Behaviors by Perpetrators," in *Sexual Abuse: An Interdisciplinary Approach*, ed. Ersi Kalfoglu and Sotirios Kalfoglou (London: Intech-Open, 2022).
4. While the term *grooming* is more recent, beginning to gain recognition outside the research world in the early 1970s, earlier descriptions identified it as romancing, relationship-building, emotional manipulation, and other terms. The patterns were characterized as seduction within the prevention community. That label changed over time as researchers learned more about how children are persuaded into targets. The change in terminology had more to do with the perception of the words than the actual behaviors.
5. Jim Tanner and Stephen Brake, "Exploring Sex Offender Grooming," KB Solutions, 2013, https://www.kbsolutions.com/Grooming/grooming.html; other frameworks, such as the Sexual Grooming Scale are valuable tools for understanding grooming.
6. Kenneth Lanning, "The Evolution of *Grooming*: Concept and Term," *Journal of Interpersonal Violence* 33, no. 1 (2018): 5–16.
7. Elizabeth L. Jeglic, Georgia M. Winters, and Benjamin N. Johnson, "Identification of Red Flag Child Sexual Grooming Behaviors," *Child Abuse & Neglect* 136 (2023): 105998.
8. Georgia M. Winters and Elizabeth L. Jeglic, "The Sexual Grooming Scale—Victim Version: The Development and Pilot Testing of a Measure to Assess the Nature and Extent of Child Sexual Grooming," *Victims & Offenders* 17, no. 6 (2022): 919–40.
9. Jeglic, Winters, and Johnson, "Identification of Red Flag."
10. Jeglic, Winters, and Johnson.
11. "Doe v. Fairfax School Board," *Amicus Brief of the National Women's Law Center* (US Court of Appeals for the Fourth Circuit: no. 19–2203, June 2021), 16.

Chapter 7

1. See chapter 2.
2. Elaine Whiteley, "Nightmare in Our Classrooms," *Ladies Home Journal*, October 1992, 81–83.
3. Patrick Boyle, *Scout's Honor: Sexual Abuse in America's Most Trusted Institution* (New York: Prima Lifestyles, 1994).
4. Luciana C. Assini-Meytin et al., "Preventing and Responding to Child Sexual Abuse: Organizational Efforts," *Child Abuse & Neglect* 112 (2021): 104892.
5. "Code of Ethics for Educators," National Education Association, September 14, 2020, https://www.nea.org/resource-library/code-ethics-educators; the first code was adopted in 1927.
6. "Model Code of Ethics for Educators," NASDTEC, 2023, https://www.nasdtec.net/page/mcee_doc.
7. Daniel Frederick Klemm, "The Evolution of Ethical Codes in the Teaching Profession in the United States" (master's thesis, Fort Hays Kansas State College, 1938).
8. Klemm, "The Evolution of Ethical Codes," 22.
9. Klemm, 30.
10. Robert Shoop and Jack Hayhow, *Sexual Harassment in Our Schools: What Teachers and Parents Need to Know to Spot It and Stop It* (Boston: Allyn & Bacon, 1994).

11. Robert Shoop, "Identifying a Standard of Care," *Principal Leadership* 7, no. 2 (2002): 48–52; Robert Shoop, *Sexual Exploitation in Schools: How to Spot It and Stop It* (Thousand Oaks, CA: Corwin, 2003).

12. Amanda L. Robertson, Danielle A. Harris, and Susanne Karstedt, "It's a Preventable Type of Harm": Evidence-Based Strategies to Prevent Sexual Abuse in Schools," *Child Abuse & Neglect* 145 (2023): 106419.

13. David Finkelhor, *Child Sexual Abuse: New Theory and Research* (New York: Free Press, 1984), 1–13.

14. "Welcome to Help Wanted," Help Wanted, https://www.helpwantedprevention.org/.

15. Adapted from Educator's Guide to Controlling Sexual Harassment, monthly newsletter, Washington, D.C., Thompson Publishing Group.

16. "Concussion Facts and Statistics," UPMC, https://www.upmc.com/services/sports-medicine /services/concussion/about/facts-statistics.

17. Tara Johnson, *From Teacher to Lover* (New York: Peter Lang, 2009).

18. Johnson makes important points about the control of women teachers and the definition of teaching, which I will return to later in this book. However, her study of women teachers who are sexually involved with male students does not provide direction on how to have an eroticized classroom without the possibility of sexual exploitation of students.

19. E. J. Mikkelsen, T. G. Gutheil, and M. Emens, "False Sexual-Abuse Allegations by Children and Adolescents: Contextual Factors and Clinical Subtypes," *American Journal of Psychotherapy* 46, no. 4 (1992): 556–70.

20. "Independent School Task Force on Educator Sexual Misconduct Report: Prevention and Response," NAIS, https://www.nais.org/articles/pages/independent-school-task-force-on -educator-sexual-misconduct-report-prevention-response/.

21. Source unknown; commonly attributed to Dietrich Bonhoeffer,

22. Assini-Meytin et al., "Preventing and Responding to Child Sexual Abuse: Organizational Efforts," *Child Abuse & Neglect* 112 (February 2021): 5.

Chapter 8

1. Billie-Jo Grant, Jeffrey Haverland, and Jessica Kalbfleisch, "Title IX Policy Implementation and Sexual Harassment Prevalence in K–12 Schools," *Educational Policy* 38, no. 2 (2023): 510–47.

2. Grant, Haverland, and Kalbfleisch, 510–47.

3. Grant, Haverland, and Kalbfleisch, 510–47.

4. Under Title IX, schools must have policies on school employee sexual misconduct. "Combatting Sexual Assault," US Department of Education, https://www2.ed.gov/about/offices /list/ocr/docs/sexhar01.html.

5. "United States Age of Consent Map," AgeOfConsent, https://www.ageofconsent.net/states.

6. Daniel Frederick Klemm, "The Evolution of Ethical Codes in the Teaching Profession in the United States" (master's thesis, Fort Hays Kansas State College, 1938).

7. See appendix 1 for organizations.

8. Patrick Boyle, *Scout's Honor: Sexual Abuse in America's Most Trusted Institution* (New York: Prima Lifestyles, 1994); Luciana Assini-Meytin et al., "Preventing and Responding to Child Sexual Abuse: Organizational Efforts," *Child Abuse & Neglect* 112 (2021): 104892.

9. Mia J. Abboud et al., "Educator Sexual Misconduct: A Statutory Analysis," *Criminal Justice Policy Review* 31, no. 1 (2019): 133–53.

10. "Prevention and Response Task Force Report 2018," National Association of Independent Schools, https://www.nais.org/getmedia/f27450cf-6737-4c6b-ab49-3c1762112b69/Prevention-and-Response-Task-Force-Report-2018.pdf.

11. "Adoption of Policies on Sexual Harassment Required," Oregon Laws, https://oregon.public.law/statutes/ors_342.704.

12. "ASM Defined," REMS, https://rems.ed.gov/ASM_Chapter1_Defined.aspx.

13. "About Us," REMS, https://rems.ed.gov/AboutUs.aspx.

14. "Policies and Procedures for Staff Interactions with Students," REMS, https://rems.ed.gov/ASM_Chapter2_Interactions.aspx.

15. Kristan Russell et al., "School District Policies Regarding Appropriate Teacher-Student Relationships: What's Missing and What Matters?" *Current Issues in Education* 23, no. 1 (2022): 1–26; this law does not apply to school employees under 21.

16. Russell et al., 5.

17. Catherine E. Robert and David P. Thompson, "Educator Sexual Misconduct and Texas Educator Discipline Database Construction," *Journal of Child Sexual Abuse* 28, no. 1 (2017): 7–25.

18. One example that provides perspective for both K–12 and higher education: Deborah L. Brake and Mariah B. Nelxon, *Staying in Bounds: NCAA Model Policy to Prevent Inappropriate Relationships Between Student-Athletes and Athletics Department Personnel* (Indiana: NCAA).

19. U.S. Department of Education, 2022, https://oese.ed.gov/offices/office-of-formula-grants/safe-supportive-schools/. Prepared by Policy Studies Associates, Magnolia Consulting , SRI International.

20. "Nondiscrimination on the Basis of Sex in Education Programs or Activities Receiving Federal Financial Assistance," Office for Civil Rights, Department of Education, final rule (unofficial version), 2024, https://www.federalregister.gov/documents/2024/04/29/2024-07915/nondiscrimination-on-the-basis-of-sex-in-education-programs-or-activities-receiving-federal?utm_campaign=subscription+mailing+list&utm_medium=email&utm_source=federalregister.gov.

21. "YRBSS Overview," CDC, Adolescent and School Health, https://www.cdc.gov/healthyyouth/data/yrbs/overview.htm.

22. Available at https://www.unh.edu/ccrc/technologyinternet-victimization.

23. Jeffrey J. Thoenes, "The Beliefs and Extent of Training of Michigan Secondary School Principals Regarding Educator Sexual Misconduct" (PhD diss., Central Michigan University, 2009).

24. Leslie Tutty, "The Relationship of Parental Knowledge and Children's Learning of Child Sexual Abuse Prevention Concepts," *Journal of Child Sexual Abuse* 2, no.1 (1993): 83–103; Leslie Tutty, "The Revised Children's Knowledge of Abuse Questionnaire: Development of a Measure of Children's Understanding of Sexual Abuse Prevention Concepts," *Social Work Research* 19, no. 2 (1995): 112–20.

25. For instance, Glenn Lipson et al., "Preventing School Employee Sexual Misconduct: An Outcomes Survey Analysis of Making Right Choices," *Journal of Child Sexual Abuse* 28, no. 2 (2019): 129–43; Melissa A. Bright et al., "Randomized Control Trial of a School-Based Curriculum that Teaches About Multiple Forms of Abuse," *Child Maltreatment* 29, no. 2 (2024): 364–74; Mengyao Lu et al., "School-Based Child Sexual Abuse Interventions," *Research on Social Work Practice* 33, no. 4 (2022): 390–412; Sunha Kim et al., "Teacher Outcomes from the Second Step Child Protection Unit: Moderating Roles of Prior Preparedness, and Treatment Acceptability," *Journal of Child Sexual Abuse* 28, no. 6 (2019): 726–44; Marisol J. Diaz et al., "Teaching Youth to Resist Abuse: Evaluation of a Strengths-Based Child Maltreatment Curriculum for High-School Students," *Journal of Child & Adoles-*

cent Trauma 14 (2021): 141–49; Eva S. Goldfarb and Lisa D. Lieberman, "Three Decades of Research: The Case for Comprehensive Sex Education," *Journal of Adolescent Health* 68, no. 1 (2021): 13–27; Amanda B. Nickerson et al., "Randomized Controlled Trial of the Child Protection Unit: Grade and Gender as Moderators of CSA Prevention Concepts in Elementary Students," *Child Abuse & Neglect* 96 (2019): 104101; Kate Guastaferro et al., "Virtual Delivery of A School-Based Child Sexual Abuse Prevention Program: A Pilot Study," *Journal of Child Sexual Abuse* 31, no. 5 (2022): 577–92.

26. Because we identified it as the overall strongest program available, we have chosen to evaluate the training with our CDC funding. That study has not been completed. A report is expected in spring 2025.
27. Payouts at $1,000,000 or more; "Praesidium Report," 2024, https://20935854.fs1 .hubspotusercontent-na1.net/hubfs/20935854/Thought%20Leadership/Praesidium%20 Report/PraesidiumReport_2022_Final.pdf?__hstc=122418196.874ea86c0d567c3a8109e bc0d87fc65c.1716066185873.1716066185873.1716066185873.1&__hssc=122418196 .1.1716066185874&__hsfp=3016618557.
28. See https://heyzine.com/flip-book/PraesidiumReport2024#page/8.
29. "The Movement to End Child Sexual Abuse Starts with a Single Word . . . Enough," Enough Abuse Campaign, https://enoughabuse.org/.

Chapter 9

1. Gene G. Abel et al., "Preventing Child Sexual Abuse: Screening for Hidden Child Molesters Seeking Jobs in Organizations That Care for Children," Sexual Abuse 31, no. 6 (2019): 662–83; Office of Justice Programs, The Importance of Background Screening for Nonprofits: An Updated Briefing (Washington DC: US Department of Justice: 2008).
2. Steve Reilly, "Broken Discipline Tracking Systems Let Teachers Flee Troubled Pasts," *USA Today*, updated October 23, 2017, https://www.usatoday.com/story/news/2016/02/14 /broken-discipline-tracking-system-lets-teachers-with-misconduct-records-back-in -classroom/79999634/.
3. Steve Reilly, "Reforms Follow the *USA Today* Network Teacher Probe," *USA Today*, updated December 22, 2016, https://www.usatoday.com/story/news/2016/12/22/reforms -follow-usa-today-network-teacher-probe/95737404/.
4. Aria Amrom, Cynthia Calkins, and Jamison Fargo, "Between the Pew and the Pulpit: Can Personality Measures Help Identify Sexually Abusive Clergy?" *Sexual Abuse* 31, no. 6 (2017): 686–706.
5. Andrew Fennell, "Study: Lying on Resumes and Fake Job References," StandoutCV, https:// standout-cv.com/usa/study-fake-job-references-resume-lies#how-many.
6. Amicus Brief of the National Women's Law Center, p 25. US Court of Appeals for the Fourth Circuit, no. 19–2203, Doe v. Fairfax School Board, 16 June 2021, p 16.
7. Brittany Shammas, "Five School Employees Arrested for Not Reporting Teen's Sexual Assault," *Washington Post*, July 26, 2023, https://www.washingtonpost.com/nation/2023 /07/26/florida-school-sexual-assault-not-reported/.
8. States where recent misdemeanor or felony charges were filed by school employees who did not report when they learned of possible sexual abuse of a student include Florida, Connecticut, Nevada, California, and Virginia.
9. See https://caselaw.findlaw.com/court/us-4th-circuit/2132555.html.
10. Johari Harris and Ann Kruger, "'We Always Tell Them, but They Don't Do Anything About It!' Middle School Black Girls Experience with Sexual Harassment at an Urban Middle School," *Urban Education* 58, no. 10, 2543–69.

11. Michael Planty et al., "School Tip Line Toolkit: A Blueprint for Implementation and Sustainability" RTI International, 2018, https://nij.ojp.gov/library/publications/school-tip-line-toolkit-blueprint-implementation-and-sustainability.
12. Eunice Magalhães et al., "Why Are Men More Likely to Endorse Myths About Sexual Abuse than Women? Evidence from Disposition and Situation-Based Approaches," *Child Maltreatment* 27, no. 3 (2022): 356–65.
13. Kurt Brundage, *After 3 PM* (New York: Morgan James, 2018), 112–17.
14. Sarah Shepherd, "Lawsuit Claims School Administration Knew Principal's Conduct," *Penobscot Bay Pilot*, April 3, 2020, https://www.penbaypilot.com/article/new-lawsuit-motion-claims-school-administration-knew-about-principal-s-alleged-miscon/132575.
15. Dana T. Hartman et al., "Childhood Sexual Abuse: A Longitudinal Study of Disclosures and Denials," *Child Maltreatment* 28, no. 3 (2023): 462–75.
16. Child USA, "Child Sex Abuse Statute of Limitations Reform," https://childusa.org/sol/.
17. See https://digitalcommons.unomaha.edu/cgi/viewcontent.cgi?article=1030&context=edad facpub.
18. Ana M. Greco et al., "Why Do School Staff Sometimes Fail to Report Potential Victimization Cases? A Mixed-Methods Study," *Journal of Interpersonal Violence* 37, no. 9–10 (2020): NP7242–67.
19. William Pelfrey (professor of criminal justice and homeland security, Virginia Commonwealth University), personal communication, December 9, 2023.
20. William Pelfrey.
21. Delfina Fernandes et al., "Forensic Interview Techniques in Child Sexual Abuse Cases: A Scoping Review," *Trauma, Violence & Abuse* 25, no. 2 (2024): 1382–96.
22. Bethany Barnes, "Mitch Whitehurst, Ex-Teacher Accused of Decades of Abuse, Wants Initial Record Erased," *The Oregonian*, December 18, 2018, https://www.oregonlive.com/education/2018/12/mitch_whitehurst_ex-teacher_ac.html.
23. "A Training Guide for Administrators and Educators on Addressing Adult Sexual Misconduct in the School Setting," US Department of Education, Office of Safe and Healthy Students, Readiness and Emergency Management for Schools (REMS) Technical Assistant Center, March 2017, https://rems.ed.gov/docs/asmtrainingguide.pdf.
24. Ida Mojadad, "Feds Demand Action on School Sexual Misconduct. Will California Heed the Call?" San Francisco Standard, April 17, 2023, https://sfstandard.com/2023/04/17/feds-demand-action-on-school-sexual-misconduct-will-california-heed-the-call/; as of June 2023, those states included Maryland, Pennsylvania, Washington, and New Jersey.
25. The San Francisco Standard published at least two investigative studies of teachers accused of sexual misconduct of students leaving the school districts; https://sfstandard.com/2023/04/17/feds-demand-action-on-school-sexual-misconduct-will-california-heed-the-call/ and https://sfstandard.com/2023/02/21/they-were-accused-of-sexual-misconduct-sf-schools-let-them-quietly-resign/.
26. Jeanne L. Surface, David Stader, and Anthony Armenta, "Educator Sexual Misconduct and Nondisclosure Agreements: Policy Guidance from Missouri's Amy Hestir Student Protection Act," *UN) The Clearing House* 87, no. 3 (May–June 2014): 130–33.
27. Jamie Satterfield, "Sevier County Hired Teacher Fired a Year Earlier for Sexually Harassing Students, Colleagues in Campbell County," *Knox News*, January 23, 2019, https://www.knoxnews.com/story/news/crime/2019/01/23/sevier-county-teacher-dan-turner-sexual-harassment/2586443002/.
28. This practice is not confined to Tennessee. Local newspaper articles across the country tell the same story. See, for instance, New Jersey: Adam Clark and Jessica Remo, "Teachers

Accused of Sexual Misconduct in N.J. Here's Why," NJ.com, updated March 8, 2024, http://www.nj.com/education/2017/12/teachers_accused_of_sexual_misconduct_keep_getting. html; Georgia: Taylor Denman, "Gwinnett Coach Resigns During Investigation of Misconduct in Chicago School System," *Gwinnett Daily Post*, November 10, 2019, https://www.gwinnettdailypost.com/local/gwinnett-coach-resigns-during-investigation-of-misconduct-in-chicago-school/article_274caeba-fffb-11e9-b9e5-3b0d852176d0.html; California: Matthew Kupfer and Ida Mojadad, "Teacher Accused of Sexual Misconduct Was Allowed to Quietly Leave Two Bay Area Schools," San Fracisco Standard, March 1, 2023, https://sfstandard.com/2023/03/01/teacher-accused-of-sexual-misconduct-was-allowed-to-quietly-leave-two-bay-area-schools/learning; Iowa: Anna Spoerre, "4 Iowa School Districts Failed to Report Coach's Misconduct, Lawyers Say in Announcing Settlement with Victim," *Des Moines Register*, October 22, 2019, https://www.desmoinesregister.com/story/news/crime-and-courts/2019/10/22/lawsuit-iowa-teacher-sex-abuse-ewinger/4062613002/; New York: "Teacher Misconduct on Long Island: Newsday Investigations," Newsday, January 23, 2024, https://www.newsday.com/long-island/investigations/teachers-resign-after-misconduct-allegations-sarvl5j; I have copies of similar issues for all states.

29. Professional Standards and Practices Commission, "Recognizing and Reporting Sexual Misconduct Under the Educator Discipline Act," https://www.pspc.education.pa.gov/Documents/Ethical%20Practices/Publications/Recognizing%20and%20Reporting%20Sexual%20Misconduct.pdf.

30. A. P. Dillon, "Former Huntersville Private School Teacher Charged with Sex Crimes," *LL1885*, March 26, 2024, https://ladyliberty1885.com/. The blog contains a listing of school employees who sexually abuse from newspapers across the country.

31. "Manchin, Toomey Urge Department of Education to Protect Students from Sexual Misconduct," Joe Manchin, https://www.manchin.senate.gov/newsroom/press-releases/manchin-toomey-urge-department-of-education-to-protect-students-from-sexual-misconduct.

32. "A Call to Action for Policymakers and Advocates," https://enoughabuse.org/get-vocal/call-to-action-report/.

33. "State Laws Mandating or Allowing Child Sexual Abuse Prevention Education in Schools," Enough Abuse Campaign, https://enoughabuse.org/get-vocal/laws-by-state/.

34. "Criminalizing Educator Sexual Misconduct Map," Enough Abuse Campaign, https://enoughabuse.org/get-vocal/laws-by-state/criminalizing-educator-sexual-misconduct-map/.

Chapter 10

1. John Dewey, *The Middle Works of John Dewey: 1899–1924* (Carbondale, Illinois: Southern Illinois University Press, 2008).

2. Judith Herman, *Truth and Repair: How Trauma Survivors Envision Justice* (New York: Basic Books, 2008).

3. "Independent School Leaders from the Independent School Task Force on Educator Sexual Misconduct," National Association of Independent Schools, https://www.nais.org/articles/pages/independent-school-task-force-on-educator-sexual-misconduct-report-prevention-response/.

4. Alec M. Smidt, Alexis A. Adams-Clark, and Jennifer J. Freyd, "Institutional Courage Buffers Against Institutional Betrayal Protects Employee Health, and Fosters Organizational Commitment Following Workplace Sexual Harassment," *PLOS One* 18, no. 1 (2023): e0278830.

5. Simona Giorgi, Christi Lockwood, and Mary Ann Glynn, "The Many Faces of Culture: Making Sense of 30 Years of Research on Culture in Organization Studies," *Academy of Management Annals* 9, no. 1 (2015): 1–54.

6. Jenny Brundin, "With Boulder Students as an Inspiration, Denver Students Push for Changes to How Schools Handle Sexual Misconduct," CPR News, April 21, 2021, https://www.cpr .org/2021/04/21/with-boulder-students-as-an-inspiration-denver-students-push-for -changes-to-how-schools-handle-sexual-misconduct/?utm_source=TNG&utm_campaign =f49c3bdf07.

7. "Activism Toolkit," SSAIS, https://stopsexualassaultinschools.org/activism/.

8. Elaine Mayer and Kathleen Mary, "Schools Are Employers Too: Rethinking the Institutional Liability Standard in Title IX Teacher-on-Student Sexual Harassment Suits," *Georgia Law Review* 50, no. 3 (2016): 909–46.

9. Jeffrey P. Metzler and Max A. Winograd, "Supreme Court Narrows Title IX Liability for Schools," Pillsbury, July 5, 2022, https://www.pillsburylaw.com/en/news-and-insights /supreme-court-title-ix-liability-schools.html.

10. "Dear Colleague Letter on ESEA Section 8546 Requirements," US Department of Education, https://www2.ed.gov/policy/elsec/leg/essa/section8546dearcolleagueletter.pdf.

11. "Dear Colleague."

12. Elizabeth J. Meyer et al., "Title IX Coordinators as Street-Level Bureaucrats in U.S. Schools: Challenges Addressing Sex Discrimination in the #MeToo Era," *Education Policy Analysis Archives* 26, no. 68 (2018), https://epaa.asu.edu/index.php/epaa/article/view/3690.

13. Kate Cimini, "What Lee County Public Schools Does to Encourage Title IX Investigations," *Naples Daily News*, updated January 9, 2024, https://www.naplesnews.com/story/news /state/2023/05/16/what-lee-county-public-schools-does-to-encourage-title-ix-investigations /70140140007/.

14. Stephanie D. Block et al., "Predictors of Prosecutorial Decision in Reports of Child Sexual Abuse," *Child Maltreatment* 28, no. 3 (2022): 488–99.

15. Alissa Anderson et al., "Who Is the Rotten Apple? Mock Jurors' Views of Teacher-Student Sexual Contact," *Journal of Interpersonal Violence* 33, no. 9 (2018): 1450.

16. Personal communication, OCR CRDC Team, 2023.

Appendix 1

1. Deborah R. Hensler et al., *Class Action Dilemmas: Pursuing Public Goals for Private Gain* (Santa Monica, CA: Rand Institute for Civil Justice, 2000).

Acknowledgments

I have worked on versions of this book since the 1990s. Many colleagues, relatives, and friends have offered ideas, support, and encouragement. I appreciate everyone sticking with me. I don't like to write. I like to read and analyze data. Unfortunately, writing is required to share one's ideas and findings. This was also a hard book for me to write. Reading about the abuse of children is soul-numbing. Not being able to stop it is rage-making. It was easy to stop working on what turned out to be a fairly short, matter-of-fact book. I ate a lot of chocolate and took many naps.

Whenever my energy flagged, I was encouraged by the dear person to whom I am married, Dale Mann. He nurtured and encouraged my sense of responsibility to those who have been abused and kept me writing. He switched from being Dale to Professor/Dr. Mann as he read many versions of all of the chapters. His insights, wordsmithing, and questions enriched this manuscript. If anything sounds smart, it's probably because Dale sharpened the language.

I'm grateful to my family for their support and encouragement. I'm shocked and surprised that I am a happy woman in a functional and loving family. Emma Shakeshaft and Sarah Meyland have been here for the whole 30-plus years I've studied sexual abuse. David Blinka and Julianne and Britton Mann added encouragement. When I started this work, I was writing to protect my daughter. Now that I've finished, I realize I am writing for my grandchildren, Coraline, Eloise, Maya, and Samuel. I hope that the things I've explored in this book never happen to them or to any child. To my friends, I regret missing our time together while doing this work. I hope to catch up.

My research team for our Centers for Disease Control and Prevention funded study on the prevention of school employee sexual misconduct kept me thinking about new ways to work with schools. Thank you, especially to my co-principal investigator Kelly Carlyle, to Emiola Oyefuga who kept things on schedule, and to AJ Ortiz, Jill Ruck, Abigail Conley, Julie Russo, and Stacie Lefeavers for their insights, hard work, and optimism. I appreciate all the help I received from Ashley Sharp, who Chicago-styled my APA references and was reliably available to proofread and help find proper citations for my references. I am deeply in debt to the doctoral students and colleagues at Hofstra University and Virginia Commonwealth University with whom I worked. They have been consistent sources of motivation.

I wish to thank all of the plaintiffs in the cases I studied who had the courage to hold schools responsible for the sexual misconduct by their employees. And, of course, I am indebted to the attorneys who took those cases and fought for their clients—children who had been abused while attending school.

It is my hope that this book—with your help—advances the safety of children.

About the Author

Charol Shakeshaft, PhD, is Distinguished Professor at Virginia Commonwealth University and has served for forty-six years as a professor of educational administration. Dr. Shakeshaft began studying the sexual abuse of students in schools in the 1980s and authored a congressionally mandated report on educator sexual misconduct published by the US Department of Education in 2004. Her research has been funded by the US Department of Education and the Centers for Disease Control and Prevention.

She has evaluated policies and practices related to preventing sexual misconduct and consulted to US schools and other professional youth-serving organizations, including the Catholic Church and the Boy Scouts of America.

Dr. Shakeshaft has been retained as an expert witness in over four hundred civil and criminal cases involving the sexual abuse of children by educators in forty-six states. She has assessed organizational compliance with Title IX and other standards related to preventing the sexual abuse of children.

She was elected a Fellow of the American Educational Research Association and has received several other academic honors. Dr. Shakeshaft is the author or coauthor of six books and three hundred refereed publications and papers. She is a cofounder and serves as director of Women Leading in Education, which has members from over forty countries.

Charol Shakeshaft lives on a farm in Virginia with her husband, Dale Mann. She advocates for women and children and is a mother and grandmother who spends her leisure time reading and gardening.

Index

AASA (The American Association of School Administrators), 138
AAUW (American Association of University Women), 22, 23, 50
Abboud, Mia J., 138–139
abusers. *See also* grooming; school employee sexual misconduct
  accountability for, 210
  childhood sexual abuse of, 55–56
  excuses by, 55
  fixed versus opportunistic, 49–50
  gender of, 14, 25, 52–54, 63, 67
  MO of, 57–64
  opportunistic versus fixated, 49–50
  overview, 47–50
  preconditions for, 117–119
  reporting by students compared to number of, 27–32
  role in school of, 50–52, 68–70, 77–81, 87
  self-harm inflicted on, 38
  training for, 117
  use of term, 47
academic vulnerability, 70–74
Adams-Clark, Alexis A., 205
administrators. *See also* bystanders
  abuser role and, 24, 51–52
  associations for, 138
  pushback from, 120–121
  tolerance or enabling by, 12, 54, 112
  training for, 154, 157
  unawareness by, 15
adverse childhood experiences (ACEs), 36
age of consent laws, 137–138
age when abusers start, 56
aiding and abetting (passing the trash), 143, 157, 194–197, 207–208

alcohol and drugs, provision of, 98
alerts versus reports, 177–178
The American Association of School Administrators (AASA), 138
American Association of University Women (AAUW), 22, 23, 50
Amy Hestir Student Protection Act, 195
annual training. *See* training and education
anonymous reports, 176–177
application forms, 164–165
arrest rates, 27
Assini-Meytin, Luciana C., 131
The Association of Boarding Schools (TABS), 130, 205
awards, abusers winning, 57–58

background checks, 108, 166–167
behaviors, as more important than demographics, 48, 50
Bensy, Mary Lou, 68
Bernier, Jetta, 196
betrayal trauma, 9–10, 37–43
blame of the victim, 12, 55, 120–123, 125, 128, 180
boarding schools, 129–130
Bouchard, Samantha, 40, 41
boundary crossings, 7–8, 84–87. *See also* abusers; grooming; school employee sexual misconduct
Bradley, Chuck, 209
Brake, Stephen, 87
Brundage, Kurt, 38
building monitoring. *See* supervision of employees
bus drivers as abusers, 68–70

bystanders
    healing of, 202
    lack of reporting by, 7, 183–186
    need to report red flags, 90
    normalized behavior and, 86
    policies for, 137
    questions to ask, 102–103

California Commission on Teacher
    Credentialing, 195
Canada, 27, 32, 38, 39–40
charisma, 48–49, 87–88
Chicago Public Schools, 28–30
childhood sexual abuse of abusers,
    55–56
Christensen, Larissa, 54
Civil Rights Data Collection (CRDC), 211
civil suits
    for accountability, 209–210
    costs due to, 40–43, 156, 209
    data collection and, 12–13
    Title IX complaints versus, 207
class helpers, 74, 97–98
climate surveys, 206
clothing of students, 62–63, 119
coaches, 51, 77–78, 122, 142
Code of Ethics for Educators (NEA), 109
codes of conduct, 109–111, 138, 143.
    See also policies
colleagues, environmental grooming and,
    88–89
community, healing of, 202
community reactions, 128–130
comprehensive ecological prevention model.
    See also policies; reporting by
    educators; training and education
    hiring, 108, 113, 133, 163–170
    investigations, 113, 133, 188–194
    overview, 130–133
    resolving/remedying, 133, 194–197
    supervision of employees, 113, 133,
    170–171
conflicts of interest, 188–190, 193
"consensual" sexual relationships
    age of consent laws and, 137–138
    as not existing, 5, 17

number of reported, 24
    trust and compliance interpreted as, 89
consequences, risk of, 112, 114
counting, importance of, 22
CRDC (Civil Rights Data Collection), 211
criminal investigations, 173, 188–190

data collection, 11–14, 21–22, 203, 211
day schools, 129–130
desensitization, 98–100
disabilities, students with, 67–70
drugs and alcohol, provision of, 98
dysfunctional home life, vulnerability and,
    74–77

economic costs of abuse, 39–40
educator sexual misconduct. *See* school
    employee sexual misconduct
Elementary and Secondary Education Act
    (ESEA), 195, 196, 207
Emens, M., 126–127
enabling, 35–36, 54, 85, 112, 210
Enough Abuse Campaign, 156, 196–197
environmental grooming, 87–89
ethical leader role, 61
ethnicity, of targets, 66–67
Every Student Succeeds Act (ESSA),
    143, 196
excuses, 55
expectations. *See* policies
extracurricular access, 77–81

false accusations, 125–127
families
    abusers acting as substitute family,
    59–61
    engaging in culture change, 206
    environmental grooming and, 88
    harm from sexual misconduct to, 38
    healing of, 202
    teacher separating targets from, 94
    threats toward, 180
    training for, 32, 155, 157
    unawareness by, 14, 57
faux investigations, 191–193
fear, lack of reporting due to, 180–182

female abuse of males, 53, 67
Finkelhor, D., 27, 117–119
firing employees, 194–197
fixated versus opportunistic abusers, 49–50
flirtation, 62–64
four-factor model of prevention, 117–119
Freyd, Jennifer, 9, 10, 37, 205
From Teacher to Lover (Johnson), 125

Gebser v. Lago Vista Independent School District (1998), 206–207
gender
    of abusers, 14, 25, 52–54, 63, 67
    child sexual abuse survivors and, 55–56
    clothing of students and, 62–63, 119
    guilt and sentencing decisions and, 210
    same-sex offending, 14, 54, 63, 183
    of targets, 14, 66–67
Gewirtz-Meydan, A., 27
gifts, 94–96
Giorgi, Simona, 205
Glynn, Mary Ann, 205
graduates, policies about, 141–142
grandiosity, 48–49, 87–88
Grant, Billie Jo, 24–25, 26, 30–31, 50, 53, 66, 136
grooming
    addressing, 101–103
    boundary crossings leading to, 7–8, 84–87
    defined, 83
    desensitization to sexual content and physical touch, 98–100
    environmental grooming, 87–89
    gifts, 94–96
    isolation of targets, 59–61, 68, 90–94
    red flag behaviors, 91
    school culture and, 83–84
    student crushes created by, 63
    trust development in, 96–98
group identity, 61
guilt, shame versus, 37
Gutheil, T. G., 126–127

harm from sexual misconduct
    betrayal trauma compounding, 37–43

financial and productivity costs, 39–43
    healing of, 201–207
    lifetime costs per victim, 39–41
    to offenders and their families, 38
    to the organization's reputation, 38
    overview, 33
    self-harm, 36, 65
    of targets, 34–37
Haverland, Jeffrey, 136
healing of harmed people, 201–207
health outcomes
    adverse childhood experiences and, 36
    betrayal and, 9, 16
    of targets, 34–37, 111
Henschel, Molly, 30–31
Hernandez, Frank, 24
Hindman, Jan, 55–56
hiring, 108, 113, 133, 163–170
homeschooling, sexual abuse risks and, 31–32
Hughes, Jamie, 24
hugs, 85

inappropriate behavior. *See* boundary crossings; grooming; school employee sexual misconduct
independent schools, 129–130
Independent School Task Force on Prevention of Educator Sexual Misconduct, 205
initial reports, 172
in loco optimae parentis, 201
in loco parentis doctrine, 108, 138
inquiries, initial, 188–189
inquiries, postincident, 190–191, 203–204
institutional betrayal, 7, 9–11, 205. *See also* comprehensive ecological prevention model
Institutional Betrayal Questionnaire (IBQ), 9
institutional courage, 205
insurance claims, 40–43, 209
internet searches, 166
interviews of job candidates, 169–170
investigations, 113, 133, 188–194
isolation of targets, 59–61, 68, 90–94

Jeglic, Elizabeth, 25, 26, 66, 90–101
job titles of abusers, 50–51
Johnson, Benjamin, 90–101
Johnson, Tara Star, 125
jurors, 210
justifications, 55, 121–122

Kalbfleisch, Jessica, 136
Klemm, Daniel, 110
Krienert, Jessie L., 37

Lanning, Kenneth, 89
law enforcement involvement, 173,
    188–190
Lee County School District, 209
legislation, resistance to, 124–125
Letourneau, Elizabeth J., 39–40, 41, 117
Letourneau, Mary Key, 53
licensure, 166–167, 173, 195
lifetime costs per victim, 39–41
Lockwood, Christi, 205
lover role, 62–64, 181–182

Martin, James, 48
masculinity, abusers and, 54
MassKids, 196–197
McPhetres, Jonathon, 24
mentor role, 58–59
Mikkelsen, E. J., 126–127
Minnesota Multiphasic Personality
    Inventory-2, 168
Model Code of Ethics for Educators
    (NASDTEC), 109–110
moral leader role, 61

narcissism, 48
National Association of Independent
    Schools (NAIS), 129–130, 139, 205
National Association of Secondary School
    Principals (NASSP), 138
National Association of State Directors of
    Teacher Education and Certification
    (NASDTEC), 109–110, 166–167
National Education Association (NEA),
    109, 138
newspaper reporting, 210

New York City Public Schools, 28, 30
"Nondiscrimination on the Basis of Sex in
    Education Programs or Activities
    Receiving Federal Financial Assis-
    tance" final rule, 151
normalized behavior, 7–8, 85–87, 101, 182.
    See also grooming
notice to districts about abuse, 151–152,
    174–175

offenders. See abusers; educator sexual
    misconduct
Office of the Special Commissioner
    (NYC), 28
official channels reports, 172–173
opportunistic versus fixated abusers, 49–50
organizational betrayal, 7, 9–11, 205. See
    also comprehensive ecological
    prevention model
outstanding teacher role, 57–58, 87

parents. See families
passing the trash, 143, 157, 194–197,
    207–208
Pelfrey, William, Jr., 188
Pennsylvania, 196
personality tests, 168
personnel management. See also policies;
    reporting by educators; training and
    education
  hiring, 108, 113, 133, 163–170
  investigations, 113, 133, 188–194
  overview, 163
  removing from employment, 194–197
  screening for interviews, 165–168
  supervision of employees, 113, 133,
    170–171
Peters, James, 55–56
photographer role, 62, 78–81
physical sexual misconduct, examples of, 20
policies
  basis for, 137–139
  enforcement of, 153
  need for, 136–137
  overview, 132, 135–136
  resistance to, 139

as safety factor, 113
what to include in, 139–153
Poole, Gerald, 203–204
postincident, local summary inquiries,
190–191, 203–204
power, 7, 54, 141–142
Praesidium, 114–115, 131, 155–156, 164
predators. *See* abusers; educator sexual
misconduct
preliminary school-based inquiries, 188–189
press, use of, 210
prevention. *See also* investigations; policies;
reporting by educators; training and
education
changing of school culture for, 119–130
comprehensive ecological prevention
model, 130–133
Finkelhor's four-factor model for,
117–119
hiring, 108, 113, 133, 163–170
need for, 111–116
overview, 107–111
principals. *See* administrators
private platforms, use of, 96–97, 100
productivity costs, 39–40
professional boundaries. *See* policies
proof as not required for reporting,
173–174
PTSD, 34

Quebec Longitudinal Study of Kindergarten
Children (QLSKC), 39–40

race, of targets, 66–67
rationalizations, 55
Ray, Brian, 31
Readiness and Emergency Management for
Schools (REMS), 140–141
reasonable belief standard for reporting,
173–174, 186
red flag behaviors, risk level and, 91
references, job, 165–166
reporting by educators
barriers to, 177–178, 182–186
lack of, 7, 112
takeaways for, 186–187

types of, 171–175
reporting by students
adults reported and investigated versus,
27–32
barriers to, 178–182
experience after, 57–58, 112, 114, 123,
127–128
language used by, 103, 133, 172,
175–176, 183–184
low rate of, 25–27
policies to increase, 136–137
reputation, concern for, 129–130
research, difficulty with, 11–12
resolving/remedying, 133
resumes, lies on, 167, 168
retaliation, 112, 122, 180–181, 184
rides, giving to students, 86
role models, 88
Rooney, Louise, 54
rules. *See* policies
Russell, Kristian, 141
Ryan, Gail, 56

same-sex offending
gender of abuser and, 63
overview, 54, 67
percentage of, 14
reporting of, 183
school board members, training for,
154–155
school culture
analysis of, 203–204
barriers to reporting and, 177–178
changing of, 119–130, 205–206
misconduct facilitation and, 83–84
preconditions for abuse and, 117–119
school employee sexual misconduct.
See also grooming
comparative data about, 27–32
complicity with, 4, 6–7
demographics about, 14
examples of, 20–21
failure to recognize, 15
federal definition versus, 23
increase in, 25–26
metrics for lacking, 21–22

school employee sexual misconduct (cont.)
  range of, 5, 17, 19–20
  rate of, 6, 22–26
  use of term, 19
school-over-student justification,
  121–122
school supplies, 95–96
school tip lines, 176–177
screening for interviews, 165–168
secondary institutional betrayal, examples
  of, 10–11
secrecy to maintain abuse, 101
self-harm, shame and, 36, 65
settlement agreements, 210
Sexual Allegations Unit (SAU, CPS), 29
sexual harassment. *See* school employee
  sexual misconduct
sexual misconduct. *See* school employee
  sexual misconduct
Shakeel, M. Danish, 31
Shakeshaft, C., 22–23, 26
shame, 36–37, 65, 178–179
Shoop, Robert, 111
Shoreham-Wading River School District,
  203–204
slut-shaming, 128, 178–180
Smidt, Alec M., 205
Smith, Cathy P., 9, 10, 37
social media, 24–25, 96–97, 100, 166
Stancik, Edward F., 28
standards of care, 108, 138. *See also*
  policies
state laws, 138–139
statutes of limitations, 182–183
stereotypes, 53
Stop Sexual Assault in Schools (SSAIS),
  206
student-athletes, 77–78, 142
student climate surveys, 206
student reactions, 127–128
students, engagement in culture change,
  206
students, training for, 154, 157
students of color, 66–67
studies on sexual misconduct, 22–26
substitute family role, 59–61

supervision of employees, 113, 133,
  170–171
survivors. *See* targets

TABS (The Association of Boarding
  Schools), 130, 205
Tanner, Jim, 87
targets. *See also* families; harm from sexual
  misconduct; reporting by students
  blaming of, 12, 55, 120–123, 125, 128,
    180
  demographics about, 65–67, 107
  extracurricular access to, 77–81
  grooming of, 89–101
  healing of, 201–202
  isolation of, 59–61, 68, 90–94
  retaliation against, 112, 122, 180–181,
    184
  vulnerability of, 67–77
  vulnerability of as factor, 67–77
teacher organizations, 123–125, 206
technology-mediated sexual abuse, types of,
  19–20
temptress myth, 62–63, 125
termination of employment, 194–197
texting, 96–97, 100
threats to prevent reporting, 180–182
tip lines, 176–177
Title IX
  history of, 138
  increasing awareness of, 207–209
  money damages under, 206–207
  passing the trash and, 194–195
  reporting and, 173–175
  retaliation prohibited by, 184
training and education
  for abusers, 117
  availability of, 155–157
  components for, 157–161
  insurance claims and, 209
  needed to investigate, 191
  overview, 132
  safety factors for, 113
  for students about acceptable educator
    conduct, 118–119
  who needs, 153–155

trust, 33, 38, 153. *See also* grooming
tutoring, 70–74, 92

unions, 123–125, 206
US Department of Education, 140–141

verbal sexual misconduct, examples of, 21
victims. *See* targets
Virginia Board of Education, 124
visual sexual misconduct, examples of, 21
volunteers, training for, 157

vulnerability of targets, 67–77

wages, impact of abuse on, 39–40
Walsh, Jeffrey A., 37
Washington Schools Risk Management Pool
(WSRMP), 40–42, 209
Winters, Georgia, 90–101

yearbook sponsor role, 79–81
Youth Risk Behavior Surveillance Survey
(YRBSS), 152